DICTIONARY
OF IDIOMS

Linda Flavell completed a first degree in modern languages and has subsequent qualifications in both secondary and primary teaching. She has worked as an English teacher both in England and overseas, and more recently as a librarian in secondary schools and as a writer. She has written three simplified readers for overseas students and co-authored, with her husband, *Current English Usage* for Papermac and several dictionaries of etymologies for Kyle Cathie.

Roger Flavell's Master's thesis was on the nature of idiomaticity and his doctoral research on idioms and their teaching in several European languages. On taking up a post as Lecturer in Education at the Institute of Education, University of London, he travelled very widely in pursuit of his principal interests in education and training language teachers. In more recent years, he was concerned with education and international development, and with online education. He also worked as an independent educational consultant. He died in November 2005.

By the same authors

Dictionary of Proverbs and their Origins
Dictionary of Word Origins
Dictionary of English down the Ages

DICTIONARY OF IDIOMS
and their Origins

LINDA AND ROGER FLAVELL

Kyle Books

This edition printed in Great Britain in 2016 by
Kyle Books, an imprint of Kyle Cathie Ltd.
192–198 Vauxhall Bridge Road
London, SW1V 1DX
general.enquiries@kylebooks.com
www.kylebooks.co.uk

First published in Great Britain in 1992 by Kyle Cathie Limited
Completely revised, updated and expanded in 2006

ISBN: 978 0 85783 409 6

A Cataloguing in Publication record for this title is available from the British Library.

Printed and bound at Gopsons Papers Ltd., Noida

INTRODUCTION

If I may be accused of encouraging or inventing a new vice – the mania, or 'idiomania', I may perhaps call it – of collecting what Pater calls the 'gypsy phrases' of our language, I have at least been punished by becoming one of its most careless and incorrigible victims. (Logan Pearsall Smith, Words and Idioms, *1925)*

Our belief is that people turn to a book on idioms for two main purposes: for reference and to browse. We have tried to cater for both.

Reference
Each phrase dealt with in the body of the book is listed alphabetically in relation to a key word in it. As idioms are by definition phrases and not single words, there is necessarily a choice to be made of which word to classify the phrase by. We have exercised our judgement as to which is the key word (normally a noun or a verb) but, in case our intuitions do not coincide with the reader's, we have provided an index of the important words in each expression.

The head words are followed by a definition. This is the *contemporary* sense or senses – an important point, given that many idioms have a long history and have undergone changes in meaning, often marked ones, during the centuries. Similarly, the comments under *Usage* are there to provide guidance on the current formality or informality of the phrase, typical contexts of its use, its grammatical peculiarities, variations in form – all necessary reference material given that idioms characteristically break the rules (see **What is an idiom?**, page 6).

A further guide to usage lies in the contemporary quotations that are a part of many entries. Quotations are listed in chronological order and the more recent provide a taste of how modern authors use idioms. We would like to thank Harper Collins for permission to use a number of quotations from their computer corpus (acknowledged in the text in each instance as 'Cobuild Corpus'). We have drawn on the traditional collections of extracts for other examples, but the great majority of the contemporary illustrations are from the serendipity of our eclectic reading over the last year. We make no claims for comprehensive coverage of today's press – the quoting of *Good Housekeeping* and the *Mid Sussex Times* simply means that we read them regularly!

The bibliography is there both to show our sources and to provide a point of extended reference. It is by no means complete: it contains *some* of the books we have referred to which are collections of idioms of one type or another. To have included them all – not to mention the hundreds of books of general language and wider reference we have consulted – would have produced a bibliography of unmanageable length. If in the text of the book we refer to a specific source, the name of the author alone may be given (e.g. Edwards); if he has more than one entry in the bibliography, the name is followed by a date (e.g. Funk 1950).

Browsing

Our own love of the curious in language is, we have observed, shared by others. For them, and for ourselves, we have written the parts of this book that aim to please the browser.

The entries have been selected because they have a tale to tell. Many idioms were rejected because there was nothing interesting to say about them. Plenty more have had to be excluded because of pressures of time and space, but we hope that what remains is a satisfying cross-section of the vast range of idioms which occur in everyday English, even if it cannot claim to be a comprehensive list.

The etymology – or etymologies, since there are often alternative accounts – tries to go back to the earliest origins. We endeavour to give dates, but it is often impossible to do this with any confidence. Phrases have literal meanings, then they generally develop metaphorical uses and ultimately, in typical cases, acquire an idiomatic sense that is separate from the literal one. The form a phrase takes may also vary considerably over the years. It is therefore extremely difficult to state accurately when the *idiom* was first used – as an idiom. Wherever possible, we make the best estimate we can. We have also sometimes selected quotations to show the historical change in the use or form of phrases, as well as for their intrinsic interest.

The stories behind the expressions are in part those that authorities suggest: Our own researches have added to or replaced these, where we felt it was necessary. Quite often it is impossible to say with certainty what is the best source; in these instances, we have not hesitated to admit that doubt exists.

There are various essays strategically situated throughout the book (usually near entries on a connected theme). These are of various kinds – linguistic, historical, just plain curious – and are intended to inform and entertain. One of them is entitled **The Old Curiosity Shop of Linguistics** (see page 108). This could also serve as the watchword for all that we have tried to provide for the browser!

In conclusion, our aim has been to provide a balance of reference information and a richer varied diet for the curious; we have striven for scholarly accuracy without falling into academic pedantry. We have certainly made mistakes and would welcome comments and corrections.

We owe a debt to many. The erudition of Stevenson and Funk, for example, is extraordinary and it is complemented in recent times by the labours of Brandreth, Manser and Rees, amongst others. Our local library has been very helpful and our children, John and Anna, extremely indulgent with their occupied parents. To these and many more, our thanks.

NOTE TO THE PAPERBACK EDITION

We were delighted to receive very well-informed comments from a number of sources on the publication of the hardback edition of this book. One correspondent even devoted much of Christmas Day to the task! On the publication of the paperback edition, we would like to extend a similar invitation to readers to comment where they feel appropriate.

MAIN ESSAYS

aback: taken aback

shocked, surprised

In the days of sailing-ships, if the wind unexpectedly whipped the huge sails back against the masts, the ship was *taken aback*, that is, its progress was abruptly halted. This could happen either through faulty steering or a swift change in wind direction. The shock involved relates now to a person's reaction when suddenly stopped short by a piece of news or a surprising event.

A short distance down the unfrequented lane, the Prime Minister's car was suddenly held up by a band of masked men. The chauffeur, momentarily taken aback, jammed on the brakes.
AGATHA CHRISTIE, Poirot Investigates, The Kidnapped Prime Minister, 1925.

'I say, can I help? I'd like to.' Willie was quite taken aback at being asked.
MICHELLE MAGORIAN, Goodnight Mr Tom, 1981.

He wasted no time with social niceties, asking her immediately how many times she had tried to commit suicide. She was taken aback, but her reply was equally forthright: 'Four or five times.'
ANDREW MORTON, Diana: Her True Story, 1992.

above board

honest, straight

If a business deal is *above board* it is honest and would bear the scrutiny of all concerned. The phrase is said to refer to the dishonest practices of gamesters who would drop their hands below the board, or table, to exchange unfavourable cards. Games played with hands above board removed at least that weapon from the cheater's armoury.

Nowadays, when young women go about in kilts and are as bare-backed as wild horses, there's no excitement. The cards are all on the table, nothing's left to fancy. All's above board and consequently boring.
ALDOUS HUXLEY, Those Barren Leaves, 1925.

I shall keep inside the gates, so no one can say I've driven on the public roads without a licence. Everything above board, that's my motto.
JOHN WAIN, Hurry On Down, 1953.

Achilles' heel, an

a weak or vulnerable spot in something or someone which is otherwise strong

According to Greek mythology, Thetis held her young son Achilles by the heel while dipping him into the river Styx to make him invulnerable. Achilles' heel, however, remained dry and was his only weakness. After years as a brave and invincible warrior, Achilles was killed during the Trojan war by an arrow which pierced his heel. His deadly enemy Paris had learned of his secret and aimed at the weak spot. The full story is told in Homer's *Iliad*.

A social climber can ill afford an Achilles heel, and this particular weakness on Hutchins' part would probably be disastrous to him sooner or later.
JOHN WAIN, Hurry On Down, 1953.

usage: As in the quotation, there may be no apostrophe. Most people would insert one, however. Originally used of people and their character, it may now be applied to projects and plans. Literary.

see also: feet of clay

acid test, the

a foolproof test for assessing the value of something

A sure way to find out whether a metal was pure gold was to test it with aquafortis, or nitric acid. Most metals are corroded away by nitric acrid but gold remains unaffected.

Although the original acid test has been known for centuries, the phrase in its figurative use is only a hundred years old. If something survives the acid test it has been proved true beyond the shadow of a doubt.

The treatment accorded Russia by her sister nations in the months to come will be the acid test of their good will.
WOODROW WILSON, Address, January 8, 1918.

usage: Bordering on a cliché

Adam's ale

water

Adam's ale is water, this being all that Adam had to drink in Eden. The phrase is thought to have been introduced by the Puritans. Hyamson refers to a work by Prynne entitled *Sovereign Power of Parliament* (1643) to support this theory.

A cup of cold Adam from the next purling brook.
THOMAS BROWN, Works, 1760.

Adam's ale, about the only gift that has descended undefiled from the Garden of Eden.
EMERY A. STORRS, Adam's Ale, 1875.

usage: Literary and jocular

Adam's apple

the lump on the forepart of the throat which is especially visible in men

The *Adam's apple* is the thyroid cartilage which appears as a lump in the throat. It is said to be there as a reminder that, in the biblical story of the Garden of Eden, Adam ate the forbidden apple, a piece of which became lodged in his throat.

Having the noose adjusted and secured by
tightening above his Adam's apple.
DAILY TELEGRAPH, 1865.

add insult to injury, to

to upset someone and then to deliver a
second insult, to make an already bad
situation worse by a second insulting act
or remark

Some authorities claim a very ancient
origin for this phrase, tracing it back to a
book of fables by the Roman writer
Phaedrus from about 25 BC. The fable in
question is *The Bald Man and the Fly* in
which a man attempts to squash an insect
which has just stung him on his bald patch
by delivering a smart smack. The fly
escapes the blow and mocks him for wanting to avenge the bite of a tiny insect with
death. To the injury of the sting he has
only succeeded in adding the insult of the
self-inflicted blow.

Other authorities, however, point out
that in past centuries, while 'injury' certainly meant physical hurt, it could also
equally well apply to wounded feelings
and was synonymous with 'insult'. French
injure (from the same Latin origin *iniuria*)
has today the predominant sense of
'insult, abuse'. The effect is therefore to
intensify the original injury by adding
'insult to insult'.

And now insult was added to injury. The
Queen of the French wrote her a formal
letter, calmly announcing, as a family
event in which she was sure Victoria would
be interested, the marriage of her son,
Montpensier.
LYTTON STRACHEY, Queen Victoria, 1921.

In an insolent proclamation from Lau-
sanne General Rapp added insult to injury
by telling the heirs of a thousand years of
ordered liberty that their history showed
they could not settle their affairs without
the intervention of France.
SIR ARTHUR BRYANT, Years of Victory, 1944.

alive and kicking

very active, lively

This is one of those expressions that lend
themselves to imaginative interpretation.
Partridge (1940) suggests that it is a fish-
vendor's call to advertise his wares. The
fish are so fresh that they are still jumping
and flapping about. Another authority
says it refers to the months of a pregnancy
following 'quickening', when the mother
is able to feel the child she is carrying
moving in her womb.

The universe isn't a machine after all. It's
alive and kicking. And in spite of the fact
that man with his cleverness has dis-
covered some of the habits of our old
earth, the old demon isn't quite nabbed.
D. H. LAWRENCE, Selected Essays, 'Climbing Down
Pisgah', 1924.

I suppose if I died you'd cry a bit. That
would be nice of you and very proper. But
I'm all alive and kicking. Don't you find
me rather a nuisance?
W. SOMERSET MAUGHAM, The Bread-Winner,
1930.

usage: colloquial

amuck: to run amuck

to be frenzied, out of control

The phrase comes from a Malayan word *amoq* which describes the behaviour of tribesmen who, perhaps under the influence of opium, would work themselves into a murderous frenzy and lash out at anyone they came across.

On its first introduction in the seventeenth century, there were varying spellings. Then *amuck* became the accepted form until well-travelled writers of this century popularised the spelling *amok*. They were accused of affectedly showing off their knowledge of the source language. Nowadays either spelling is acceptable.

So that when the policeman arrived and found me running amuck with an assegai apparently without provocation, it was rather difficult to convince him that I wasn't tight.
P. G. WODEHOUSE. Uncle Fred in the Springtime. 1939.

see also: to go berserk

angel: to write like an angel

to have beautiful handwriting; to be a gifted writer of prose or poetry

Isaac D'Israeli gives the origin of the expression in *Curiosities of Literature:*

There is a strange phrase connected with the art of the calligrapher which I think may be found in most, if not in all, modern languages, *to write like an angel!* Ladies have frequently been compared with angels; they are beautiful as angels, and sing and dance like angels; but however intelligible these are, we do not so easily connect penmanship with the other celestial accomplishments. This fanciful phrase, however, has a very human origin. Among those learned Greeks who emigrated to Italy, and some afterwards into France, in the reign of Francis I, was one Angelo Vergecto, whose beautiful calligraphy excited the admiration of the learned. The French monarch had a Greek fount cast, modelled by his writing. The learned Henry Stephens, who was one of the most elegant writers of Greek, had learnt the practice from Angelo. His name became synonymous for beautiful writing, and gave birth to the phrase *to write like an angel.*

From this explanation it is evident that the phrase is descriptive not of a person's style of writing, but of his handwriting. This critic, therefore, shows a modern shift of meaning for the idiom:

Tell-tale clichés 'She writes like an angel' (it is usually a 'she'; William Trevor is an exception): this means almost nothing, except that the critic doesn't really know what else to say; I've probably done it myself. Used about: Anita Brookner, Hilary Mantel, Elizabeth Smart, Penelope Fitzgerald, Mary Wesley, A.L. Barker.
OBSERVER, April 19, 1992.

Here lies poet Goldsmith, for shortness called Noll,
Who wrote like an angel, but talked like poor Poll.
DAVID GARRICK. c1774.

usage: literary

angels: to be on the side of the angels

to agree with the Great and the Good, the orthodox authorities

The phrase is from a speech given by Benjamin Disraeli at Oxford in 1864. Addressing the vexed issue of evolution, Disraeli declared himself opposed to the theory that our early ancestors were apes and maintained that man was descended from God: 'Is man an ape or an angel? I, my lord, am on the side of the angels.'

He had an idea that by bawling and behaving offensively he was defending art against the Philistines. Tipsy, he felt himself arrayed on the side of the angels, of Baudelaire, of Edgar Allan Poe, of De Quincey, against the dull unspiritual mob.
ALDOUS HUXLEY, Point Counter Point, 1928.

He will flit through eternity, not as an archangel, perhaps, but as a mischievous cherub in a top hat. He is cherub enough already always to be on the side of the angels.
ROBERT LYND, 'Max Beerbohm', c1920.

The war brought its dividends, however. Iran and Syria, the two key players in the hostage saga, who had been regarded as virtual international pariahs for their links with terrorism and had no diplomatic relations with Britain, found themselves back on the side of the angels.
THE SUNDAY TIMES, August 11, 1991.

apple of discord

something which causes strife, argument, rivalry

In a fit of pique because she had not been invited to the marriage of Thetis and Peleus, Eris, the goddess of Discord, threw a golden apple bearing the inscription 'for the most beautiful' among the goddesses. Pallas, Hera and Aphrodite each claimed the apple and a bitter quarrel ensued. Paris, who was chosen to judge between them, decided upon Aphrodite, whereupon Pallas and Hera swore vengeance upon him and were instrumental in bringing about the fall of Troy.

It [the letter] was her long contemplated apple of discord, and much her hand trembled as she handed the document up to him.
THOMAS HARDY, c1895.

The apple of discord had, indeed, been dropped into the house of the Millbornes.
THOMAS HARDY, Life's Little Ironies, 'For Conscience Sake', 1894.

usage: Infrequent, with a literary feel

apple of one's eye, the

someone who is much loved and protected

Originally, because of its shape, the apple was a metaphor for the pupil of the eye. As one's eyesight is precious, so is the person described as the *apple of one's eye*.

The phrase as we use it today is a literal translation of a Hebrew expression that occurs five times in the Old Testament. The earliest reference is in Deuteronomy 32:10, before 1000 BC. Through the immense influence of the 1611 Authorised Version of the Bible it has become common in the English of recent centuries. Incidentally, there is some doubt that the original Hebrew word (*tappuah*) actually means apple – perhaps we should be referring to the apricot, Chinese citron or quince of one's eye!

What is an idiom?

Language follows rules. If it did not, then its users would not be able to make sense of the random utterances they read or heard and they would not be able to communicate meaningfully themselves. Grammar books are in effect an account of the regularities of the language, with notes on the minority of cases where there are exceptions to the regular patterns. Nearly all verbs, for example, add an *s* in the third person singular, present tense (*he walks, she throws, it appeals*). There are obvious exceptions to this basic 'rule' (*he can, she may, it ought*).

One of the interesting things about idioms is that they are anomalies of language, mavericks of the linguistic world. The very word *idiom* comes from the Greek *idios*, 'one's own, peculiar, strange'. Idioms therefore break the normal rules. They do this in two main areas – semantically, with regard to their meaning, and syntactically, with regard to their grammar. A consideration, then, of the semantic and syntactic elements of idioms leads to an answer to the question *What is an idiom?*

Meaning

The problem with idioms is that the words in them do not mean what they ought to mean – an idiom cannot be understood literally. A *bucket* is 'a pail' and *to kick* means 'to move with the foot'. Yet *to kick the bucket* probably does not mean 'to move a pail with one's foot', it is likely to be understood as 'to die'. The meaning of the whole, then, is not the sum of the meaning of the parts, but is something apparently quite unconnected to them. To put this another way, idioms are mostly phrases that can have a literal meaning in one context but a totally different sense in another. If someone said *Alfred spilled the beans all over the table*, there would be a nasty mess for him to clear up. If it were *Alfred spilled the beans all over the town*, he would be divulging secrets to all who would listen.

An idiom breaks the normal rules, then, in that it does not mean what you would expect it to mean. In fact the idiom is a new linguistic entity with a sense attached to it that may be quite remote from the senses of the individual words that form it. Although it is in form a phrase, it has many of the characteristics of a single word.

Grammar

The second major way in which idioms are peculiar is with regard to their grammar. There is no idiom that does not have some syntactic defect, that fails to undergo some grammatical operation that its syntactic structure would suggest is appropriate.

Different types of idioms suffer from different restrictions. With *a hot dog*, the following are not possible: *the dog is hot, the heat of the dog, today's dog is hotter than yesterday's, it's a very hot dog today*. Yet with the superficially identical phrase *a hot sun* there is no problem: *the sun is hot, the heat of the sun, today's sun is hotter than yesterday's, it's a very hot sun today*. Idioms that include verbs are similarly inflexible in the manipulations that they will permit. For instance, why is it that you can't take the separate parts of *to beat about the bush* and substitute for them a near synonym? There's no way you can say *hit about the bush*, or *beat about the shrub*. Nor can you change the definite article to the indefinite – you can't *beat about a bush*. It's not possible to make *bush* plural. Who ever heard of *beating about the bushes*? *The bush was beaten about* is as strange as the passive in *the music was faced*. Some idioms go further, exhibiting a completely idiosyncratic grammatical structure, such as intransitive verbs apparently with a direct object: *to come a cropper, to go the whole hog, to look daggers at*.

The best examples of idioms, therefore, are very fixed grammatically and it is impossible to guess their meaning from the sense of the words that constitute them. Not all phrases meet these stringent criteria. Quite often it is possible to see the link between the literal sense of the words and the idiomatic meaning. It is because a route by which many phrases become idioms involves a metaphorical stage, where the original reference is still discernible. *To skate on thin ice*, 'to court danger', is a very obvious figure of speech. The borderline between metaphor and idiom is a fuzzy one. Other idioms allow a wide range of grammatical transformations: *my father read the riot act to me when I arrived* can become *I was read the riot act by my father when I arrived* or *the riot act was read to me by my father when I arrived*. Much more acceptable than *the bush was beaten about!*

In short, it is not that a phrase is or is not an idiom; rather, a given expression is more or less 'idiomaticky', on an cline stretching from the normal, literal use of language via degrees of metaphor and grammatical flexibility to the pure idiom. To take an analogy, in the colour spectrum there is general agreement on what is green and what is yellow but it is impossible to say precisely where one becomes the other. So it is hard to specify where the flexible metaphor becomes the syntactically frozen idiom, with a new meaning all its own.

*George was the apple of his father's eye.
He did not like Harry, his second son, so
well.*
W. SOMERSET MAUGHAM, First Person Singular,
'The Alien Corn', 1931.

Adam, the apple of her eye.
HEADLINE, MID SUSSEX TIMES, September 6,
1991.

apple pie order, in

with everything neatly arranged, in its
proper place

Where there is uncertainty, the suggestions proliferate. For this phrase there is
a veritable smorgasbord of international
choice: French, Greek and American
origins are the main theories.

Two folk corruptions are suggested
from the French. The idea of the Old
French *cap à pié*, meaning 'clothed in
armour from head to foot', is that of an
immaculately ordered and fully equipped
soldier. Other researchers, Brewer
included, suggest the idiom may come
from the phrase *nappe pliée* (folded
linen), which conveys the idea of neatness
and tidiness.

In the nineteenth century, a learned
discussion in *Notes and Queries* con-
cluded that *in apple-pie order* was a corruption of *in alpha, beta order*, i.e. as
well-ordered as the letters of the (Greek)
alphabet.

Our Transatlantic cousins have also
tried to lay claim to the phrase by tracing
its origins to New England, where it is
said that housewives made pies of unbe-
lievable neatness, taking much time and
trouble to cut the apples into even slices
before arranging them just so, layer upon
perfect layer, in the crust.

The New England story may be true,
and Colonial women may indeed have

had nothing more worthwhile to do than
make patterns with the pie filling, but the
phrase was current in Britain long before
it was in America and belongs to the
British.

*Susan replied that her aunt wanted to put
the house in apple pie order.*
CHARLES READE, c1850.

*In the hall, drawing-room and dining-
room everything was always gleaming and
solidly in apple-pie order in its right place.*
DAVID GARNETT, The Golden Echo, 1953.

usage: Apple-pie may be hyphenated.

see also: spick and span, all shipshape and
Bristol fashion

apple-pie bed

A practical joke in which a bed is made
using only one sheet, folded over part
way down the bed, thus preventing the
would-be occupant from stretching out.

The phrase may be a folk corruption from
the French *nappe pliée* (folded cloth).
Alternatively, the expression may well
refer to an apple turnover, which is a
folded piece of pastry (just as the sheet
is folded over in the bed), with an apple
filling in the middle.

*No boy in any school could have more
liberty, even where all the noblemen's sons
are allowed to make apple pie beds for
their masters.*
R. D. BLACKMORE, c1870.

usage: Restricted to a context where
schoolboy japes are the norm.

augur well/ill for, to

to be a good/bad sign for the future

See *under the auspices of*

Bradford Grammar School won the final of the Daily Mail under-15 Cup with a display of maturity which augurs well for the school's senior side. They beat King Edward VII, Lytham St Anne's, 30–4 at Twickenham, conceding only one try.
COBUILD CORPUS.

auspices: under the auspices of

with the favour and support of a person or organisation; under their patronage or guidance

Auspices is made up of two Latin words: *avis*, 'a bird', and *specere*, 'to observe'. In ancient Rome it was customary to consult an augur or soothsayer before making weighty decisions. Affairs of state and military campaigns were thus decided. The augur would interpret natural phenomena (known in the trade as *auspices*) such as bird flight and bird song, and examine the entrails of victims offered for sacrifice, to make his predictions. In war, only the commander in chief would have access to this military intelligence from his advisers, so any victory won by an officer of lower rank was gained 'under the good auspices' of his commander.

The expressions *augur well* and *augur ill* have the same origin.

The French dispute therefore boils down to a straight decision between our right to teach and be taught in English, and the French right to set their own teaching standard. To side-step this dilemma, a small

but increasing number of British instructors are taking the French exam and then teaching English clients under the auspices of the Ecole de Ski Française.
WEEKEND TELEGRAPH, November 2, 1991.

Sunday's Olivier Awards, under the auspices of the Society of West End Theatre, round off the thespian prize-giving season; Matt Wolf argues that the ground-rules need to be clarified.
THE TIMES, April 24, 1992.

The mere knowledge that the Americans, under the auspices of the UN, were serious would, in any case, probably be sufficient to stop the majority of the fighting.
DAILY EXPRESS, May 25, 1992.

usage: Generally written, except in radio and TV journalism.

see also: augur well/ill for

AWOL, to go

to take leave without permission (an acronym for *absent without leave*)

Rees attests that during the American Civil War any soldier who absented himself without permission was forced to wear a placard bearing the inscription AWOL. During the First World War it was used to describe a soldier who was not present for rollcall but was not yet classified as a deserter. At this time, the four letters were pronounced individually but, sometime before the Second World War, the pronunciation 'aywol' became current.

According to Kouby, thousands of service men and women are now absent without leave, or AWOL. For them one recourse is to seek sanctuary, a place of refuge from

the authorities while considering their options.
COBUILD CORPUS.

The troops went AWOL to express their complaints about food, work, and leave time.
COBUILD CORPUS: Washington National Public Radio. 1991.

usage: Older usage inserts full stops between each letter, to indicate an abbreviation. This is a progressively less common practice. The acronym itself is nearly always written in capitals, not in lower case characters. It can now be applied to a range of situations, such as absent husbands, missing office workers, etc.

---

axe: to have an axe to grind

to have a selfish, usually secret, motive for doing something; to insist upon one's own fixed belief or course of action

All the authorities are agreed that the phrase originates in a moral tale of a boy who is flattered by a stranger into sharpening his axe for him. The problem comes in deciding which story and which author.

The *OED* and most other etymologists ascribe the phrase to American diplomat Benjamin Franklin, in an article entitled 'Too Much for your Whistle' – his early career was that of a journalist. The story concerns a young man who wants his whole axe as shiny as the cutting edge. The smith agrees to do it – provided that the man turns the grindstone himself. Of course, he soon tires and gives up, realising he has bitten off more than he can chew.

A similar story, *Who'll turn the grindstone?*, is popularly associated with

Franklin. However, it was published some twenty years after his death and was in fact written by Charles Miner. There is doubt as to its place of publication: some say in the *Luzerne Federalist* of 7/9/1810, others in the *Wilkesbarre Gleaner* of Pennsylvania in 1811.

The story itself clearly draws on Franklin's tale. It is about Poor Robert, who is talked into turning the grindstone for a man wanting to sharpen his axe. The story continues:

Tickled with the flattery, like a little fool, I went to work, and bitterly did I rue the day. It was a new ax, and I toiled and tugged, till I was almost tired to death. The school bell rung, and I could not get away; my hands were blistered and it was not half ground. At length, however, the ax was sharpened, and the man turned to me with, 'Now, you little rascal, you've played the truant – scud to school, or you'll rue it.' Alas, thought I, it was hard enough to turn grindstone, this cold day; but now to be called 'little rascal' was too much. It sunk deep in my mind, and often have I thought of it since.

Poor Robert concludes with a moral about over-politeness and excessive persuasion: '*When I see a merchant over-polite to his customers, begging them to taste a little brandy and throwing half his goods on the counter thinks I, that man has an ax to grind.*'

The true originator of the phrase is undoubtedly Charles Miner, not Benjamin Franklin.

The first essential is to examine the source of the testimony. Did the person reporting the fact observe it himself? If so, was he in a position to observe accurately? Had he any motive for reporting falsely, or for embellishing what he saw? Was he a

credulous person, or a trained scientist?
Had he an axe to grind, or was he a propa-
gandist?
I. LEVINE (ed), Philosophy, c1923.

You may fear that I am about to use my
column inches as a whetstone on which to
grind a very private axe, but I can assure
you that, so far as I can remember, I have
no personal reason to dislike this ludicrous
figure . . .
DAILY TELEGRAPH, November 22, 1991.

usage: The contemporary sense emphasises making sure one's own fixed, selfish
ideas or plans are victorious. When used
with a negative (as is often the case), the
meaning is 'impartial, neutral': *He made*
the perfect chairman as he had no axe to
grind.
    The original American spelling of *ax* is
always anglicised.

see also: to have a bee in one's bonnet

backroom boys

researchers, scientists, etc., whose hard
work is essential but is not brought to
public attention

The phrase was coined by Lord Beaver-
brook, then British Minister for Aircraft
Production, in a speech in honour of the
'unsung heroes' of the war effort, made
on March 24, 1941: *'To whom must praise*
be given? I will tell you. It is the boys
in the back room. They do not sit in the
limelight but they are the men who do the
work.'

The other detective said, 'We've got evi-
dence you don't know about yet. You'd be
surprised at what the backroom boys can

do.' I said, 'What's that supposed to
mean?' and he replied, 'You'll find out.'
First evidence that the backroom boys had
been active came when he heard from Mr
Beltrami that the police were claiming to
have found pieces of paper there.
COBUILD CORPUS.

usage: Usually plural. *One of the back-*
room boys, rather than the simple *a back-*
room boy, is the more natural singular
form. *Backroom* is normally one word,
unhyphenated.

bacon: to bring home the bacon

to succeed, to win a prize; to earn enough
money to support one's family

Two delightful possibilities are suggested
as origins of this idiom.
    For centuries, catching a greased pig
was a popular sport at country fairs. The
winner kept the pig, as the prize, and
brought home the bacon. Funk (1950)
quotes the 1720 edition of Bailey's dictionary, in which *bacon* is defined in the
narrower context of thieves' slang as 'the
Prize, of whatever kind which Robbers
make in their Enterprizes'. This implies
that at the least *bring home the bacon*
would have been understood at that
period.
    Alternatively, there could be a connec-
tion with the Dunmow Flitch. In AD1111
a noblewoman, Juga, wishing to promote
marital felicity, proclaimed that a flitch,
or side of bacon, should be awarded to
any person from any part of England who
could humbly kneel on two stones by the
church door in Great Dunmow, Essex
and swear that 'for twelve months and a
day he has never had a household brawl
or wished himself unmarried'. Between

1244 and 1772 only eight flitches were bestowed, for as Matthew Prior remarked, 'Few married folk peck Dunmow-bacon' (*Turtle and Sparrow*, 1708). Sadly, with the recent closure of the local bacon factory, the custom, revived at the end of the nineteenth century, has ceased.

None of this historical evidence is conclusive, but it is convincing enough to discount, in all probability, the attribution to Tiny Johnson. Her son, boxer Jack Johnson, defeated James J. Jeffries on July 4, 1910. She said after the fight in Reno, Nevada, 'He said he'd bring home the bacon, and the honey boy has gone and done it.' Her use of the idiom may well have popularised it, rather than originated it.

Many a time I've given him a tip that has resulted in his bringing home the bacon with a startling story.
ERLE STANLEY GARDNER, The DA Calls a Turn, 1954.

American women wanted men in whom kindness and aloofness would be so subtly blended that a relationship with them could never become a routine; but they wanted these men in a daydream situation – not as any actual substitute for the reliable bringer home of the bacon.
H. OVERSTREET, The Mature Mind, 'What We Read, See and Hear', 1977.

usage: informal

both an Old Dutch word for 'bacon' and Anglo-Saxon for 'back'. There is another connection between back and bacon: it is the pig's back which is usually cured for bacon, while the legs become hams.

This said, Brewer suggests the phrase might allude to guarding the bacon stored for the winter months from the household dogs.

As the entry *to bring home the bacon* explains, in the colloquial language of the early 1700s *bacon* meant 'prize'. Bailey comments on *to save one's bacon*: '*He has himself escaped with the Prize, whence it is commonly used for any narrow Escape.*' Grose in 1811 also defined *bacon* as thieves' cant for 'escape'. This third option appears to be the best, and earliest, source for the expression.

It was a sad and sober Oswald who that evening beheld the fairy world of Russian Ballet. True, he had the check in his pocket. True, he had saved his bacon for the time being, but at what a cost! Somehow the glory had faded from the Ballet.
RICHARD ALDINGTON, Soft Answers, 'Yes, Aunt', 1932.

These pigs could save our bacon. A European research project into the genes of pigs to improve breeding, could help to fight human ills.
THE TIMES, September 12, 1991.

usage: informal

bacon: to save one's bacon

to escape injury or difficulty; to rescue someone from trouble

Saving one's bacon is, perhaps, the same as saving one's back from a beating – a reasonable assumption, given that *baec* is

baker's dozen, a

not twelve but thirteen

The first, quite plausible suggestion for *baker's dozen* concerns medieval sales techniques. Bakers (and other tradesmen such as printers), when not selling direct to the public, gave a thirteenth loaf (or book) to the middleman. This constituted his profit.

The most popular suggestion, however, is that in thirteenth-century England, bakers had a bad reputation for selling underweight loaves. Strict regulations were therefore introduced in 1266 to fix standard weights for the various types of bread, and a spell in the pillory could be expected if short weight was given. So bakers would include an extra loaf, called the 'vantage loaf', with each order of twelve to make sure the law was satisfied.

Such was the medieval baker's unpopularity that he became the subject of a traditional puppet play in which he was shown being hurried into the flames of hell by the devil for keeping the price of bread high and giving short weight.

Mrs Joe has been out a dozen times, looking for you, Pip. And she's out now, making it a baker's dozen.
CHARLES DICKENS, Great Expectations, 1861.

It's all very well for you, who have got some baker's dozen of little ones and lost only one by the measles.
R. D. BLACKMORE, c1870.

---

bandwagon: to climb on the bandwagon

to support a plan or cause for personal profit or advantage

Electioneering in the USA has always been a noisy affair. In days gone by, especially in the southern States, a political rally would be heralded by a band playing on board a huge horse-drawn wagon which would wind its way through the streets of the town. The political candidate would be up there with the band and, as the excitement mounted, he would be joined by members of the public who wished to show their allegiance. Needless to say, only some of those who jumped on the bandwagon were loyal supporters; others were looking for reward if the candidate were elected. Although the practice is long-standing, the idiom itself is first recorded about the presidential campaign of William Jennings Bryan early this century. Familiarity with the phrase was undoubtedly helped by the considerable success of the first comedy show specially written for radio, *Band Waggon*. It ran in the UK for two years in 1938 and 1939, starring Arthur Askey and Dickie Murdoch.

Sir has been on a course . . . So back he bounces, bursting with it. The latest thing. A new bandwagon. We fear the worst.
TIMES EDUCATIONAL SUPPLEMENT, September 6, 1991.

'Fewer and fewer people are pulling the economic wagon and more and more people jumping on it.'
DAVID DUKE, candidate for governor of Louisiana, November 1991.

Inevitably, many have jumped on the bandwagon. Companies like Rhodes Design have done very nicely, producing what they admit is Shaker pastiche: dressers, bookshelves and wall cupboards from as little as £33.
WEEKEND TELEGRAPH, January 18, 1992.

Many companies hustled into the Eighties hotel boom, ignoring the principle of the old-established 'personalised' proprietor. They assumed they would make megabucks out of country-house hotels whose managing directors sat in an office block somewhere, leaving managers to run them all. Long established hotels also have the edge over the bandwagon crowd in that

they have 'customer muscle' – in other words, return business.
SUNDAY TELEGRAPH, May 17, 1992.

usage: *Waggon* is a British spelling of *wagon; bandwaggon*, however, would be unusual, even in England. It is written as one word in contemporary usage, not two. By extension, a *bandwagon* as a simple noun means a fancy, fad or vogue – see *flavour of the month*. The verb can vary: *to jump, to board*, etc.

So common as to make it a cliché.

see also: on the wagon

bandy something about, to

to spread unfavourable or untrue ideas

Bandy originated from a French word *bander*, which was a term in an early type of tennis meaning 'to hit a ball to and fro'.

In the early seventeenth century the word *bandy* became the name of an Irish team game from which hockey originated. The ball was 'bandied' (hit) back and forth from player to player, rather as rumours are spread from person to person. The same metaphor is evident in the phrase *to bandy words with someone*, meaning 'to argue'.

The shape of the crooked stick bandy players used has given rise to the description *bandy-legged*.

'*People should be careful when they bandy about words like freedom,*' said Dr Kovacs bitterly, *after well-meaning social workers moved the old ladies out into the community.*
DAILY EXPRESS, August 30, 1991.

Sex, I'm afraid, is the topic to be aired, bandied and thrashed out at the third of the Sunday Times literary evenings.
THE SUNDAY TIMES, March 22, 1992.

bandy words with someone, to

to argue, quarrel

See *to bandy something about*

Alexander did not join Lodge, Crowe and the rest. He sat on one end, high up in tree shadows, listening to Spenser and Ralegh bandying words, his own, their own, to unseen melodies in the bushes.
COBUILD CORPUS.

usage: Often found in the negative: let's not bandy words, I'm not going to bandy words with you.

bandy-legged

having legs which curve outwards from the knee

See *to bandy something about*

When they put on cheap versions of the sack suit they looked misshapen, even deformed. As Berger puts it, they seemed 'uncoordinated, bandy-legged, barrel-chested, low-arsed . . . coarse, clumsy, brutelike.'
COBUILD CORPUS.

bank on something, to

to count or depend on something

Few people today would keep their life savings hidden under the mattress; a bank is generally reckoned to be a safer place. Similarly, we *bank on* people or institutions that we consider dependable. The first banks were in medieval Venice, then a prosperous centre for world trade. They were no more than benches set up in main squares by men who both changed and lent money. Their benches would be laden with currencies from the different trading countries. The Italian for bench or counter is *banco*. The English word 'bank' comes from this and here we have the origin of this phrase.

'I can put this entire structure at your disposal for assistance purposes.'

'No, thank you. I prefer to bank on my own complete anonymity. It is the best weapon I have.'
COBUILD CORPUS.

The Super-Pocket may at last accept the fact that you have been a good loser and give you a wintry smile. But don't bank on it.
COBUILD CORPUS.

usage: I'm banking on . . . is current but the negative phrase *I wouldn't bank on it* is just as common. *A banker* is used in racing and gambling circles to mean a sure bet.

beliefs. The phrase was used figuratively by Napoleon whilst in exile on St Helena in 1817: '*I love a brave soldier who has undergone the baptism of fire*' (O'Meara, *Napoleon in Exile*), and later by Napoleon III in a letter to his wife, the Empress Eugénie, about their young son's first experiences of war at the battle of Saarbruck on August 10, 1870: '*Louis has just received his baptism of fire.*' It must have been a terrifying ordeal for a boy of fourteen.

The phrase is still used in military contexts for a soldier's first experience of hostile fire, but also much more widely for any sudden and demanding initiation.

We do not blood young cricketers for long enough in Test cricket. This year a new, young team is chosen. The West Indies are beaten for the first time in 30 years in England. Now after two defeats the youth policy is cracked, with, for example, Graeme Hick dropped. The youngsters have been given a baptism of fire. We desperately need stability. We should leave the side alone, give them the winter tour together, and I bet within a year or two we would have a strong batting line up.
DAILY MAIL, August 7, 1991.

Diana admits that she was not easy to handle during that baptism of fire. She was often in tears as they travelled to the various venues, telling her husband that she simply could not face the crowds.
THE SUNDAY TIMES, June 7, 1992.

baptism of fire

a harsh initiation into a new experience

Baptism of fire describes the horrific death by burning suffered by multitudes of sixteenth- and seventeenth-century Christians who were martyred for their

barge pole: wouldn't touch it with a barge pole

used of someone or something one loathes or distrusts, from which one wants to keep one's distance

'*Without a payre of tongs no man will touch her*,' protested an unknown author in the seventeenth century (*Wit Restor'd*, 1658), and in the mid-nineteenth century Dickens wrote: '*I was so ragged and dirty that you wouldn't have touched me with a pair of tongs*' (*Hard Times*, 1854). This was the original expression and the allusion is clear: tongs are used to pick up objects which are dirty or potentially harmful. Our present-day expression, *wouldn't touch it with a barge pole*, is much more recent, originating from the turn of the century, and emphasises one's detestation for someone or something by the desire to keep it at a great distance.

A third former Foreign Secretary could stroll into the post to everyone's delight at Westminster, Hong Kong and Peking. But the ever-popular Lord Carrington has let it be known he would not touch it with a barge pole.
DAILY MAIL, October 11, 1991.

Meanwhile, the mere mention of a leasing company is likely to see the average City fund manager reaching for the nearest barge pole, after earlier well-publicised disasters in the sector typified by the foundering of the once highly-regarded British and Commonwealth financial services combine under the weight of the Atlantic Computers leasing business.
THE TIMES, April 30, 1992.

usage: Informal. Where both expressions were originally used to refer to people one disliked or distrusted, the modern idiom can just as easily apply to a make of car or even a business proposal.

bark up the wrong tree, to

to follow a wrong line of enquiry

This is an early nineteenth-century American phrase from racoon hunting. Racoons are hunted at night because of their nocturnal habits. Hunting dogs chase the quarry up a tree and then wait down below barking until the huntsman arrives with his gun. A dog who mistakes the tree in the darkness, or is outwitted by the prey scrambling across to an adjacent tree, wastes time and energy barking up the wrong one.

He reminded me of the meanest thing on God's earth, an old coon dog, barking up the wrong tree.
DAVY CROCKETT. Sketches and Eccentricities. 1833.

Pisces. *Have a bit of faith in yourself this weekend. Ignore the voice of self doubt that is trying to suggest you're barking up the wrong tree.*
TODAY, September 14, 1991.

usage: informal
see also: on the right/wrong tack

barrel: over a barrel

helpless to act, at the mercy of others

At one time a person who had almost drowned would be draped, face down, over a barrel which would then be gently rocked back and forth until all the water had drained from the victim's lungs. The person was, of course, in no fit state to act for himself and was totally dependent on his rescuers. In the same way, someone experiencing business difficulties might find himself powerless to act and forced to accept another's terms.

Then you'd be over a barrel.
RAYMOND CHANDLER, The Big Sleep, 1939.

Tenants are having their tenancies terminated. The brewers have got their former partners over a barrel.
BBC RADIO 4, Face the Facts, October 1991.

usage: The formulation *to have someone over a barrel* suggests a malicious intent.

battle axe, a

an overbearing and belligerent (usually middle-aged or old) woman

This originated in America in the early years of the women's rights movement. *The Battle Axe* was a journal published by the movement and the expression is thought to come from it. The term was obviously not originally meant as an insult but as a war cry. The fact that it soon came to refer to a domineering and aggressive woman of a certain age could well be a reflection on what many people thought of the movement's members.

The days when secretaries refused to work for women are I hope on the way out. Mainly, I think, because the old-fashioned 'battle-axe' type of lady executive, like the old-fashioned dedicated secretary, is disappearing from the scene.
COBUILD CORPUS.

usage: colloquial

beam: broad in the beam

having wide hips

See *to be on one's beam ends*

beam ends: on one's beam ends

having nothing left to live on, in a difficult financial position

In a wooden sailing ship the beams were the vast cross-timbers which spanned the width of the vessel, to prevent the sides from caving inwards and to support the deck. So, if a ship was on its beam ends it was listing at a dangerous angle, almost on its side. The sense of a ship being in an alarming predicament transfers to a person in financial jeopardy.

Broad in the beam refers to a ship which is particularly wide, and is now put to unflattering use to describe a woman with ample hips.

'One of his boots is split across the toe.'
  'Ah! of course! On his beam ends. So – it begins again! This'll about finish father.'
JOHN GALSWORTHY, In Chancery, 1920.

You see how all this works in. He is on his beam ends before the murder. He decides on the murder as his only chance of keeping above water.
FREEMAN WILLIS CROFTS, The 12.30 from Croydon, 1934.

bean feast, a

a social event, a party

Once a year it was customary for employers to hold a dinner for their workers. Opinions differ as to what was offered to eat. One authority says that it was a bean-goose (the bird's name coming from a bean-shaped mark on its beak) and others that beans made up the main dish. Whatever the feast consisted of, it was a rowdy and somewhat vulgar occasion but much looked forward to throughout the year.

An abbreviation of *beanfeast* passed into the language and so we have *beano*, also meaning 'a spree .

'*Oh sure. You just go up top and take a crowsnest at the scenery. All you'll get is a beanfeast of bulrushes.*' *Sally climbed on top of the cabin and scanned the horizon.*
COBUILD CORPUS.

usage: Informal. Sometimes written as one word.

beat a (hasty) retreat, to

to leave, usually in a hurry; to abandon an undertaking

Drums were formerly very much a part of the war machine as soldiers marched to the drum and took their orders from its beat. Retreat was one such order and would sound each evening. It was a signal for the soldiers to get behind their lines as darkness fell and for the guards to present themselves for duty. Of course, if fighting were taking place but things were not going well, the retreat would sound to signal to the army to withdraw.

The postman handed it to me with a nervous smile – and a parcel – and beat a hasty retreat to his van.
GOOD HOUSEKEEPING. September 1991.

Mr Kelly told how his team found a lead casket containing radioactive cobalt 60 in a bunker, but left hurriedly in case of health risks.
  '*We beat a hasty retreat then waited until we had a geiger counter,*' *he said.*
DAILY MAIL. August 7, 1991.

. . . foreign correspondency, at least on television, remains fundamentally a male preserve and when the drums for war beat, women, it is felt, should, in response, beat a retreat.
SUNDAY TELEGRAPH. April 26, 1992.

usage: Hasty commonly intensifies the original expression. *To beat retreat* is a military musical expression only.

beat about the bush, to

to express oneself in a round-about way; to avoid coming to the point.

In a hunt beaters are employed to thrash the bushes and undergrowth in order to frighten game from its cover. It is they who beat about the bush; the huntsman is more direct or, in the words of George Gascoigne (1525–77), 'He bet about the bush whyles others caught the birds.'

My mother came round one day and said, 'My God, you're growing so boring! All you talk about is children and schools – you have to do something, dear.' She didn't beat about the bush, she was lovely.
GOOD HOUSEKEEPING. April 1991.

Creativity

Language is a very productive thing. New words – neologisms – are coming into existence all the time, to such an extent that there are now several dictionaries of just new words, and new editions and supplements to long-established dictionaries. Many of the neologisms, though, die out fairly quickly. Catchphrases, fads, gimmicks hold the popular fancy for a short while and then disappear. Others meet a particular need and survive whilst they have a function to fulfil. For instance, verbs come from nouns quite commonly. This process has been going on for centuries. If we go back as early as 1606, there's 'to eavesdrop', which comes from 'eaves-dropper', and right back to 1225 when 'to beg' came from the word 'begard' or 'beggen'.

These are new words derived from existing words, a phenomenon that applies to idioms as well. For instance, the expression *to be in the red* means 'to be in debt and to have an overdraft'. It comes from the accountancy and bookkeeping practice of using red ink to indicate debts. It was first found around 1920. By analogy, amounts in credit are indicated *in the black*.

The iron curtain of the post-war era, popularised by Churchill in a speech on March 5, 1946, in its turn gave rise to *the bamboo curtain*, metaphorically dividing the West from mainland China.

There is another phrase which is productive in the same sort of way. In Victorian times, the 'uniform' of an office worker was a black coat. So the phrase grew a *black-coated worker*. This referred to his social status and security in a good job – perhaps as a clerk in an office. That was in Victorian England, and it has been suggested that in the turmoil of the First World War period an American counterpart of the British phrase arose: *the white collar worker*. The synonym could perhaps have been formed by analogy.

It is interesting to see how in more recent years there have been other extensions to this phrase. We find now the *blue collar worker*. There is an example in Webster's American dictionary of this: *They refer to warehousemen, longshoremen, farmers, miners, mechanics, construction workers and other blue collar workers*. It was first found in about 1950 in America and came across the Atlantic in about 1958. There is at least one more stage in the story. Since then, people have begun to refer to *pink collar jobs* – low-paid jobs mainly for women, such as cleaners, hair-dressers, waitresses.

The desire to be creative and productive with language permeates every aspect of it: idioms are no exception.

Kim said: 'Dad kicked me into shape
when I needed it most. He told me what I
didn't want to hear and didn't beat about
the bush – he was brutally honest.'
SUN, May 18, 1992.

usage: Beat around the bush is also found.

beaten track: off the beaten track

away from the normal, the ordinary; geo-
graphically removed

The countryside is criss-crossed by many
footpaths and bridleways trampled down
and beaten hard with the passage of time
and many feet. This phrase is now a
favourite with holiday tour operators,
who exhort potential clients to take a
long-haul holiday away from the over-
crowded European resorts.

To . . . Pace the Round Eternal?
To beat and beat The beaten Track?
EDWARD YOUNG, Night Thoughts, 1742.

As leader I was also navigator-in-chief and
felt it would be good for the group to dis-
cover parts of the island well off the beaten
track.
MID SUSSEX TIMES, August 16, 1991.

usage: The phrase may be applied geo-
graphically in a more literal way, but also
commonly refers figuratively to thoughts,
courses of action, etc. It may be shortened to *the beaten track.*

bed: to get out of bed on the wrong side

to be bad tempered, grumpy

The wrong side of the bed is the left.
According to a superstition that goes back
to Roman times, it is unlucky to get out
of bed on the left side because that is
where evil spirits dwell and their influence
will then be with you through your wak-
ing hours. Someone who is expecting to
be the butt of a malevolent spirit's whims
throughout the day is thrown into an irri-
table frame of mind from the outset and
so, when a person is in a bad temper, he
is accused of *getting out of bed on the*
wrong side.

You rose on the wrong side of the bed
today.
RICHARD BROME, The Court-Beggar, 1653.

Someone got out of bed on the wrong side
this morning!
GEORGETTE HEYER, Envious Casca, 1941.

usage: To get up on the wrong side of the
bed is a less common alternative.

see also: to set off on the wrong foot

bee: to be the bee's knees

to be or consider oneself superior to
others in some way

When bees climb inside the cup of a
flower, pollen sticks to their bodies. The
bees then carefully comb this off and
transfer it to pollen sacks on their back
legs. Some authorities believe that the
expression refers to the delicate way bees
bend their knees as they perform this
operation.
  Rees, however, makes a strong case for
an alternative theory. He argues that,
although there has long been a preoccupation with bees and their knees, which
has given rise to a variety of expressions

over the last two hundred years or so, the phrase under discussion here only dates back as far as the 1920s when it was coined as an amusing rhyme. He points to the importance of rhyme, assonance and alliteration in the origins of many expressions and a vogue in the twenties for combining features of the body or articles of clothing with parts of animals, to bizarre effect. Thus we also find *the cat's miaow, the cat's pyjamas, the eel's heel, the elephant's instep,* and many more.

The Royalton, re-opened by Steve Rubell of Studio 54 and designed by Philippe Starck, has been the bee's knees of the New York hotel world for the past year or two. There is simply no equivalent to it in Britain, where a hotel is marketed as chic if it can boast an electric kettle in each room, a fruit machine in the bar and a full-colour photograph of an under-manager in the hallway.
THE SUNDAY TIMES, August 11, 1991.

usage: informal

bee: to have a bee in one's bonnet

to be obsessed by an idea

The phrase has been in popular use for over three hundred years. Whether the metaphor alludes to the frenetic buzzing of thought, like the protests of the trapped bee, or the frenzied behaviour of the wearer of the bonnet, convinced that he will be stung at any moment, is up to the reader to decide.

Like all specialists, Bauerstein's got a bee in his bonnet. Poisons are his hobby, so, of course, he sees them everywhere.
AGATHA CHRISTIE, The Mysterious Affair at Styles, 1920.

The new Spanish ambassador, with the bee of an economic blockade buzzing in his head, advised Alva to seize English shipping and goods before he knew that Elizabeth intended to appropriate the treasure.
J. E. NEALE, Queen Elizabeth, 1971.

usage: informal

bee line: to make a bee line for

to use the shortest route between two places

In days gone by it was thought that bees were single minded in their work and always flew in a straight line back to the hive. Unfortunately, this piece of country lore has since been proved untrue.

There is a similar snippet of country wisdom about crows, who are supposed to fly directly to their intended destination, hence the expression *as the crow flies*.

I'm going to get home as soon as I can – strike a bee line.
W. D. HOWELLS, c1880.

You can make a bee-line for the South of France, or slip into the Low Countries within minutes.
SALLY LINE brochure, 1991.

usage: The hyphen is usually omitted.

see also: as the crow flies

bell the cat, to

to undertake a difficult mission at great
personal risk

An ancient fable, related by Langland in
Piers Plowman (1377), tells of a colony
of mice who met together to discuss how
they could thwart a cat who was terroris-
ing them. One young mouse suggested
hanging a bell around the cat's neck so
that its movements would be known. This
plan delighted the rest until an old mouse
asked the obvious question, 'Who will
bell the cat?'

Scottish history records a very perti-
nent instance of the expression in action.
Members of the nobility at the court of
James III were suspicious of the king's
new favourite, an architect named Cochran. The nobles met together secretly
and determined to get rid of him, whereupon Lord Gray asked, 'Who will bell the
cat?' Archibald Douglas, Earl of Angus
was prompt with his reply: 'I shall bell the
cat.' He did as he had promised, seizing
Cochran and hanging him over the bridge
at Lauder, an act which earned him the
nickname 'Bell-the-Cat Douglas.'

'Mrs and Miss Jennynge must bell the cat.'
'What have I to do with cats?' inquired
Mrs Jennynge wildly. 'I hate cats.'
'My dear madam, it is a well-known
proverb,' explained Mrs Armytage. 'What
I mean is, that it is you who should ask
Mr Josceline to say grace this evening.'
JAMES PAYN, c1880.

A fine manly fellow, who has belled the
cat with fortune.
WALTER SCOTT, Journal, 1890.

usage: dated

berserk, to go

to be in a state of wild and uncontrollable
fury

Berserk is a nineteenth-century
borrowing from Norse mythology which
tells of a fierce warrior who, casting aside
weapons and armour, would work himself into a murderous frenzy before plunging into battle clad only in his bearskin
coat. This earned him the name Berserker (from *bern*, 'a bear' and *serkr*, 'a
coat'). Twelve sons succeeded him, each
named Berserker and each as furious and
reckless in battle as he.

Some Viking warriors who emulated
the example of Berserker and his sons
earned recognition of their prowess by
being referred to as berserkers. For the
story of a berserk Italian warrior, see *like
billio*.

A few years ago, we gave a teenage party.
It was very memorable. Gatecrashers
crashed. Boys vomited. Girls had hyster-
ics. The police were called. The neigh-
bours went berserk.
GOOD HOUSEKEEPING, November 1991.

Five more victims were hurt, two seri-
ously, as the 44-year-old went berserk in
front of screaming children including his
own son and two daughters.
DAILY MAIL, January 2, 1992.

The Medusa Touch *Tedious hokum about*
a famous author who discovers an ability
to will disasters by remote control.
Richard Burton plays the novelist who
goes berserk and beyond the control of
psychiatrist Lee Remick.
WEEKEND TELEGRAPH, January 8, 1992.

see also: to run amuck

Betty Martin: all my eye and Betty Martin

A lot of nonsense

There are several suggested etymologies for this phrase. Partridge found mention of an actress, a certain Betty Martin, in the eighteenth century. She apparently used the exclamation 'My eye!' regularly. Conveniently, she lived around the time of the first written version of the full expression, as recorded in the *OED* Supplement: '*Physic, to old, crazy Frames like ours, is all my eye and Betty Martin – (a sea phrase that Admiral Jemm frequently makes use of).*' Perhaps Betty Martin's part was to help popularise an originally nautical idiom.

The sea plays a role in another possible derivation. Radford relays the tradition that the nonsensical English represents a British sailor's garbled version of words heard in an Italian church, '*Ah mihi, beate Martini*', meaning 'Ah grant me, blessed St Martin'. In favour of this supposition is the well-attested practice of Englishmen turning the unfamiliar into something that is at least superficially recognisable. The *Elephant and Castle*, for example, is reckoned to have come from the Spanish *Infanta de Castilla*.

In yet another story Betty Martin was a gypsy woman who had been taken before a magistrate. After the policeman responsible for her arrest had given his evidence, the woman flew at him, dealing him a hefty blow to the face and screaming all the while that what he had said was *all my eye*. The officer's eye was badly bruised in the incident and he was then forced to endure much teasing from the public, who would call after him, '*My eye and Betty Martin.*' Responsibility for this story lies with Dr Butler, one-time head-

master of Shrewsbury school and later Bishop of Lichfield.

A final possibility is suggested by Rees. The linguistic device of rhyming slang may account for the phrase's popularity – *Martin* does rhyme with *fartin*'! The idiom's negative sense of 'nonsense' fits quite well with the scatological *fartin*'.

The decision rests with the reader but, as a last word, a certain Mr Cuthbert Bede claimed in the December 1856 issue of *Notes and Queries* that he had come across the phrase in an old black-letter volume bearing the title *The Ryghte Tragycal Historie of Master Thomas Thumbe*. If this is so, then the phrase could be some four hundred years old.

I'm not such an oaf as to think that these things are all my eye or anything of that sort. But psychoanalysis was after all conceived in the old days of Vienna, when the Hapsburgs, pretty women, and neat ankles were going to last to eternity.
ANGUS WILSON, Hemlock and After, 1952.

I do wonder whether L'Inglese come si parla was published in a spirit of mischief by someone obsessed with Ealing Films, because actually the story that emerges from its pages is rather like an Ealing plot. Poor guileless foreigner (played by Alec Guinness, perhaps) works hard to overcome loneliness by using authentic popular slang such as 'nose-rag', 'old horse', and 'cheese it!' and nobody knows what the hell he is talking about. 'Dhets ool mai ai end Beti Maarten!' he exclaims jocularly ('That's all my eye and Betty Martin'), amid general shrugs.
LYNNE TRUSS, The Times, April 23, 1992.

usage: Spoken, colloquial. As one of the quotations above shows, it is now rather dated. Generally used as an exclamation, rejecting another speaker's statement. As with all longer idioms, it is often reduced in length, to *It's all my eye* or even *My eye*. This last form is particularly likely to be an exclamation.

bib: best bib and tucker

one's best clothes

Bib brings to mind the cloth tied under a baby's chin to absorb the dribbles. In the late seventeenth century, bibs of a sort were also worn by adults to protect their clothes from spills. A tucker was a woman's garment, this time a flimsy piece of lace or muslin tucked into the top of low-cut dresses and ending in a lacy frill at the neck. Some authorities think that in the expression *best bib and tucker*, the bib referred to a man's attire and the tucker to a woman's. Others consider that the entire expression was originally only used to describe a lady, dressed in all her finery for a special occasion. The passage of time and changes in fashion meant that no one remembered what bibs and tuckers were any more and so gradually the term came to be applied to men as well.

His host warns him when he gets to the threshold: 'Sorry, we have a silly rule here. Shoes off. Brings mud in.' If Super Country's house happens to be large, enormous sections of it, the best, will be shut off and unheated. 'We only open these up when we have to put on our best bib and tucker.'
COBUILD CORPUS.

usage: Informal. *To wear* or *be in one's best bib and tucker* are common alternative formulations.

Proverbs and idioms

Proverbs exist in all languages and written collections of them date back to the earliest times. A good example is the Book of Proverbs in Jewish sacred writings, which is of course also found in the Old Testament of the Christian Bible.

Proverbs are universally held in high esteem, whereas idioms have had to struggle for recognition. Perhaps this is a little surprising, as there's some overlap between idioms and proverbs. Proverbs can be defined as 'memorable short sayings of the people, containing wise words of advice or warning'. Many idioms share at least some of these characteristics. For example, are *a stitch in time saves nine* and *more haste, less speed* better considered as proverbs or idioms? Or *better late than never, the more, the merrier, out of sight, out of mind, seeing is believing*? Idioms or proverbs? Proverbs, probably, but two idiom experts feel that they can class them as idioms without, as they put it, 'stretching the definition too far'.

A further cause for confusion is the capacity of an idiomatic phrase – idioms are normally phrases, whereas proverbs are whole sentences – to be adapted into proverbial form. For example, the phrase (idiom?) *to cry for the moon* (see **Moonshine**, page 130), meaning 'to ask for the impossible', can easily become the full sentence (proverb?) *Don't cry for the moon* or, better, *Only fools cry for the moon*.

big wig, a

someone of importance

This expression goes back to the seventeenth and eighteenth centuries when all gentlemen wore wigs. Some wigs, however, were bigger than others. Bishops, judges and aristocrats, for instance, were attired in the full-length wigs that present-day high court judges still wear. Thus people of importance came to be known as *big wigs*.

Some contemporary *big wigs*, however, are becoming disenchanted with their headgear. The first woman Speaker of the House of Commons refused to wear her wig on the grounds of comfort at work and Lord Chief Justice Taylor thinks that wigs and robes make the judiciary seem out of touch and remote. Perhaps the time is coming when, like other figures of importance, they will be *big wigs* in name only.

The biggest wig in the most benighted Chancery.
THOMAS CARLYLE, Frederick the Great, 1858.

Some big-wig has come in his way who is going to dine with him.
ANTHONY TROLLOPE, The Belton Estate, 1865.

So, while the Government – which means you and me, the taxpayers – spends a mint on preserving our heritage, our big-wigs apply themselves to dismantling our traditions.
DAILY EXPRESS, April 30, 1992.

So far, so good. After all, if someone is producing food for commercial sale from their own kitchen, it seems only right that it should be inspected to make sure it is not a health hazard. But the EC wants to go much further. The Brussels bigwigs have decided that by the end of 1992 we

should operate under common legislation. So the dreaded directives have come into being . . .
GOOD HOUSEKEEPING, July 1992.

usage: Can be written as one word, two words or hyphenated.

see also: to pull the wool over someone's eyes

billio, like

with enthusiasm, with gusto

This expression of exuberance seems to have originated in the nineteenth century, according to Brandreth. Two appropriate theories have been advanced. The first is that it makes reference to the action of Stephenson's steam engine, the Puffing Billy. The second links the phrase to Nino Biglio, a lieutenant under Garibaldi, who would plunge into the fray exhorting his men to 'follow me and fight like Biglio'.

A third theory, that the phrase comes from the name of Joseph Billio (a particularly zealous Puritan and founder of the Independent Congregation at Maldon, Essex in 1682), is perhaps inappropriate for a nineteenth-century term unless the energetic Joseph managed to inspire a revival in Maldon from beyond the grave.

'*But, Bertie, this sounds as if you weren't going to sit in.*'
    '*It was how I meant it to sound.*'
    '*You wouldn't fail me, would you?*'
    '*I would. I would fail you like billy-o.*'
P. G. WODEHOUSE, The Code of the Woosters, 1938.

usage: spoken, colloquial

bird: a little bird told me

a secret source told me

Most authorities subscribe to the view that this phrase is a biblical one and can be found in Ecclesiastes 10:20: '*Curse not the King, no not in thy thought; and curse not the rich in thy bedchamber: for a bird of the air shall carry the voice, and that which hath wings shall tell the matter.*'

There is a story which is an unlikely origin but is worth telling for its charm. All the birds were summoned to appear before Solomon. Only the Lapwing did not appear. When questioned on his disobedience, Lapwing explained that he was with the Queen of Sheba and that she had resolved to visit King Solomon. The King immediately began preparations for the visit. Meanwhile Lapwing flew to Ethiopia and told the Queen that King Solomon had a great desire to see her. The magnificent meeting, as we know, then took place. Idiomatic little birds have been English messengers since the middle of the sixteenth century.

'*Now just how did you know that? I only fixed it up this morning.*'
'*Ah – a little bird. One bird, little, pretty: to wit, your cousin Margot. Met her outside the office this morning.*'
F. W. CROFTS. The 12.30 from Croydon. 1934.

usage: jocular

biscuit: to take the biscuit

to win the prize; to be the most outstanding or outrageous instance of something

See *to take the cake*

'*I've known some pretty cool customers in my time and particularly since they stopped hanging but this one takes the biscuit. If you ask me he's a raving psychopath.*' Flint dismissed the idea. '*Psychopaths crack easy,*' he said.
COBUILD CORPUS.

usage: Mostly used today in a tone of exasperation, with the sense of *That's too much, That's going too far.*

bit: to take the bit between one's teeth

to be so keen to do something that one cannot be restrained, to pursue one's own course relentlessly

The 'bit' is the metal mouthpiece on a horse's bridle that enables the rider to direct the animal. The horse is only sensitive to the rider's direction while the bit is in the right place in his mouth. If he takes the bit between his teeth he can no longer feel the pull of the reins and the rider has lost control of him.

The expression is a very old one, dating back in Greek culture to Aeschylus in 470 BC: '*You take the bit in your teeth, like a new-harnessed colt.*' It is in the Hebrew Wisdom literature of the Old Testament: '*Be ye not like the horse, or like the mule, that have no understanding, whose mouth must be held in with bit and bridle, lest they come near unto thee.*'

The meaning through millennia has been of obstinate self-will. Comparatively recently, it has developed the sense of determinedly setting out on a task, without necessarily negative overtones.

On the Sunday morning old Heppenstall fairly took the bit between his teeth, and gave us thirty-six minutes on Certain

Popular Superstitions. I was sitting next to Steggles in the pew, and I saw him blench visibly.
P. G. WODEHOUSE, The Inimitable Jeeves, 1924.

I can see no particular virtue in writing quickly; on the contrary, I am well aware that too great a facility is often dangerous, and should be curbed when it shows signs of getting the bit too firmly between its teeth.
NOEL COWARD, Future Indefinite, 1954.

bite off more than one can chew, to

to try to do more than one can manage or is capable of

An American phrase of late nineteenth-century origin. It probably refers to the offering of a bite from a plug of tobacco. A greedy man would naturally bite off as much as he could but was then unable to chew his mouthful comfortably.

According to Mark Twain, a humorous ritual built up around tobacco chewing in which a plug of tobacco would be offered for a free bite. The biter would then take off as much as he could fit into his mouth, whereupon the owner of the plug would gaze at the stump of tobacco which remained and invite his friend to exchange the plug for the piece he had bitten off. One can easily imagine the playful prohibition 'Now, Tom, don't bite off more than you can chew' as part of the ritual conversation.

'What did the voice say?'

'It said – only it sounded much more apocalyptic in the middle of the night – "You've bitten off more than you can chew, my girl."'
GRAHAM GREENE, Our Man in Havana, 1958.

Babies born this weekend have, if born before 10.11 p.m. tomorrow, the Moon in adventurous, enthusiastic, optimistic Sagittarius. With the Sun in easy-going Libra too, they will have a regular tendency to bite off more than they can chew – but will learn a lot and go a long way as a result.
TODAY, 12 October, 1991.

Virgo – Hard work is only too familiar to you, so do not bite off more than you can chew now, even if career matters seem a haven of calm compared with your emotional life. Your health will need more care over the next four weeks.
DAILY EXPRESS, January 20, 1992.

usage: informal

bite the bullet, to

to show courage in facing a difficult or unpleasant situation

On the battlefields of the last century, wounded men, operated on without the benefits of pain-killing drugs and anaesthetics, were encouraged to bite on a bullet to help them forget their intense pain.

Taking a longer term view of personal computing, Apple is also following new technology directions in speech and character recognition, speech synthesis and artificial intelligence to make Macs easier to use . . . But all of these enhancements will require more power . . . To follow these initiatives, Apple has had to bite the bullet and move to a high-performance RISC technology, even though it is incompatible with current Motorola 680XO CISC devices.
MACUSER, May 1, 1992.

usage: The phrase has been a favourite with politicians who have the unenviable task of encouraging the public to face up to hardship with fortitude.

Bite on *the bullet* is sometimes found.

bite the dust, to

to be finished, to be worn out; to die

Although it was popularised by the American western genre, especially in the *Nick Carter Library* at the turn of the century, the phrase has a classical origin going back to Homer's *Iliad* (c850 BC). We have the translation of the American poet William Cullen Bryant (1870) to thank for the modern expression:

. . . his fellow warriors, many a one,
Fall round him to the earth and bite the dust.'

English writers and translators before Bryant used other words for 'dust': *ground* (John Gay, Lord Byron, Cowper) and *sand* (Pope).

The original meaning of the expression was 'to fall in battle' but modern usage has extended this and now almost anything that has succumbed to disrepair or failure, from a lawn-mower to a business, is said to have *bitten the dust*.

And so another hero is about to bite the dust – is nothing sacred? This time it's Columbus, the intrepid navigator who, as we all know, stumbled across the New World after braving the unknown ocean. Or did he?
DAILY MAIL, October 16, 1991.

usage: A cliché. Used very much in tongue-in-cheek humorous fashion today.

bitter end, to the

to the very last, until overtaken by death or defeat

The anchor cable on sailing ships was coiled around the bitts, stout posts set in the deck. The last portion of cable, which was attached to the bitts themselves, was known as *the bitter end*. Captain John Smith explains it thus in his *Seaman's Grammar* of 1627: '*A Bitter is but the turne of a Cable about the bitts, and veare it out by little and little. And the Bitters end is that part of the Cable doth stay within boord.*' If it were necessary to let out the anchor cable to the bitter end, the likelihood of disaster would be much greater, since there would be nothing left in reserve. It is probable, however, that the phrase was influenced by a verse in the Old Testament book of Proverbs, chapter 5, verse 4: 'But her end is bitter as wormwood, sharp as a two-edged sword.'

Stockmar had told him that he must 'never relax' and he never would. He would go on, working to the utmost and striving for the highest, to the bitter end. His industry grew almost maniacal.
LYTTON STRACHEY, Queen Victoria, 1921.

My correspondent assures me that I can sire little children right up until the bitter end if I have the inclination, although this is hardly likely. Our problem is not ability, it is simply that we lose our 'get up and go'.
MID SUSSEX TIMES, August 16, 1991.

And by the way, the plan did work – nearly everyone did stay to the bitter end.
NATIONAL ASSOCIATION OF PENSION FUNDS, EC Bulletin, January 1991.

usage: Although *bitter* with the meaning 'sharp to the taste' is unconnected historically, the connotations of *to the bitter end* go beyond the basic sense of 'to the last extremity' and suggest a sticky and unpleasant last act. There is undoubtedly a coalescence of meaning.

usage: The original high seriousness has weakened dramatically today. The phrase is now used mainly in unimportant social contexts. It takes various forms: *book* can be singular; a verb *to black* or *declare black* derives from the main expression.

see also: to blacklist

black books: to be in someone's black books

to be out of favour with someone, to be in disgrace

Black books have a very long history. The earliest ones seem to be collections of the laws of the times or of accounts of contemporary practice. The *black books* referred to in the idiom are reports on monastic holdings and allegations of corruption within the church, compiled by Henry VIII during his struggle to sever his kingdom from Papal authority. The first one listed monasteries that were alleged to be centres of 'manifest sin, vicious, carnal, and abominable living'. In the light of this 'evidence', Parliament was persuaded in 1536 to dissolve them and assign their property to the king.

In roughly the same period, black books were also held by medieval merchants who kept records of people who did not pay for goods. Black lists were compiled of men who had gone bankrupt. In 1592 Robert Greene wrote in his *Black Bookes Messenger*, 'Ned Browne's villanies are too many to be described in my Blacke Booke.'

Later, Proctors of the Universities of Oxford and Cambridge took to keeping black books which listed the names of students guilty of misconduct. So did military regiments. No one in them could go on to a degree or higher rank.

black sheep of the family, the

a member of a family who has fallen foul of the others, who is in disgrace

Shepherds dislike black sheep since their fleece cannot be dyed and is therefore worth less than white. Shepherds in earlier times also thought that black sheep disturbed the rest of the flock. A ballad of 1550 tells us that 'The blacke shepe is a perylous beast' and Thomas Bastard, writing in 1598, accuses the poor animal of being savage:

Till now I thought the prouerbe did but iest,
Which said a blacke sheepe was a biting beast.

Market forces, superstitions and prejudices have prevailed and the term is now applied to anyone who does not behave as the rest of the group thinks fit.

We're poor little lambs who've lost our way,
Baa! Baa! Baa!
We're little black sheep who've gone astray,
Baa – aa – aa!
Gentleman rankers out on the spree,
Damned from here to Eternity,
God h'mercy on such as we,
Baa! Yah! Baa!
RUDYARD KIPLING, Ballads and Barrack Room Ballads, 'Gentleman Rankers', 1892.

In black and white

In some areas of life, in art or the church for instance, black symbolises evil. This is reflected in such idioms as the *black arts, black magic, a black-hearted villain*, and we say something is *as black as the devil* or *as black as hell*. They all have overtones of evil and wrong-doing.

Black is also associated with illegality. There's the *black market*, of course, and an ever-increasing *black economy* where transactions are never declared to the Inland Revenue. Much older expressions, such as to *fly the black flag* and *blackmail* (originally an illegal protection racket), contain the same idea of breaking the law.

Evil and illegality obviously bring moral censure and disgrace. Not surprisingly then there are plenty of phrases expressing this idea: **to be in someone's black books, to blacklist, to blackball** or just to *black someone, a blackleg,* **the black sheep of the family**, *a black mark*, and so on.

Black is associated with death in most cultures and this probably explains the gloomy connotations of the word in relation to human feelings. You can be *in a black humour* or *mood, look on the black side of things, paint things in black colours* and claim that *things are looking black*. Other expressions connecting black with feelings aren't much better. *To give somebody a black look* and *to look as black as thunder* suggest anger and threat.

On the other hand, white has had generally positive connotations: a *white wedding*, for instance, or that old phrase *That's white of you*, meaning 'That's fair of you'. White has the power to turn something bad into something good. Lying, witches and magic all have negative associations, yet add the positive word *white* and they are rendered harmless, even beneficial: *a white lie, a white witch* and *white magic*.

Conversely, there are quite a few negative expressions connected with white. A coward may be *white-livered*, be shown the white feather or surrender by *waving the white flag*.

None the less, it is generally true to say that in English black indicates bad whilst white indicates good.

Every privileged class tries at first to whitewash its black sheep; if they prove incorrigible, they're kicked out.
RICHARD ALDINGTON, Soft Answers, 'Now Lies She There', 1932.

'May I speak frankly to you, sir? About your nephew? I do not wish to offend you, but I fancy he is more the black sheep of your family than you are!'
GEORGETTE HEYER, Black Sheep, 1966

There is one black sheep in every family, but what about the idea that there is one very white one?
DAILY MAIL, August 8, 1991.

usage: Usually used of a family member; by extension it can refer to any member of a close-knit group or very generally to a ne'er-do-well. In these senses it is often abbreviated to *black sheep.*

see also: to have a skeleton in one's cupboard

blackball, to

to exclude someone from a social group or club

In the eighteenth century applicants for membership of exclusive clubs were voted upon by the existing members. A white or black ball was put into an urn. If just one black ball was found at the count, then the candidate was not admitted. Today the means of voting might be different – as the quotation from the *Daily Mail* shows – but the term is still around, as is the exclusivity it represents.
See *to spill the beans* for voting methods.

I shall make a note to blackball him at the Athenaeum.
BENJAMIN DISRAELI, Vivian Grey, 1826.

There has been a campaign of vilification against the Duke of Roxburghe culminating in the falsehood that he had been 'blackballed' by the Jockey Club . . . Roxburghe's name was circulated to the 115 or so members of the Jockey Club for approval. The election will take place later this month and the Marquis of Hartington, the Senior Steward, informed members

that unless he heard from nine or more against a nomination, these four [nominated] would go forward, but the Jockey Club did receive letters opposing Roxburghe's candidacy.
DAILY MAIL, October 2, 1991.

But at the Garrick these delicate matters are transacted in a blaze of gossip paragraphs. When Bernard Levin was blackballed by the lawyers (for a posthumous denunciation of the Lord Chief Justice Goddard's bigotry and boorishness), it was the talk of two continents. When Anthony Howard was in danger of being blackballed for a second time, allegedly by someone he had fallen out with at school, his brother-in-law Alan Watkins, un uomo di rispetto, ensured that his name was re-submitted and approved – again in the spotlight. A BBC rival is said to have engineered the blackballing of Brian Wenham. Anything less clubbable than these publicised stabbings it is hard for outsiders to conceive.
OBSERVER, July 5, 1992.

usage: The phrase can be applied to situations wider than entry to exclusive clubs, with a sense closer to *give someone the cold shoulder.* However, it retains connotations of upper class snobbery.

see also: to blacklist, to spill the beans

blacklist, to

to list the name of someone contravening rules or conventions; to ostracise

The history of *blacklist* is closely connected with that of *to be in someone's black books.* One American authority suggests its first use was in the reign of Charles II, with reference to a list of persons implicated in the trial and execution of his father, Charles I. On his accession to the throne, Charles II hunted them out, executing thirteen and imprisoning many others.

Particularly in the twentieth century, the principal use has been in relation to management and union affairs. The *OED* gives J. D. Hackett's 1923 definition in his *Labor Terms in Management Engineering*: *'Black List. A list of union workmen circulated by employers to prevent such workers from being hired.'* Conversely, unions have produced blacklists of firms they refuse to deal with. Laws, litigation and considerable industrial strife have regularly resulted. Wider uses are reasonably common, e.g. libraries can have blacklists of borrowers who abuse the system.

The Maritime Unions have threatened to declare 'black' all the government liners.
DAILY MAIL, March 17, 1928.

Rock star Rod Stewart has been blacklisted by an 80,000-strong entertainment union over an unpaid bill. The union is threatening to take the 47-year-old singer to court if he fails to pay £2,350 for clothes he wore on a tour almost five years ago. The singer has now been added to a BECTU warning list sent out to all members.
DAILY EXPRESS, May 25, 1992.

usage: Blacklist is both a noun and a verb. It is most commonly written as one word nowadays, though hyphenated or two-word versions persist. In the abbreviated form *to black*, the use is only in the restricted context of union affairs.

see also: to be in someone's black books

blanket: born on the wrong side of the blanket

illegitimate

This is a delicate euphemism for an illegitimate child. The allusion could be to the consequences of hurried moments of illicit sexual pleasure on the top of the blankets, whereas legitimate children would have been conceived in more leisure and with due propriety underneath them.

Alternatively, it might refer to the shame of illegitimate births that forced mothers to have their children in secrecy outside the marriage bed rather than in the comfort of it.

My mother was an honest woman. I didn't come in on the wrong side of the blanket.
TOBIAS SMOLLETT, Humphry Clinker, 1771.

Psychiatrists will tell you . . . that none of it is accidental, but a subconscious compulsion to confront the truth, and to puncture pomposity . . . it would certainly explain the way my husband (a kindly and usually mildly spoken man) was heard telling a colleague that he was a lucky bastard one day, a silly bastard the next, and a clever bastard on the third. My husband put this down entirely to having been warned so repeatedly of the man's immense sensitivity about having been born on the wrong side of the blanket that it was the only thing he could remember about him.
GOOD HOUSEKEEPING, May 1992.

usage: Derogatory, but becoming less common as society's attitude to illegitimacy changes.

Blighty: dear old Blighty

England

Soldiers serving in India adopted and adapted the Hindi word *bilayti*, meaning 'foreign', to refer to their distant homeland. The expression became widely used among forces in the First World War and a variation, *blighty-one*, meant a wound that was serious enough to cause the injured man to be sent home to England.

During the First World War, quite a number of British soldiers were affected by an incurable disease that was a sure-fire guarantee for a one-way ticket to Blighty. DAH it was called – Disorder Affecting the Heart.
COBUILD CORPUS: Alistair Maclean, San Andreas, 1984.

usage: Very high in emotional content, hence its use and new lease of life in moments of national crisis, such as the Falklands Campaign and Gulf War.

blue: like a bolt from the blue

totally unexpectedly

The reference here is to a bolt of lightning coming from a cloudless blue sky. If atmospheric conditions had not led one to suspect that it might happen, such an event would be shocking and unexpected indeed. It is not known how long the phrase has been in the spoken language, but Thomas Carlyle used it in *The French Revolution* in 1837: 'Arrestment, sudden really as a bolt out of the blue, has hit strange victims.'

In the Summer Term of '93 a bolt from the blue flashed down on Oxford. It drove deep, it hurtlingly embedded itself in the soil. Dons and undergraduates stood around, rather pale, discussing nothing but it. Whence came it, this meteorite? From Paris. Its name? Will Rothenstein. Its aim? . . .
MAX BEERBOHM, Seven Men, 'Enoch Soames', 1912.

see also: out of the blue

blue: out of the blue

suddenly and surprisingly, totally unexpectedly

See *like a bolt from the blue*

We cannot live in a permanent state of religious rapture, but there are those special disclosure moments when, out of the blue, God meets us, refreshes us and restores us.
MID SUSSEX TIMES, August 16, 1991.

Then, out of the blue, I started to suffer hot flushes. I would experience a strange sensation in my stomach, and could count the seconds before this terrible gush of heat consumed my body.
WOMAN'S OWN, September 16, 1991.

usage: Can be good or bad news.

see also: like a bolt from the blue

blue moon, once in a

very rarely, occasionally

Blue moons really do occur but only under extremely rare atmospheric conditions. Collins (1958) lists the occurrences of recent blue moons and explains them as dust particles (the eruption of Krakatoa in 1883, or a forest fire in Alberta in September 1920).

The allusion to the moon being blue goes back at least to a 1528 rhyme:

If they saye the mone is belewe,
We muct beleve that it is true.

The earliest reference to the phrase in the form we know it today is in J. Burrowes' *Life in St George's Fields* (1821).

That indefinite period known as a 'blue moon'.
EDMUND YATES. Wrecked in Port. 1869.

A fruit pasty once in a blue moon.
MISS BRADDON. Joshua Haggard's Daughter. 1876.

If Mr Gladstone had only become visible once in a blue moon to a patient watcher, and even then had torn his way back into darkness in frenzied haste, Lord Morley could hardly have written three volumes about him.
ROBERT LYND. The Blue Lion. 'Going for a Walk'. 1923.

usage: informal

Blue Ribbon, the

the highest distinction, the pick of the bunch

The most desired Order of Knighthood in Britain is the blue ribbon of the Garter. It is conferred by the Sovereign. By extension, the expression *the blue ribbon* connotes excellence and the highest honour. It is usually used in conjunction with something quite outstanding.

The Blue Ribbon of the Turf, for instance, is the Derby. Lord Beaconsfield apparently originated the phrase in the splendid quotation from his *Biography*

of Lord George Bentinck, given below.

The Blue Ribbon of the Atlantic has the alternative form *the Blue Riband of the Atlantic* – see **The Old Curiosity Shop of Linguistics** (page 108).

Less common forms are *the Blue Ribbon of the Law* (the office of the Lord Chancellor) and *the Blue Ribbon of the Church* (the Archbishopric of Canterbury).

There is an interesting parallel case in French. *Cordon bleu* means 'blue ribbon'. Honours conferred on knights of the Order of the Holy Spirit (*L'Ordre du Saint Esprit*) were suspended from this ribbon. The development of meaning took a rather different path in France, however. These *chevaliers* by association became known as *cordons bleus*. They had a reputation for excellent food, so *un repas de cordon bleu* was really out of the ordinary. English has since borrowed the term, such that we now refer to *cordon bleu* cooking and chefs.

Lord George had given up racing to become the leader of the Conservative party, and was defeated in Parliament a few days before the horse Surplice, which he had sold, won the coveted prize. The two events troubled him greatly.

'It was in vain to offer solace,' says Disraeli.

He gave a sort of stifled groan. 'All my life I have been trying for this, and for what have I sacrificed it? You do not know what the Derby is,' he moaned out.

'Yes I do; it is the Blue Ribbon of the Turf.'

'It is the Blue Ribbon of the Turf,' he slowly repeated, and sitting down at a table he buried himself in a folio of statistics.
LORD BEACONSFIELD. Biography of Lord George Bentinck. 1870.

In 1840 he was elected to a fellowship at Oriel, then the blue ribbon of the university.
THE ATHENAEUM, 1887.

usage: The phrase is now more passively recognised than actively used, though it was popular enough in the 1970s for the marketing men to name a chocolate bar a Blue Riband. With this exception, *riband* is not used outside the phrase *the Blue Riband of the Atlantic*. Initial capitals are usual, except adjectivally, where a hyphen is also common.

see also: blue-chip

blue stocking, a

an erudite woman

In Venice in 1400, a society was founded by erudite men and women. It was named *Della Calza*, 'of the stocking', and had blue stockings as its emblem. The idea was copied in Paris in 1590 when a club called *Bas-bleu*, 'Blue-stocking', was begun and proved very successful among ladies of learning. It was not until about 1750 that London had a similar society. This was founded by Lady Montagu who, tired of the trivial social round of cards and gossip, opened her house to like-minded intellectuals and invited prominent literary figures of the day to share their ideas. Emphasis was on learning and discussion, not on fashion and it was soon noticed by smart society that one member of the circle, Benjamin Stillingfleet, habitually wore his everyday blue worsted stockings to the gatherings instead of the black silk favoured for evening wear. The group, already the

subject of derision and ridicule, was promptly labelled 'the Blue Stocking Society'.

Today the term continues to have derogatory overtones. According to one journalist *'Bluestocking is now a man's term of abuse when faced with the ugly possibility that a woman may be cleverer than he is.'* (*The Times*, February 5, 1992)

For someone now hailed as being so extraordinary, it is fascinating to discover that Hawking's formative years and influence were so very ordinary. We learn about his 'slightly bluestocking' family life in Hillside Road, St Albans; his studies at St Albans School; and his circle of close schoolboy friends . . .
TIMES EDUCATIONAL SUPPLEMENT, January 17, 1992.

Something of value is being lost with the passing of our blue-stocking colleges . . . There is something to be said for the fun, and freedom, and privacy, and sensible feminism of an all-women's college . . . Equality means equal opportunities, not compulsory shared bathrooms for all.
THE TIMES, February 5, 1992.

blue-blooded

born into a royal or aristocratic family

The phrase is a direct translation from the Spanish *sangre azul* (blue blood). AD 711 saw the first invasion of Spain by the Moors and, for centuries, vast areas of the country were under Moorish influence and rule. Spanish aristocrats had fairer complexions than the dusky-skinned Moors, who were considered their social inferiors, and their veins showed more blue beneath their paler skin.

A question of colour

Some years ago there was a fascinating piece of research done by two anthropologists in America. After looking at ninety-eight different languages they found that contrary to contemporary views there were universal basic colour terms. Some languages had as few as two basic colour terms, whereas others could have up to eleven. Not only that, but languages acquire colour terms in a fixed order. For instance, any language with only two basic colour terms, such as Jale in New Guinea, must have black and white. A language with three basic colour terms must have black, white and red. One with five colour terms must have black, white, red, green and yellow, and so on.

The evidence seems strong that this is how languages in general acquire their basic colour terms. Idioms including colour terms, however, show some characteristics that are difficult to explain in terms of universals of language. Perhaps that's not surprising, since one fundamental characteristic of an idiom is that it breaks the rules of language. Rather, the evidence from them points to each language expressing a unique world view by the way it slices up reality into its own relative categories. For instance, why do we say *to be in the red* in English, yet *to be in the green* in Italian? Why is a *blackleg* in English a *yellow* in French and Spanish? And why is **to be in someone's black books** in English *to be in the green book* of somebody in Spanish?

One particularly interesting example is that of the *blue joke* or 'dirty story'. In Spanish this can be a *red story* or a *green joke*. Yet in French a *blue tale* means a 'fairy story'. However, still in French, a *green story* or even a *green* as a noun does mean our *blue story*. But a German who tells *blue tales* is lying – perhaps telling *a white lie*?

So individual are languages, so much do things change from language to language, that several authorities have suggested that a good test to decide if a given phrase is an idiom or not – and this applies to all idioms, not just colour idioms – is to see if it translates directly into another language. If it does, it's not an idiom. If it doesn't, it is.

Better ways to decide what constitutes an idiom are considered in **What is an idiom?** (see page 6). However, the translation test highlights the peculiarity and idiosyncrasy of different languages as a basic criterion for definition, which in turn lends support to what is known technically as the Sapir-Whorf hypothesis. This argues that languages – and, it seems from the limited evidence above, idioms also – are the unique product of their immediate context and do not obviously obey universal rules.

And the girl – what of her? To which side of the house did she belong? To the blue blood of the Clintons, or the muddy stream of the Carews?
MRS E. LYNN LINTON, Pastor Carew, 1886.

Before long there was an endless stream of customers and a new class of clientèle beginning to tread the path to our door. The advance party were the fashion journalists, and then came the wives of pop stars and the junior league blue bloods. The success was phenomenal.
DAILY MAIL, October 16, 1991.

Most of the other 10 queens are on European thrones, but the thin blue-blooded line reaches as far as Queen Aishwarya of Nepal, and Queen Mata-aho of Tonga.
GOOD HOUSEKEEPING, February 1992.

usage: A fuller form is *to have blue blood (in one's veins)*.

blue-chip

reliable, giving the highest return

This phrase comes from the gaming tables. Chips are the coloured counters used to represent money in games like poker. The blue chip has the highest value, so *a blue-chip investment* is one that promises to be most lucrative. *A blue-chip company* is financially secure, with high profits. *A blue-ribbon company*, on the other hand, is judged principally in terms of honour and excellence, not simply of the size of its bank balance.

The group still has a blue-chip client list, however, and serves more than 300 of the Fortune 500 companies.
NATIONAL ASSOCIATION OF PENSION FUNDS, EC Bulletin, January 1991.

BTR poised for Blue Chip bid
HEADLINE, OBSERVER, September 15, 1991.

usage: Although gambling is clearly a risky business, the connotations of blue-chip are much more positive: good returns with security is the sense conveyed, in an interesting shift of meaning. There is varied initial capitalisation – on the whole it is better not to. It is progressively more common to omit the hyphen.

see also: Blue Ribbon

blue-eyed boy, a

a favourite, a protégé

Some of the varying applications of the word *blue* are discussed in **Giving it to them hot and strong** (page 117) **and A question of colour** (page 36). Here we are concerned with fair hair and blue eyes, which have long been connected with chastity and innocence.

Rating standards differ from manager to manager in a single company. There is also the 'blue-eyed boy' syndrome. If a manager likes you, you are well paid.
DAILY TELEGRAPH, May 21, 1992.

usage: For all its positive associations, *blue-eyed boy* is often used deprecatingly, with implications of favouritism and nepotism.
   The form *blue-eyed girl* is occasionally found.

see also: the apple of one's eye

board: to go by the board

to be cast aside; to be irretrievably lost

A 'board' is the side of a ship, and something which *goes by the board* falls over the side (over*board*) into the sea and is probably lost forever. The phrase is often applied to ideas, projects or values which are discarded through impracticality or in favour of something else.

Measures affecting a particular class or a particular locality would be apt to go by the board. They might command a large and enthusiastic majority among those primarily affected by them, but only receive a languid assent elsewhere.
L. T. HOBHOUSE, Liberalism, c1920.

There are times, Madame, when pride and dignity – they go by the board! There are other – stronger emotions.
AGATHA CHRISTIE, Death on the Nile, 1937.

bombshell: to drop a bombshell

to disclose disturbing news or information

Various metaphors have taken root from the basic military term. One concerns a piece of news that has an impact like that of a bomb going off. Another, in the expression *a blonde bombshell*, suggests that the stunning good looks of a woman with blonde hair (not usually any other colour) have a startling effect on those who see her.

Our golden years were just about to begin when Peter dropped a bombshell: all our married life he had been having affairs.
DAILY MAIL, October 16, 1991.

usage: *Bombshell* can never be shortened to the virtual synonym *bomb* and retain the same sense. *Blonde* is rarely spelt *blond* – appropriately since in this case it is borrowed from the French feminine form and refers to a woman.

boot: the boot is on the other foot

there has been a reversal of circumstances or opinion

The end of the eighteenth century saw a revolution in shoemaking: for the first time cobblers were beginning to make 'right' and 'left' shoes. Before then shoes could be put on either foot, so if one boot pinched and rubbed excessively the obvious thing to do was to try it out on the other foot to see if it suited better.

Here . . . the boot is on the other leg, and Civilisation is ashamed of her arrangements in the presence of a savage.
WINSTON CHURCHILL, My African Journey, 1908.

A few years ago Speelman – then ranked number five in the world – caused something of an upset when he beat number three-ranked Short. This time the boot was on the other foot. 'We all suspected that Nigel hadn't developed the degree of ruthlessness he needed to beat a friend,' says Black. 'Now he obviously has.'
DAILY EXPRESS, April 30, 1992.

usage: *The boot is on the other leg* is less common, so is *the shoe is on the other foot*.

boot, to

in addition, as well

The etymology ought to be more exciting but has nothing to do with stylish footwear. Boot in this phrase comes from the Anglo-Saxon *bot* which means 'advantage' or 'profit'. The word was current until the early nineteenth century but has since fallen out of use, surviving only in this phrase meaning 'in addition' or, literally, 'for a profit'.

Mrs Mackridge had no wit, but she had acquired the caustic voice and gestures along with the satins and trimmings of the great lady. When she told you it was a fine morning, she seemed also to be telling you you were a fool and a low fool to boot.
H. G. WELLS. Tono-Bungay, 1909.

Unkind though it sounds, he was even more boring than the last one and 5ft 2in to boot. We had dinner in a brightly-lit restaurant and he ordered cottage cheese and lettuce. I was clearly expected to do the same. After that, I decided to give up on men for a while.
GOOD HOUSEKEEPING, November 1991.

usage: literary

brand new

entirely new, completely new

Here *brand* has nothing to do with the mark of workmanship, but means 'firebrand, piece of burning wood'. *Brand new* comes from the smith's trade and so was originally used only of objects made of metal which were literally fire-new, fresh from the furnace.

A man of fire-new words.
WILLIAM SHAKESPEARE, Love's Labour's Lost, 1595.

usage: The addition of *brand* intensifies the basic sense of *new*, as did *spanking* in the very dated *spanking new*. Occasionally written as one word, more frequently hyphenated. Now most commonly as two words.

see also: spick and span

brass tacks: to get down to brass tacks

to bring the essential facts under discussion, to get to the heart of the matter

The phrase would seem to be American and, probably, nineteenth century, although its origins are obscure. The most common suggestion is that the wooden countertop in a draper's store would have brass-headed tacks hammered into it at carefully measured intervals. The customer who had got to the point of having her cloth measured out against the tacks was about to make a purchase and was really getting down to business.

The expression, however, seems to suggest a removal of layers in order to reveal the tacks. Two suggestions from different American authorities cover this implication.

The first is that the brass tacks may refer to those used by upholsterers to fix the fabric and wadding in place. Any defect in the furniture or renewal of the upholstery meant stripping it down to the brass tacks to sort the problem out.

The second suggestion is that the expression originated in the shipyard and referred to the cleaning of a ship's hull, a process which involved scrubbing off all the barnacles to reveal the bolts which held the structure together. The exponent of this theory admits that such bolts would be of copper and not brass and that a tack is rather a flimsy fastening with which to secure a ship, but puts this down to American understatement for humorous effect.

Rhyme might also come into the story, if only to reinforce the meaning: 'hard facts' conveniently is similar in sense and rhymes with 'brass tacks'. However, it is unlikely that rhyming slang is the full explanation of the etymology.

Highbrow sermons that don't come down to brass tacks.
SINCLAIR LEWIS, Our Mr Wrenn, 1914.

usage: It is common to find this idiom used after a period of *not* talking about the important point, after *beating about the bush!* Colloquial.

bread: the best thing since sliced bread

the best innovation for some time

Rees (1990) mentions a clever advertisement of Sainsbury's from 1981: 'Sainsbury's brings you the greatest thing since sliced bread. Unsliced bread.'

These days we pour scorn on the tastelessness and spongy texture of the product which we take so much for granted, but when it first appeared, in 1925, it caused quite a stir. The loaves, neatly and hygienically wrapped in waxed paper, were produced by a bakery founded in 1840 by Henry Nevill. When sample loaves from the Nevill bakery were put on show at the Wembley Exhibition, they were greeted with such excitement that other businesses were swift to board the bandwagon and invest in the machinery required. The 1950s brought the formation of large bakery groups which started to produce vast quantities of sliced bread to meet a growing demand. Loaves now came in a plastic wrapper and were sold through supermarket outlets.

It is not known when the phrase *the best thing since sliced bread* first became popular. It may have been during the early years of the product or perhaps when sales started to boom in the 1950s and the work of the housewife was made just that little bit easier.

I work as a technician in a secondary school where we have 21 Macs. The staff think the machines are the best thing since sliced bread and use them all the time for their work.
MACUSER, May 1, 1992.

The greatest thing since sliced bread, they say . . . Quite an accolade, when the only great thing about sliced bread is that it fits easily into a toaster and makes neat sandwiches.
DAILY MAIL, May 11, 1992.

usage: It can be *the greatest, best* or even *hottest thing since sliced bread.* Informal.

breadline, on the

very poor, having almost nothing to eat

On the breadline originated in America during the last century. Poor people queued for free or cheap bread (*line* is American for 'queue'), so the phrase gained the general meaning of 'destitute, bordering on starvation'. A specific story about the possible origin concerns the Fleischmann family and the bakery business they ran in New York, in the 1870s. The bakery was renowned for the freshness of its fare, a reputation won by the fact that all the bread left on the shelves at closing time was given away to the poor. The queue of hungry people which stood outside the shop each evening became known as *the breadline.*

Mr David Fryer of the University of Stirling interviewed people who had recently lost their jobs and found that even those far from the breadline felt cut off from their peer groups.
GOOD HOUSEKEEPING, September 1991.

break: a good/bad/lucky break

a good/bad opportunity, chance

The most likely origin seems to come from pool, though the source suggested for *to give someone a break* is also a possibility here. In pool, the game begins with the balls arranged in a set position. The first player then uses the cue ball to break this formation. The 'break' is largely a matter of chance, the skill coming into subsequent play. With *a good break* a skilful player can go on to pocket many of the balls and build towards a winning position; *a bad break* gives the other player an opportunity to play. *A lucky break* is easy to understand as an extension of the basic idea.

Even with the girl's full co-operation the description of the two men was sketchy. The first lucky break the homicide officers got on the Lustig killing was a direct result of the killers' haste.
COBUILD CORPUS.

break: to get/give someone a break

to get/be given a good opportunity; to be let off

The phrase may well be a piece of underworld slang. A *break* was an interruption in a street performer's act during which he would pass round the hat for the audience to show their appreciation. The term was taken up by the vagrant and criminal community and by the nineteenth century a *break* had come to mean a collection or whip-round made for a felon on his release from prison. The lucky man had been *given a break*, he had not been left

to face the world completely penniless.

It is also possible that the source could be in the pool room, as detailed in *a good break*.

Bogart: Initially, when I started my own thing, it was difficult to get work. Actually, the first place to give me a break was Ethel's Place.
COBUILD CORPUS: Washington National Public Radio. 1991.

usage: Often said pleadingly and easily becomes a cliche: 'Give me a break, Guv'nor!'

buck: to pass the buck

to pass the responsibility on to someone else

A poker term which refers to the marker (buck) which was placed in front of a player as a reminder that it was his turn to deal. The dealer has the unenviable task of declaring the first stake and may choose to pass the marker on, thus avoiding the responsibility. Some say that the original marker was a buckhorn knife, hence the word buck. An alternative explanation – perhaps a complementary one – is that in the early West of America a silver dollar was used as the marker. As everyone knows, the informal term for dollar is buck, so the passing on of the dollar was literally *passing the buck*. This monetary use of buck has been widespread since the mid-1800s. John Bakeless in *Master of the Wilderness* (1939) explains why: '*Skins were classified [around 1800] as "bucks" and "does", the former being larger, and more valuable. Americans still refer to dollars as "bucks" . . . echoing the business terminology of their ancestors.*'

US President Truman had a sign on his desk in the White House which read, 'the buck stops here', indicating that he was prepared to take full responsibility for every decision made under his presidency. Later presidents, Ford and Carter among them, have echoed his intent by quoting the phrase after announcing weighty decisions. Gerald Ford used it, for example, when deciding to pardon Richard Nixon.

In straits like these, the wrestler with destiny is tempted to look for bugbears and scapegoats to carry the burden of his own inadequacy. Yet to 'pass the buck' in adversity is still more dangerous than to persuade oneself that prosperity is everlasting.
A. J. TOYNBEE, Civilization on Trial, 1948.

Dear X, I'm not going to tell you to forget your childhood, because you carry it with you to the grave. You can't exorcise the past; all you can do is learn from it. You can say, 'I'm here. I survived.' You can make sure that the buck stops right there, that you break the cycle and say, 'That's how it was for me but I'm going to make my child the happiest child in the whole world.'
COSMOPOLITAN, July 1989.

I consulted my Handbook of Psychiatry about all this. If I understood it correctly, it all comes down to the female capacity to feel guilt and accept blame . . . The hand that rocks the cradle stops the buck; and it's not an entirely ignoble thing to do. After all something has to halt the damn thing in its tracks . . .
GOOD HOUSEKEEPING, July 1992.

usage: Informal, with an American flavour.

bull: to take the bull by the horns

to face up to a difficulty with boldness

Although bull-running once took place in England it was made illegal in 1840, so since the phrase has only been in use from the beginning of the nineteenth century, it probably alludes not to this but to the Spanish sport of bull-fighting. Early in the fight the bull is tormented and enraged by the banderilleros who pierce his neck muscles with darts. As a result, the bull's head droops, making it easier for the matador to play him along with his cape, sometimes grasping his horns before finally killing him.

Nora would have faced the difficulty, and taken the bull by the horns.
ANTHONY TROLLOPE, He Knew He Was Right, 1869.

I have often been told to be bold, and take the bull by the horns.
C. H. SPURGEON, John Ploughman's Talk, 1869.

To hang our heads in private and not be seen about anywhere would only make our ultimate emergence more embarrassing, and it seemed much more sensible to take the bull, however fetid its breath, by the horns at the outset.
NOËL COWARD, Present Indicative, 1937.

Cresson takes the bull by the horns in picking IBM as France's partner.
HEADLINE, THE TIMES, February 7, 1992.

burn one's boats/bridges (behind one), to

to be so committed to a course of action that it is impossible to withdraw

The phrase refers to the practice Roman generals sometimes employed of setting fire to their own boats after mounting an

Like a load of old bull

Similes are figures of speech which compare two things, using the words *as* or *like*. Sometimes the comparison is very unflattering or redolent with negative connotations. There are plenty of idiomatic English similes that fit into this category. The two that follow have overseas associations and to some extent reflect the chauvinism implicit in many idioms. For much more overt dislike of foreigners, see **National rivalries** (page 76).

like a red rag to a bull: Spanish bull fights are well-known throughout the world. The brave matador shakes his cape in front of the bull's nose, enraging it. It was believed that the red lining of the cape excited the bulls and made them even more fearful opponents. Sad to say, it appears that bulls are colour blind and react to the movement of the cape, not to its colour. However, that was not widely known when the Spanish bull-fighting practice found its way into our simile *like a red rag to a bull*.

   The phrase is used to mean 'likely to cause great annoyance or anger', as in this example from a nineteenth-century magazine: '*George II hated books, and the sight of one in a drawing room was as a red rag to a bull.*' It is often used in connection with people who get angry very quickly.

like a bull in a china shop is also uncomplimentary. The *china shop* refers to shops which have existed since the sixteenth century when traders started bringing back fine porcelain from China. The power of the image lies in the juxtaposition of the clumsy bulk of the bull with the delicacy of the china. The phrase applies to somebody who is very awkward physically and keeps knocking things to the floor and breaking them. By extension it can be used of anyone behaving in a rough, assertive way.

---

invasion. This was to remove any idea of retreat from the minds of their soldiers. Similarly, as the Roman army advanced, they would burn bridges behind them, forcing the soldiers to move forward.

Then he took the perforated cardboard and tore that likewise into small pieces. 'Now I have burned my boats with a vengeance,' he added grimly.
JAMES PAYN, c1880.

He thought of his past, its cold splendour and insouciance. But he knew that for him there was no returning. His boats were burnt.
MAX BEERBOHM, Zuleika Dobson, 1911.

'This'll make it pretty hard for you to come back.'

   'Come back?' Robert asked incredulously, as if I were mad. So he was really going it. Putting a match to his boats and bridges right in front of my eyes.
JOHN WAIN, The Contenders, 1958.

usage: Burning one's *boats* is probably more frequent than one's *bridges*. The phrase emphasises the high risk element: a daring venture in the first place, made still more hazardous by an 'all or nothing' action.

see also: to cross the Rubicon

burn the midnight oil, to

to stay up late, usually to study or write

The idea of burning away oil in the pursuit of learning and creativity is not uncommon in classical literature. In his *Life of Demosthenes*, Plutarch speaks of the orator's meticulous care in composition, then writes: 'For this many of the orators ridiculed him, and Pytheas in particular told him, "That all his arguments smelled of the lamp." Demosthenes retorted sharply upon him: "Yes, indeed, but your lamp and mine, my friend, are not conscious to the same labours." '

The phrase as we know it today has been in use since at least the mid seventeenth century and, in the following century, Gay had occasion to use it more than once, as in this passage from *Trivia* which describes bookstalls in London streets:

Walkers at leisure learning's flowers may spoil,
Nor watch the wasting of the midnight oil.

Even in these days of electricity and light bulbs the phrase has remained current to describe those, especially students, who write or study far into the night.

I burn the midnight oil, and the early black-bird – the first of our choir to awake – has often saluted me on my way home. Therefore I lie in bed in the morning looking at the ceiling and listening to the sounds of the busy world without a twinge of conscience.
A. G. GARDINER ('Alpha of the Plough'), 'On Early Rising', c1910.

Would not the expenditure of a little more midnight oil have given you the accepted form? Forgive this captiousness. For the
rest of the book I have only the most cordial praise.
E. V. LUCAS, 'The Test', 1938.

burton: to go for a burton

to be killed, ruined, completely spoiled

During the Second World War, the RAF used this euphemism to speak of colleagues who were killed or missing in action. A *Burton* is thought to be a reference to strong beer made in Burton-on-Trent. Some even say that the slogan 'Gone for a Burton' featured in advertisements of the period. Friends were not said to have gone to their deaths, they had just gone out for a beer.

Nowadays the phrase has lost its association with death. Instead it is commonly used to refer to objects which are broken beyond mending (vases, lawn-mowers, cars) or to hopes, dreams and plans that are shattered.

And in case that didn't knock Eros for a Burton, he adds that the lover should examine his lady closely, in the light, when he will be sure to discover 'crooked nose, bad eyes, prominent veins, concavities about the eyes, wrinkles, pimples, red streams, frechons, hairs, warts, neves, inequalities, roughness, scabridity, paleness, yellowness, frowns, gapes, squints'.
-COBUILD CORPUS.

usage: Just as *a hoover, a xerox* lose touch with the Hoover and Xerox companies that introduced them, so *a burton* is today found more often than *a Burton*.

bury the hatchet, to

to restore a relationship after a long quarrel, to make up

When American Indians negotiated the cessation of hostilities, each party would ceremonially bury a tomahawk to seal the pact. In the *New England Historical Register* of 1680 Samuel Sewall writes of one such ceremony, this between Indians and white men: '*Meeting with the Sachem they came to an agreement and buried two Axes in the Ground; . . . which ceremony to them is more significant and binding than all Articles of Peace, the Hatchet being a principal weapon.*'

Of course, the tomahawks could always be dug up again, and this meant renewed aggression.

I don't know what you'll think sir – I didn't come to inquire –
But I picked up that agreement and stuffed it in the fire;
And I told her we'd bury the hatchet alongside of the cow;
And we struck an agreement never to have another row.
WILL CARLETON'S Farm Ballads, c1830.

The chiefs met; the amicable pipe was smoked, the hatchet buried, and peace formally proclaimed.
WASHINGTON IRVING, Captain Bonneville's Adventures, 1837.

Yet even to-day despite his appreciation and love of England, Chaudhuri is unwilling to bury the hatchet. He condemns what he regards as ingratiating gush on the part of English and Indians alike and recommends instead an attitude of 'honourable taciturnity'.
JOHN RAYMOND, England's on the Anvil, 'A Prophet in Bengal', 1958.

usage: Very much a cliché today.

busman's holiday, a

spending one's holiday doing the same thing one would be doing at work

At the turn of the century when buses were horse-drawn, it was not uncommon for a driver to spend his day off riding on his own bus to check that the relief driver was treating his horses properly. Such devotion must surely have played its part in confirming the British as a nation of animal lovers. The first use in print, according to Brandreth, in *The Times* of 1921 referred to the expression's proverbial nature, suggesting it had been in common currency for some while.

It was the kind of hair, he could see, which would always be coming down: too much of it, and too heavy. ''Ere,' she said, kicking off her shoes, 'aren't you gunner take yer duds off? A busman's holiday don't last for ever. I sometimes get a client as early as the milk.' In her enthusiasm and hurry a roselight had begun to pour out of the straining camisole. Her natural, moist mouth had worked off the cheap veneer; the whites of her eyes were rolling.
COBUILD CORPUS.

usage: informal

by and by

presently, in due course

This little phrase has been in use for many centuries. Originally *bi and bi* meant 'in order, neatly spaced'. Chaucer writes of 'Two yonge knightes, ligging *by and by*', meaning 'side by side'. Sometimes it referred to a succession of separate happenings as in this example from Robert of Brunne: 'Whan William . . . had taken homage of barons *bi and bi*', meaning 'one by one'. From here the phrase took on its present-day meaning of 'after a while' or 'in a little while, eventually'.

I was a little stumbled and could not tell what to do, whether to thank him or no; but I by and by did, but not very heartily.
SAMUEL PEPYS, Diary, 1660.

You will eat bye and bye
In that glorious land above the sky;
Work and pray, live on hay,
You'll get pie in the sky when you die.
JOE HILL, The Preacher and the Slave, 1906.

by and large

in general, generally speaking, on the whole

A nautical term referring to a sailing ship being steered slightly off the direction of the wind to reduce the likelihood of its being *taken aback*. *By and large* is the combination of two old sailing terms, each with a specific meaning. *By* means 'close-hauled', 'to within six points of the wind', where the wind is before the beam – as in the old phrase *full and by*. *Large* means 'with the wind on the quarter', 'abaft the beam', as in the seventeenth-century phrase *to sail large*. So, the joining of these two technical nautical expressions suggests the wind both before and behind ('abaft') the beam: a little of each, an average of them. There is also the implication of taking the rough with the smooth. Hence, someone who speaks *by and large* is taking a broad perspective on a topic and coming to a general conclusion.

Taking it by and large, I thought, it's not so bad to be fat. One thing about a fat man is that he's always popular. There's really
no kind of company, from bookies to bishops, where a fat man doesn't fit in and feel at home.
GEORGE ORWELL, Coming Up for Air, 1939.

By and large, mothers and housewives are the only workers who do not have regular time off. They are the great vacationless class.
A. M. LINDBERGH, Gift from the Sea, 'Moon Shell', 1955.

Children in the primary years, by and large, do not reach the point of being able to use and develop concepts at a high level of abstraction.
WYNNE HARLEN, Developing Science in the Primary Classroom, 1989.

But in the vast middle ground – among the thousands of business hotels, country house hotels, provincial inns and modest guesthouses – children remain, by and large, an unmentionable problem.
AA MAGAZINE, Issue 1, 1992.

cake: to take the cake

to deserve honour or merit; to be outrageous

Many authorities believe that the phrase has its origins in a late nineteenth-century amusement devised by black slaves in Southern US plantations in which participating couples promenaded about the room arm in arm. The pair judged as walking and turning most gracefully were given a cake as a prize. The admiring cry 'That takes the cake' meaning 'That wins the prize' gave rise not only to the expression but also to the name of the entertainment, the cakewalk.

However, Stevenson quotes Aristophanes as far back as the fifth century BC, who writes in *The Knights*: '*If you surpass him in impudence, we take the cake.*' A cake, a confection of toasted cereal sweetened and bound together with honey, was an award given to the most vigilant man on a night watch. The phrase became idiomatic and was then used to refer to any prize for any event. Nevertheless, it is probable that Mark Twain had the cakewalk in mind when he wrote: '*I judged that the cake was ours.*' (*A Connecticut Yankee in King Arthur's Court*, 1889.)

You Yankees assuredly take the cake for assurance.
O. HENRY, Helping the Other Fellow, 1908.

He rose, clapped him on the shoulder, and burst out laughing. 'Not so bad for an old dog! Upon my word, you take the cake! Come out and have a spot of lunch?'
AGATHA CHRISTIE, Murder in the Mews, 1927.

usage: The original sense of *that takes the cake* was 'that deserves the prize or the special mention'. Today it is often said of a clever or amusing remark and is sometimes used slightly sarcastically to express exasperation, especially when the word *biscuit* is substituted. Colloquial.

see also: to take the biscuit

call someone's bluff, to

to test someone's claims

In a poker game, when a player makes a bet on the cards he holds, he might try to bluff or trick the other players into believing that his hand is better than it really is. If his bluff is called, he is forced to expose his cards and show himself true or false.

O'Connell was resolved, as always, to have no bloodshed, and this time Peel would not give way before mere agitation as in 1828. Peel called O'Connell's bluff.
G. M. TREVELYAN, British History in the Nineteenth Century, 1922.

Franco's simply a German agent. They tried to put him in to prepare air bases to bomb France. That bluff has been called, anyway.
EVELYN WAUGH, Brideshead Revisited, 1945.

cards: to be on the cards

to be possible, to be likely to happen

The expression is from the beginning of the nineteenth century and refers to the practice of fortune telling with Tarot cards.

I don't want to get married yet awhile, but it's distinctly on the cards that I might marry Christine in a couple of years or so.
KINGSLEY AMIS, Lucky Jim, 1954.

Then there is the question of remarriage. Given the age of the two protagonists – both 32 – it must be on the cards. Andrew would once again have his pick of the aristocracy and foreign royalty.
DAILY EXPRESS, May 26, 1992.

cat: no room to swing a cat

very cramped

The picture which springs to mind is that of a cat being whirled round by its tail. One suggested etymology is scarcely less horrific. It seems that it was not uncommon in the sixteenth century to put a cat inside a sack of some sort and then string it up as a moving target for archery practice – Shakespeare refers to the practice in *Much Ado about Nothing*. *No room to swing a cat*, therefore, meant that there was not enough space available for this activity.

A more common theory is that the 'cat' in question was the cat-o'-nine-tails, a whip with nine knotted thongs which was used as a punishment in the British navy. *No room to swing a cat* refers to the cramped conditions on board ship which made the lashing difficult to administer properly. Funk (1950), however, rejects this explanation, since the phrase was in use a hundred years before this particular punishment.

He found Joe in the liner in a little cabin with three other men where there was not room to swing a cat.
DAVID GARNETT, Beany-Eye, 1935.

There is the proud possession of a garden, however diminutive; if the Little Baron cannot swing that inexplicable but proverbial cat indoors, he can ply a spade without.
IVOR BROWN, The Heart of England, 1935.

The cosy little flat didn't have enough room to swing a cat, let alone a racquet. But for nine years it was a very happy home for Virginia, and she will always remember it with affection – not least because it was here, on 1 July 1977, that she enjoyed her first sips of victory champagne after winning Wimbledon at her 16th attempt.
HOUSE BEAUTIFUL, July/August 1992.

usage: colloquial

cat: to grin like a Cheshire cat

to smile constantly and foolishly

The mysterious Cheshire cat makes an unforgettable appearance and disappearance in Lewis Carroll's *Alice's Adventures in Wonderland*. In the story, the Cheshire cat is seen completely but then gradually fades away until all that remains is its grin. Carroll's book is so well-known that it is inevitable that the invention of the remarkable animal should be attributed to him. However, the Cheshire cat existed long before Carroll wrote about it and stories about its origin abound.

Cheshire is famous for its cheeses, and some say that long ago the cheeses were either made in the shape of a grinning cat, or had the head of a cat stamped on them.

Alternatively the Cheshire cat might refer to the unsuccessful efforts of a Cheshire sign painter to represent the lion rampant on the coat of arms of an influential county family. The results looked more like a grinning cat than a roaring lion and became the subject of much hilarity.

Finally, Ewart tells the story of one of Richard III's gamekeepers named Caterling, a burly monster of a man with a wide and unpleasant grin. Originally the simile was 'to grin like a Cheshire Caterling' but, as time went by, economy of effort reduced 'caterling' to 'cat'.

A faint trace of God, half metaphysical and half magic, still broods over our world, like the smile of a cosmic Cheshire Cat. But the growth of psychological knowledge will rub even that from the universe.
JULIAN HUXLEY, Man in the Modern World, 1947.

I was standing beside her, grinning like the Cheshire Cat, in a white suit and holding my broad-brimmed round straw hat.
CECIL DAY-LEWIS, The Buried Day, 1960.

cat: to let the cat out of the bag

to divulge a secret inadvertently

Unscrupulous vendors in medieval markets would display a sample of their wares openly then give the customer a bag, already packed, tied and ready to take away. If a hare or a pig were shown for sale, the bag might contain a cat. The wary customer who opened his bag to check his purchase would discover the deception and *let the cat out of the bag*. The secret would be out.

See *a pig in a poke*.

Reading one's own poems aloud is letting the cat out of the bag. You may have always suspected bits of a poem to be over-weighted, overviolent, or daft, and then, suddenly, with the poet's tongue round them, your suspicion is made certain.
DYLAN THOMAS, Quite Early One Morning, 'On Reading One's Own Poems', 1954.

He was afraid, being a little affected with wine, [he] would 'let the cat out of the bag'.
FREDERICK MARRYAT, Mr Midshipman Easy, 1836.

Penny Vincenzi's recent article 'Q: What Do You Do? A: I'm Just A Housewife' was excellent but has she let the cat out of the bag? Perhaps we should continue to let 'them' think what hell it is to be one's own boss; occupy each day according to one's mood or the weather; be as lazy or as busy as one wishes and not answerable to anyone!
GOOD HOUSEKEEPING, December 1991.

usage: informal

cheek by jowl

in close intimacy; close together

At the beginning of the fourteenth century the idea of being nice and close to someone was expressed by 'cheke by cheke'. It was not until the second half of the sixteenth century that 'cheek by iowle' put in an appearance. Jowl means 'jaw' or 'cheek', so the phrase changed only in form, not meaning. The expression has had a number of dialectal forms over the centuries (Norfolk has *jig-by-jole* and Ayrshire *cheek for chow*) and it is likely that the ultimate origin lies in one of these regional uses. There is another school of thought that prefers a French origin, but evidence for it is scarce.

Books have a way of influencing each other. Fiction will be much the better for standing cheek by jowl with poetry and philosophy.
VIRGINIA WOOLF, A Room of One's Own, 1929.

In London, neighbourly relations are culturally unacceptable. People contrive to live cheek by jowl for half a century without acknowledging each other's existence.
GOOD HOUSEKEEPING, September 1991.

cheek: to turn the other cheek

to have an attitude of patience or forgiveness when one is wrongly or unkindly treated

This is a phrase from the Bible. In Matthew 5:39 Jesus exhorts his followers with these words: '*But I say unto you, that ye resist not evil: but whosoever shall smite thee on thy right cheek, turn to him the other also.*'

If you throw away your weapons, some less scrupulous person will pick them up. If you turn the other cheek, you will get a harder blow on it than you got on the first one.
GEORGE ORWELL, Shooting an Elephant, 'Lear, Tolstoy and the Fool', 1950.

Drivers are advised to 'turn the other cheek' and make allowances for other motorists' mistakes or aggression in a new version of the Transport Department's driving manual.
DAILY TELEGRAPH, May 20, 1992.

usage: literary

cheesed off

fed up

Cheesed off is one of a long list of expressions with the general sense of 'fed up': browned off, brassed off, pissed off, ticked off. As for its origin, no one knows. There is considerable speculation, but nothing substantial.

Pour on parmesan when you're cheesed off with potatoes.
ADVERTISEMENT for Batchelors Pasta and Sauce, Good Housekeeping, September 1991.

usage: colloquial

chestnut, an old

a tired old joke; any overly familiar topic

Although its origins are in an English melodrama, it was an American actor who coined its usage. The actor, William Warren, found occasion to quote from *The Broken Sword*, a rather mediocre play by William Dillon. One of the characters has the irritating habit of telling and retelling the same stories and jokes. He is embarking upon one such tale about a cork tree when his companion, Pablo, interrupts crying, '*A chestnut. I should know as well as you, having heard you tell the tale these twenty-seven times, and I'm sure it was a chestnut.*' Warren, who played the part of Pablo in the melodrama, was at a dinner one evening when a fellow guest started to recount a well-worn and rather elderly anecdote, whereupon Warren murmured, '*A chestnut. I have heard you tell the tale these twenty-seven times.*' The rest of the company was delighted with Warren's very appropriate quoting of the play and it was not long before news of the incident had spread amongst their acquaintances and beyond.

The problem concerns that old chestnut the professional foul, and the new guidelines issued by FIFA in July that affect not only British football but the game the world over.
MID SUSSEX TIMES, September 6, 1991.

Yet Susannah wriggles with understandable discomfort at the very idea that she and Iain are the latest manifestation of that old media chestnut, the perfect theatrical couple.
COSMOPOLITAN, September 1991.

usage: Although the phrase originally referred only to often repeated jokes, songs, anecdotes, etc., its use has spread to include any topic that is considered hackneyed – from nationalisation to the royal family's exemption from taxation. Can be intensified to *a hoary old chestnut*.

chip: a chip off the old block

a child who is very like its father in character or appearance, or both

The reference here is to a chip hacked from a block of wood. The chip is from the same wood as the block, as the child is of the same stock as the parent. The metaphor is age-old: Theocritus in 270 BC preferred a *chip of old flint* for the same concept, which hints that one variant or other of the phrase might go back to the Stone Age.

John Milton used one English form in 1642: '*How well dost thou appear to be a chip of the old block?*' Edmund Burke commented on the occasion of William Pitt the Younger's first speech in Parliament, on 26 February 1781, that he was 'not merely a chip off the old block, but the old block itself'. Pitt was just twenty-one years old. Some three years later he was to become Prime Minister.

The plots of enough modern novels are about the agony and the ecstasy of creation. The central character is invariably a novelist with an angst to grind, or else a chip off the old writer's block sitting in the Hotel du Lac or a flat next to London Fields.
OBSERVER, August 25, 1991.

The West End's Eve Club, owned by Romanian émigrée Helen O'Brien, has fallen victim to the recession and closed its doors for the last time. Its heyday was in the pre-free love Fifties and early Sixties. Errol Flynn dropped by with son, Sean, then aged 14. He was, Helen recalls, 'a real chip off the old block. He disappeared and we found him in dressing room Number 2 ogling the girls.'
DAILY EXPRESS, February 19, 1992.

usage: Usually used (approvingly) of the likeness between father and son, rather than mother and daughter. It can be used jocularly, and is close to being a cliché. *Off* has generally replaced *of*, though not necessarily in American English, where *out of* may be found.

chip in, to

to contribute; to interrupt

The allusion is to poker, where players place their chips (money tokens) in the pot, thus contributing to the sum to be won. This explains the sense 'to contribute' but it is unclear how the further meaning 'to interrupt' came about.

The crew chipped in and bought him a . . . chair.
SYRACUSE POST-STANDARD, September 29, 1949.

Her school friends would chip in with their pocket money so Samantha could eat.
TODAY, September 14, 1991.

chip: to have a chip on one's shoulder

to display anger or resentment because of feelings of inferiority or grievance

The phrase is of American origin. A youth who was spoiling for a fight would put a chip of wood upon his shoulder daring someone to accept the challenge and knock it off. G. Gorer explains in *The Americans*:

Boys in the country and small towns who are validating their manhood sometimes walk around with a literal chip of wood balanced on their shoulder, the sign of a

readiness to fight anyone who will take the initiative of knocking the chip off.

Competition can take many forms – athletics is one. The British team captain, Linford Christie, had this to say about the 4×400m relay squad:

'*They are not my sort of guys . . . I don't like their attitude.*'

One of the relay quartet, Derek Redmond, responded: '*There's a saying among the athletes that Linford is the most balanced runner in Britain because he's got a chip on both shoulders. You can understand why with comments like that.*' (*Daily Telegraph*, May 18, 1992)

Macho men obviously compete on and off the track.

The earlier physical applications of the phrase have now largely given way to those of grievance, aggression, etc., which probably stem from a deep-seated, imagined inferiority.

In spite of these transpositions, the general pattern of the experience was preserved, because only that experience was fertile to the author's mind. Where would Mr Goodrich be without his chip on the shoulder, his grievance against women? It was that that made him tick, to use a vulgarism.
L. P. HARTLEY, A Perfect Woman, 1955.

These men and women, although some of them no doubt had chips on their shoulders or personal axes to grind, had also an admirable devotion to a Cause they could get nothing from in the foreseeable future except victimisation.
CECIL DAY-LEWIS, The Buried Day, 1960.

Titmuss is contemptuous, hooded-eyed, vindictive; he staggers visibly under the weight of a giant chip on the shoulder.
THE TIMES, September 4, 1991.

They are an uneasy listening band who come across with chips on their shoulders. No one likes us and we don't care. Their problem is that they are still groping for a personality.
DAILY MAIL, November 5, 1991.

chips: the chips are down

the situation has reached crisis point; the moment of truth, of trial, of testing has come

In gambling, *the chips are down* when all the bets have been placed but the outcome of the game is not yet known. It is the moment of high tension, when much could be gained – or lost.

When the chips are down, a man shows what he really is.
MARTIN KANE, Private Eye (NYC radio programme, September 4, 1949).

When the chips are down, if anybody criticises either of them, they cling together.
BBC Radio 4, October 2, 1991.

usage: colloquial

chips: to have had one's chips

to be close to failure or defeat; to have had one's last chance

Chips are the coloured tokens which represent money on the gaming tables. A player who has placed and lost all his chips has therefore lost all his money.

usage: colloquial

Splitting one's sides

Did you hear the story about the dog that went to the local flea market and stole the show? Or perhaps you heard of the young man who stayed up all night, trying to work out where the sun went when it went down. It finally dawned on him.

Comedians are very grateful for one characteristic of idioms, for they get a lot of laughs from its operation. Just about all idioms have a quite straightforward, literal meaning and an idiomatic meaning.

Part of the art of the comedian lies in leading you to expect one interpretation and then suddenly forcing you to switch over to the other. For instance, we hear of the dog going down to the local open-air flea market. A little unusual, perhaps, but quite possible in the context of a comedian's 'patter'. But the addition of *stole the show* completely changes things. Here we have to decide whether the dog *stole the show*, that is, 'captured the limelight, became the centre of attention' (the idiomatic sense), or whether the whole sentence now becomes literal. The dog went to a market where fleas were on display and stole that display, stole the show of them.

Similarly with the second story. Is the meaning 'the sun finally came up at dawn' or is it 'the solution finally came to him'? Again, the humour comes from the ambiguity of interpretation that the listener is faced with.

If those were two terrible plays on words, there are others that are even worse:

'I've got my husband to the point where he eats out of my hand, it saves such a lot of washing up.'

'Waiter, bring me something to eat, I could eat a horse.'
'You couldn't have come to a better place, sir.'

'What goes "Ha Ha Bonk"?'
'A man laughing his head off.'

'What lies on the sea bed and twitches?'
'A nervous wreck.'

On the same principle, the poet gets his effects by playing on the tension between the literal and idiomatic in humorous verse, as in this limerick:

> *There was a young lad of Montrose*
> *who had pockets in none of his clothes.*
> *When asked by his lass*
> *where he carried his brass,*
> *he replied, 'I just pay through the nose.'*

choc-a-bloc

crowded, crammed full

A nautical term used when the two blocks of a tackle are hard together so that they cannot be tightened any more.

[The kennel] started from scratch 14 years ago. Mr Quibell said: 'I am nearly always choc-a-bloc. I am licensed for 23 dogs and 16 cats.'
MID SUSSEX TIMES, August 16, 1991.

usage: Informal. There are varying spellings: *chock a block, chockablock.* Hyphenation is also variable. A colloquial shortening in speech is *chocker,* e.g. 'It's absolutely chocker in there.'

cleaners: to be taken to the cleaners

to lose all one's money, to be ruined

In the last century people were 'cleaned out' when they were stripped clean of everything of value, either through gambling or as victims of dishonest practice. This use is still current. *To be taken to the cleaners* is a more recent term which expresses exactly the same thing.

Prices that won't take you to the Cleaners. *Advertisement from Superdrug for various domestic cleaners.*
DAILY MAIL, October 2, 1991.

I was taken to the Cleaners, sobs Royal Designer. *'She took me to the cleaners,' Miss Cierach said. 'I trusted her with everything as a friend, business associate and employee . . . Can't you see what she has done? She has stolen goods, a car,* cheques, enormous sums of money. What's the point of going on?'*
DAILY MAIL, October 2, 1991.

usage: To take someone to the cleaners is found, but the passive form is equally common.

cleft stick, in a

in a predicament, unable to decide which way to go

This expression has been current since the turn of the century. It probably alludes to the trapping of snakes and the like by pinning them down behind the head with a forked stick.

If you are only a voter you are caught in the same cleft stick. It may be plain to you that the candidate of your Party is a political imbecile, a pompous snob, a vulgar ranter, a conceited self-seeker, or anything else that you dislike, and his opponent an honest, intelligent, public-spirited person.
G. B. SHAW, The Intelligent Woman's Guide to Socialism, 1928.

The war party looked to the King rather than Clarendon, and believed that they had the Chancellor in a cleft stick. If the war went well, they, as the instigators, would take the credit for it. If it went badly they would put all the blame on Clarendon.
R. LOCKYER, Tudor and Stuart Britain, 1964.

Pensioners . . . are complaining the switch has left them without an easy way to reach a general store – and they cannot afford to pay bus fares to the new superstore. Mrs Gooding, 73, said: 'We are a very vulnerable section of the community and they have got us in a cleft stick.'
MID SUSSEX TIMES, September 27, 1991.

close your eyes and think of England

Advice to succumb to unwanted sexual intercourse; to put up with any unpleasant action

Partridge's *Dictionary of Catch Phrases* ascribes the phrase to the 1912 Journal of Lady Hillingdon:

I am happy now that Charles calls on my bedchamber less frequently than of old. As it is, I now endure but two calls a week and when I hear his steps outside my door I lie down on my bed, close my eyes, open my legs and think of England.

The original use concerns sexual intercourse but it is widely used humorously as advice to someone faced with any unpleasant task.

Now the bad news: immigration will not divulge the names of the schools. So when it comes to choosing your school it's a case of shut your eyes and think of England.
EFL GAZETTE, 1991.

Adding insult to injury, Gold Spot, the breath freshener who commissioned the most kissable lips survey, point out that although as the song has it 'a kiss is just a kiss' there's much more to it than puckering up and thinking of England.
MID SUSSEX TIMES, September 13, 1991.

It is bizarre to call a television programme Think of England, for that phrase is invariably preceded by the words 'Close your eyes and . . .' which really won't do for so visual a medium. And in any case, it denotes having to engage in something unpleasant.
DAILY MAIL, October 16, 1991.

usage: Colloquial, often jocular. A common variant is to *think of the Empire*; another is *to lie back and think of England*.

clothes line: I could sleep on a clothes line

I am so tired I could fall asleep anywhere

This phrase has its roots in the poverty of the nineteenth century amongst those who slept rough. For just two pence each, poor people could buy a night's lodging on the two-penny rope. This was a bench where these unfortunates would sleep sitting up, their bodies slumped over a clothes line stretched taut before them. The morning brought a rough awakening, for the landlord would often cut the rope to wake his impoverished guests before sending them on their way.

Occasionally, if we stop to think, we are aware of the story behind an idiom. The Bible tells us how Pontius Pilate gave way before the pressure of the mob and handed Christ over to be crucified: *He took some water, washed his hands in front of the crowd, and said, 'I am not responsible for the death of this man, this is your doing.'* (Matthew 27:24).

The same sense of refusing to accept any sense of responsibility, of withdrawing from a situation, occurs commonly today, as in this extract from Angus Wilson: *'If, of course, you are going to regard every suggestion I make as a criticism,' he said, 'then I wash my hands of the whole matter.'*

See **The Bible and Shakespeare** (page 180) for more expressions from these prolific sources.

cloud cuckoo land, in

divorced from the reality of ordinary life

This evocative phrase is a translation of the Greek *Nephelococcygia* from the comedy *The Birds* by Aristophanes (fifth century BC). *Nephelococcygia* is an imaginary city which the birds built in the air.

Anyone who believes the US produces fewer talented scientists, engineers, accountants, novelists or academics than we do is living in cloud-cuckoo-land.
OBSERVER, August 25, 1991.

Last night Mr Peter Dawson, secretary of the no-strike Professional Association of Teachers said: 'If they think they'll get a pay rise of that order they are living in cloud cuckoo land.'
DAILY MAIL, October 16, 1991.

If Mr Benyon were to look at the methods Chatset used to arrive at their forecast for the particular points just mentioned, he might understand why I took issue with them . . . it is abundantly clear that Mr Benyon has joined Chatset in 'cloud cuckoo Land'!
THE TIMES, June 15, 1992.

usage: A hyphenated version is common: *cloud-cuckoo-land.* Informal.

see also: an ivory tower

cloud nine, on

supremely happy

Two possibilities present themselves for this phrase. In the USA *on cloud seven* is sometimes still heard. This, according to some, was the original expression and it referred to the seventh heaven, the dwell-

ing place of Almighty God (see *in the seventh heaven*). It is unclear why the number nine should have been substituted. Supporters of this theory say that it is because of the ancient significance given to the number three – nine being the square of that number. This overlooks, however, the prominence given to the number seven in the Mohammedan and Jewish cultures, an importance reflected in the *seventh* heaven.

A less spiritual and more scientific explanation is also offered. It seems that meteorologists hold that the thickest clouds are up to eight miles high. Being *on cloud nine* then is to go one better and find oneself in ecstasy. This leaves us with the uncomfortable question as to why some US citizens should be content with cloud seven.

Dawn French is a marshmallow of emotion – a mum in love. Dawn, 34, and husband Lenny Henry, 33, have been on cloud nine since Billie arrived last September.
TODAY, May 6, 1992.

Hawaiian actress Tia Carrere is on cloud nine. Her first major role, in the US smash hit comedy Wayne's World, *has catapulted her into the spotlight and she is about to appear with Sean Connery in* Rising Sun. *Her career is going so well the 25-year-old has even had to postpone her marriage to property developer Elie Samaha until October.*
DAILY EXPRESS, May 23, 1992.

usage: informal

clue: not to have a clue

to have no idea, to lack inspiration; to be perplexed

For this phrase we need to look to the ancient Greek story of Theseus and the Minotaur. The Minotaur was a terrible beast, half-man and half-bull, which lived in a huge and complicated Labyrinth on the island of Crete. The king wished to be rid of the monster but no champion ever came out of the Labyrinth alive. They were either killed by the Minotaur or lost in the maze of corridors. Theseus determined to slay the Minotaur. When he entered the maze he took with him a ball of thread which he unwound and let out as he groped his way down the dark corridors. After a mighty struggle, Theseus killed the monster and was able to find his way safely out of the Labyrinth by rewinding the ball of thread.

Originally, *clue*, or *clew*, meant 'ball of yarn' but, as the story of the Minotaur gained popularity, the word took on a new meaning, that of a means to solving a puzzle.

'I want to look my best, but I haven't a clue where to start. Should I wear make-up or go without? Should I wear my hair up or down? I really could do with some help.'
WOMAN'S OWN, September 16, 1991.

But if the dish is to be made commercially for Marks & Spencer, it will be his task as technologist to find the fish. The red mullet has not been sourced before – 'I haven't a clue where we would get it' – and as for the lobster tails, well . . . you can get them frozen from Canada, but now is not the season.
GOOD HOUSEKEEPING, December 1991.

usage: informal

cock a snook at someone, to

to show defiance, contempt or opposition

The phrase describes *snooks*, the disdainful gesture of putting the end of the thumb of one hand on the tip of the nose and spreading out the fingers. Although this sign of contempt only came about during the last century its origins are unknown. Today the expression can be applied to any show of contempt and need not be accompanied by the gesture.

Suzannah Jackson broke down in tears when she was convicted of stealing £25,000 worth of designer clothes and cheques from her former boss. But Jackson still managed to cock a snook at her old employer by wearing a suit designed by Miss Cierach, who created the Duchess of York's wedding dress.
DAILY EXPRESS, October 8, 1991.

My more considered verdict is that he is demonstrating, by a gesture of heroic dottiness, his unquenchable confidence in the future. By similar token, it could be argued that he is cocking a snook at the industry's Cassandras.
SUNDAY TELEGRAPH, May 17, 1992.

cock-a-hoop, to be

to be delighted, jubilant

During medieval drinking bouts the ale literally flowed freely. The spigot, or *cock*, would be removed from the barrel and placed upon the hoop at the top, leaving the contents to run down in an unregulated stream whilst the assembled company made merry. This is certainly how Sir Thomas Moore and his contemporaries seem to have used the phrase:

'*They . . . sette cocke a hoope, and fyll in all the cups at ones.*' (*A Dialogue of Comforte Against Tribulation*, 1529.) It is easy to see how the meaning might have moved from alcoholic merriment to rowdy elation of any kind.

An alternative but much less favoured suggestion is that *hoop* is a corruption of the French *houppe* or *huppe* meaning 'crest of feathers', the allusion being to a strutting game-cock.

You'll make a mutiny among my guests?
You will set cock-a-hoop.
WILLIAM SHAKESPEARE, Romeo and Juliet, 1594.

Your eyes, lips, breasts are so provoking
They set my heart more cock-a-hoop
Than could whole seas of cray-fish soupe.
JOHN GAY, Poems, 1720.

Harland & Wolff, the Belfast shipyard, was rightly cock-a-hoop about landing a £230 million order for six new bulk carriers which, given the state of British shipbuilding, suggests that the yard's sales staff probably walk on water in their spare time.
THE TIMES, August 31, 1991.

Corky the cockerel was cock-a-hoop last night after a court ruled he should not be silenced.
TODAY, May 12, 1992.

codswallop: a load of codswallop

a lot of nonsense, something of no value
rubbish

Codswallop is an interesting blend of 'Codd' and 'wallop', 'Codd' being the name of a Victorian businessman, Hiram C. Codd, and 'wallop' a nineteenth-century slang term for beer. In 1872 Mr Codd went into business selling lemonade in green glass bottles with marble stoppers. The brew was humorously referred to as *Codd's wallop*. Just how good the lemonade really was can only be guessed at from the derisory tone of the term.

Codswallop may be making a comeback, however, and this time as 'the ultimate designer water'. The *Daily Mail* (October 16, 1991) carried an article about the Yawl Spring, a source once enjoyed by the Romans and monks of Glastonbury Abbey. The spring was reopened by local businessmen who found the sales gimmick they were looking for literally under their feet:

When the Victorian bottling plant closed, its stock of Codd bottles was buried on the slopes of Knoll Hill, Uplime. Director Chris Hallett said: 'We were playing marbles with the stoppers when we realised that we'd found a container that made Coke, Perrier, and Grolsch bottles look boring'.

The original plant and moulds were tracked down to India. And now Bate's Mineral Water, the new Codswallop, is sold in top people's stores and restaurants.

The phrase can now be applied to anything at all of no value, not simply a drink.

The world's most beautiful and most talented people we are told are walking bean poles. Luciano proves this to be a load of codswallop and he doesn't have to sing in the rain in order to prove it.
MID SUSSEX TIMES, August 16, 1991.

The Astronomer Royal, Professor Arnold Wolfendale of Durham University, struck a cautionary note. 'It's either the discovery of the decade or pure codswallop,' he said. 'We really do need confirmation before people get too excited.'
THE TIMES, April 24, 1992.

usage: Colloquial. The phrase can be expanded or abbreviated in a variety of ways: *a load of old codswallop, a load of codge.*

see also: mumbo jumbo, to talk gibberish

cold feet, to get

to feel anxious and uncertain about an undertaking, to the point of wanting to withdraw

According to an old Lombard proverb known in England in the seventeenth century through Ben Jonson's play *Volpone* (1605), *to have cold feet* signifies 'to be without means or resources', a reference, perhaps, to the fact that the destitute cannot afford shoes. If this is the root of our modern idiom, it is not evident how the expression came to mean 'nervous and uncertain', although it has been proposed that a novel by Fritz Reuter (1862), in which a card-player pleads 'cold feet' as his excuse for backing out of a game, might have influenced this shift in meaning.

Instead of 'getting cold feet', as the phrase for discouragement ran, and turning back, they determined to cover as many as possible of the seventeen hundred miles.
ELIZABETH ROBINS, The Magnetic North, 1904.

Swollen head, weak nerves, cold feet.
H. C. BAILEY, Mr Fortune Finds a Pig, 1943.

'We always planned to have four children . . . I wouldn't mind having one more, but Robert isn't keen. Probably if he said "Go ahead", I'd get cold feet.'
GOOD HOUSEKEEPING, July 1992.

usage; informal

cold shoulder: to give someone the cold shoulder

to behave in an unfriendly way towards someone, to snub someone; to be unenthusiastic about an idea

In medieval times the welcome guest to the family home would naturally be treated to a warm reception and a lavish meal. On the other hand, the unwanted visitor who was just passing by or the guest who had stayed rather too long would be served from a cold shoulder of mutton, probably the leftovers from dinner the night before.

The performance has placed Yeltsin at the pinnacle of popularity at home and won him admiration in the West, where he has until recently been cold-shouldered, even insulted, as a dangerous populist and troublemaker . . .
OBSERVER, August 25, 1991.

I recently purchased a very expensive cat-accessory, which has somehow failed to elicit huzzahs of appreciation. In fact, it has been completely cold-shouldered. Called a 'cat's cradle', it is a special fleecy-covered cat-hammock which hooks on to a radiator. The cat is suspended in a cocoon of warmth.
THE TIMES, January 1992.

The City of Coventry finds itself in a delicate position as the result of the war in Yugoslavia: it is twinned with both Sarajevo, capital of Bosnia, and Belgrade, the Serbian capital. David Edwards, the outgoing Lord Mayor, has been trying, unsuccessfully, to fax a message of sympathy to his opposite number in Sarajevo . . . But Coventry is giving Belgrade the cold-shoulder. A council spokesman says: 'It's just that Sarajevo is the city that's suffering.'
DAILY TELEGRAPH, May 29, 1992.

usage: The derivative *to cold-shoulder* is growing in frequency.

cold turkey, to go

to come off (hard) drugs abruptly, rather than gradually and more easily

Although drug-world terminology changes quickly, this particular phrase goes back at least to the early 1930s. Partridge gives several quotations from the period in his *Dictionary of the Underworld*. It caught on more widely in the 1960s with the spread of drug-taking.

The best explanation for the use of cold turkey in this context is that it was a plain dish, served without frills or ceremony. By analogy, the withdrawal method was the most basic and straightforward.

Cold turkey – instantaneous withdrawal – is the method usually used in jails to take a boy off narcotics. We used it partly because we had no choice; we could not administer the withdrawal drugs they use in hospitals. But we prefer cold turkey on its own merits, too. The withdrawal is considerably faster; three days as against three weeks. The pain is more intense, but it is over sooner.
DAVID WILKERSON, The Cross and the Switchblade, 1963.

usage: Applied metaphorically to any situation that involves painful withdrawal by an act of will. Colloquial.

see also: to sign the pledge

cold water: to pour/throw cold water on something

to discourage, to quench enthusiasm for something

Plautus used the expression in 200 BC in the sense of 'to slander', but it is only since the beginning of the nineteenth century that it has been current and with the changed sense of 'to discourage'. The origin of the term is unknown, but it brings to mind the dousing of brawling cats, mating dogs or even ardent suitors in cold water, thus bringing their intentions to an abrupt end.

As he walked across the room to the veranda, to escape her angry accusing face, it seemed to her that it was not a tall, spare, stooping man whom she saw, only; but also a swaggering little boy, trying to keep his end up after cold water had been poured over his enthusiasm.
DORIS LESSING, The Grass is Singing, 1950.

Officially, Dr Owen has dismissed such talk as speculation, but I understand the main person likely to pour cold water on his application would be current Foreign Secretary Douglas Hurd.
DAILY MAIL, October 11, 1991.

Conspiracy theories abounded . . . However appealing, none of these scenarios bear much resemblance to the truth. The Daily Mail *had its story ready to run last Monday, but held it over, not only because Nigel Dempster, the paper's diarist, continued to pour cold water on it, but because John Smith's Labour budget had to be savaged in the Tory cause.*
THE SUNDAY TIMES, March 22, 1992.

colours: to nail one's colours to the mast

to be resolute, unwavering in one's opinions or principles; to declare one's allegiance publicly

Battleships always fly their colours, that is, their national ensign. If the flag were taken down, it was a sign of surrender. A flag literally nailed to the mast, however, showed the determination of the crew to fight on, come what may. Today the phrase is used to show a person's determination to stand by his opinion or principles, a stand which is not always easy to maintain, as Sir Robert Peel showed:

I never heard him [Ashburton] make a speech in the course of which he did not nail, unnail, renail and unnail again his colours. (Croker Papers, 1844)

She could not conceive in what ignominy the dreadful affairs would end, but she was the kind of woman that nails her colours to the mast.
ARNOLD BENNETT, The Matador of the Five Towns, 'Hot Potatoes', 1912.

In that famous Romanes Lecture, 'Evolution and Ethics', which contained his greatest single contribution to moral and religious thought, he nailed his colours to the mast.
JULIAN HUXLEY, Essays in Popular Science, 'Huxley and Religion', 1926.

colours: to sail under false colours

to be hypocritical, dishonest

In this expression, as in *to nail one's colours to the mast*, 'colours' are a ship's national flag which every vessel is obliged by law to fly. In the days when piracy was rife on the high seas it was a common deception of pirates, on sighting a likely treasure ship, to hoist the ensign of a friendly nation. In this way, *sailing under false colours*, the pirate vessel was able to approach its target without exciting suspicion, and then attack.

After his first visit to the bank over which Addison presided, and an informal dinner at the latter's home, Cowperwood had decided that he did not care to sit under any false colors so far as Addison was concerned.
THEODORE DREISER, The Titan, 1914.

Mr Stanley Baldwin simply had to be called Stanley Baldwin. Mr Ramsay MacDonald with any other name but Ramsay MacDonald would be sailing under false colours.
R. LYND, In Defence of Pink, 'Christian Names', 1939.

usage: Rather dated and not as common as a synonym *a wolf in sheep's clothing*.

colours: to show oneself in one's true colours

to make one's true opinion known, to show one's real self

Getting close to its prey by *sailing under false colours*, the pirate ship would at the last moment unfurl its own flag, the skull and crossbones, revealing its true identity and nefarious designs. This at least is the stereotype nurtured in endless Hollywood swashbuckling adventure epics, starring romantic heroes like Errol Flynn. The phrase itself long pre-dates its popularity in the first half of this century – it is found in the eighteenth century and in Dickens' *Old Curiosity Shop*.

*He showed me New York in its true
colours. He showed me the vanity and
wickedness of sitting in gilded haunts of
vice, eating lobster when decent people
should be in bed.*
P. G. WODEHOUSE, Carry On, Jeeves, 1925.

*Most Brazilians may sport Copacabana-
style suntans, but underneath it all they
want to be white . . . As Brazil begins its
first demographic census in over a decade,
an apparently straightforward question
seems to be fraught with difficulty for some
of the country's estimated 153 million
inhabitants. It is: Describe yourself
in terms of race or colour. Are you black,
white, or of mixed, Asiatic or indigenous
blood? The question is part of a campaign
to persuade Brazilians to reveal themselves in their true colours.*
OBSERVER, September 15, 1991.

usage: Too dramatic and romantic for
common use today.

see also: sail under false colours

couch potato, a

someone living life with minimum effort;
an inactive TV addict

A recent American idiom that has rapidly
caught on in the UK. This is probably
because of the colourful metaphor of the
stereotypical TV addict who leads a veg-
etable-like existence in front of the 'box',
sitting on his couch. As for the choice
of potato as the vegetable, one can only
hazard the guess that it has a reputation
of a dull, inert and shapeless mass – just
like the obese TV watcher.

New uses are proliferating – *Competitor's Companion* has a section called

'Couch Potato Comping'. This involves a
list of competitions where the absolute
minimum of effort is required to enter.

*Television can be blamed for many things
but not, apparently, for making you fat.
Scientists in Britain are sceptical of a
suggestion from an American psychologist
that couch potatoes are the shape they are
because television slows their metabolic
rate, rather than as a result of the quantities of food they eat and their lack of
exercise.*
THE TIMES, April 24, 1992.

usage: Used disapprovingly.

Coventry: to send someone to Coventry

to ignore someone totally, to refuse to
speak to someone

There are several suggestions as to why
this Midland town lends its name to the
idiom.

The first claims that during the English
Civil War (1642–1649) supporters of
Parliament in Birmingham rose against
small groups of their fellow citizens who
were known to have pledged allegiance
to the Crown. Some they killed, others
were sent as prisoners to neighbouring
Coventry, a town which was staunchly
pro-Parliamentarian. This story comes
from a passage in Clarendon's *True Historical Narrative of the Rebellion and Civil
Wars in England*. Whether the facts can
be relied upon or whether they are
coloured by the author's own royalist persuasion, the description of the events
includes the words 'and sent them to Coventry'. The literal sense has since become
a figurative expression of ostracism.

A transatlantic duo

In my office I have a little device for heating water in a cup so I can have a cup of coffee whenever I feel like it. It's not very solid, so I have got a couple of elastic bands round it to hold it together. It's very much of *a Heath Robinson contraption*. That expression comes from William Heath Robinson, who specialised in the first half of this century in drawing cartoons of elaborate and ingenious machines.

Across the Atlantic the same sort of fantastic invention, a needlessly complicated gadget, is known as a *Rube Goldberg*, after the Pulitzer prize-winning cartoonist. He, too, worked in the first half of the twentieth century.

A second theory is that the townspeople of Coventry so disliked having soldiers garrisoned in their town that if a woman was caught speaking to one she would instantly be shunned by her neighbours. The soldiers, of course, had no desire to be sent to Coventry where social contact was so difficult. No one knows at what period this aversion to soldiers is supposed to have arisen but the phrase was well known by 1777. It has been suggested that this also happened during the turbulent period of the Civil War.

Collins (1958) suggests that the term might be linked to the 'covin-tree', an oak which supposedly stood in front of a former castle in Coventry in feudal times and was used as a gallows. Those to be executed were *sent to the covin-tree*. The town's name, Coventry, may derive from 'covin-tree'.

In fact that solemn assembly a levy of the school had been held, at which the captain of the school had got up and given out that any boy, in whatever form, who should thenceforth appeal to a master, without having first gone to some propositor and laid the case before him, should be thrashed publicly, and sent to Coventry.
THOMAS HUGHES, Tom Brown's Schooldays, 1856.

The smaller fry among the courtiers were in a fury at Voltaire's appointment as gentleman-in-ordinary, a post hitherto reserved for the nobility. His new colleagues decided that when he came to dine with them they would send him to Coventry.
NANCY MITFORD, Voltaire in Love, 1957.

crocodile tears

a show of hypocritical sorrow; insincere tears

According to ancient belief the cunning crocodile arouses the curiosity of its unsuspecting victims with pitiful sighs and groans. Once its prey is within reach of its powerful jaws, the crocodile snaps it up and devours it, shedding insincere tears of sorrow all the while. Pliny and Seneca both give rather fanciful accounts of the crocodile's wiles and *crocodile's tears* is used figuratively to refer to a show of false emotion in both Greek and Latin. It is not surprising that, before travel and exploration became commonplace, people were prepared to accept the ancient belief. In 1356 Sir John Maundeville wrote his *Voiage and Travaile*. This account of things strange and fantastic mentions '*in a certain countree . . . cokadrilles*', adding, '*Theise Serpentes slen men, and thei eten hem wepynge.*' Two centuries later, in 1565, Sir John Hawkins wrote of a voyage he had undertaken and repeated the information. Small wonder then that Shakespeare and his audiences were well aware of the creature's supposed deceit:

> *Gloster's show*
> *Beguiles him as the mournful crocodile*
> *With sorrow snares relenting passengers.*
> (*Henry VI Part II*, 1590)

Not until the seventeenth century did belief in crocodile's tears wane and the phrase become purely idiomatic.

And George did chief mourner. I suppose he blubbered freely; he always could blubber freely when a lad. I remember how he used to take folks in as a lad, and then laugh at them; that's why they called him 'Crocodile' at school.
H. RIDER HAGGARD. c1900.

I'm told that tattoos can be removed, but it's an even more painful process. Remain undecorated – whether your boyfriend cries crocodile tears or not!
TV QUICK. September 28. 1991.

---

cross one's fingers, to

to be hoping for luck or a happy outcome

Crossing one's fingers is a quick and easy way of making the sign of the cross to shield oneself from diabolic power. It is also easy to *keep* them crossed, thus ensuring lasting protection from the devil's tricks.

Funk (1950) says that the expression is certainly American, probably originating among the black slave population.

Fingers are crossed for the South of England Traditional Youth Marching Band Contest . . . but it's the fifth time the 2nd Burgess Hill Boys and Girls Brigade have organised the event and they've got it off pat.
MID SUSSEX TIMES. September 6. 1991.

When I got back a colleague informed me that a large proportion of our Cabinet was on holiday in France. Keep your fingers crossed. They might learn something.
MID SUSSEX TIMES. August 9. 1991.

Tony plans to plant another 1,000 vines in the spring – and will keep his fingers crossed there are no late frosts.
DAILY MAIL. October 11. 1991.

usage: The phrase is still often accompanied by the physical sign of crossed fingers. The expression is very flexible and can be used in a variety of forms.

---

crow: as the crow flies

the shortest distance between two places, the measure of the straight distance between two points

See *to make a bee line for.*

I think the pots are rather attractive . . . The one I dug up is in Somerset. I don't like to separate it from the house which is, as the crow flies, about 15 miles from Bridport.
TELEGRAPH MAGAZINE. April 25. 1992.

usage: informal

---

cry wolf, to

to (habitually) sound a false alarm

One of Aesop's fables tells of a shepherd boy who kept himself amused by crying 'wolf, wolf' to alarm the villagers and make them rush to his rescue. One day wolves really did come among his flock, but when he cried out for help no one took any notice.

Time and again the economists and fore-casters had cried wolf, wolf, and the wolf had made only the most fleeting of visits. Time and again the Reserve Board had expressed fear of inflation, and inflation had failed to bring hard times.
F. L. ALLEN, Only Yesterday, 1931.

On that January day in 1982, the first new year within the royal family, she threatened to take her own life. Charles accused her of crying wolf and prepared to go riding. But she was as good as her word. Standing on top of the wooden staircase she hurled herself to the ground, landing in a heap at the bottom.
ANDREW MORTON, Diana: Her True Story, 1992.

---

cup of tea: not one's cup of tea

not to one's taste

Tea is reputedly the national beverage of the British and has been enjoyed by them since it was brought into the country in the seventeenth century. This rapturous eulogy from Colley Cibber's *The Lady's Last Stake* (1708) gives us a glimpse of the tea drinker's heaven:

Tea! thou soft, thou sober, sage, and ven-erable liquid,
thou female tongue-running, smile-soothing,
heart-opening, wink-tipping cordial, to whose glorious
insipidity I owe the happiest moments of my life.

Later that century, Cowper gave expression to the British affection for and dependence upon tea when he wrote: *'The cups That cheer but not inebriate.'* (*The Task*, 1785)

A misquotation of this is still frequently and contentedly murmured over the nation's tea cups. For a British citizen to declare, therefore, that something is *not his cup of tea* is a damning statement showing distaste or even detestation. On the other hand the statement *That's just my cup of tea* brings with it an aura of satisfaction and approval.

Broadway by night seemed to be my cup of tea entirely. Its splendours and its noise and its crowds haunted my imagination. Its gigantic sky-signs dazzled my dreams, flashing in a myriad lights, with unfailing regularity, the two words 'Noël Coward'.
NOËL COWARD, Present Indicative, 1937.

Ghoulish actor Peter Cushing could soon hit new heights as a pop star – at the age of 78. He was originally asked to recite a war poem with traditional backing music for Christmas release but now the poem has been set to a funky dance beat. 'When I first heard it I was a bit taken aback. It's not quite my cup of tea,' says Cushing.
DAILY MAIL, October 16, 1991.

Novels adapted for the stage have never really been my cup of tea . . .
THE JOURNAL, November 7, 1991.

usage: The phrase implies a strong liking (*just my cup of tea*) or, perhaps more commonly, the converse with a negative.

---

curate's egg: like the curate's egg – good in parts

something which is a haphazard mixture of good and mediocre

See bad/good egg

There was just as much protein in the curate's half-bad egg as in a fresh egg, but no one would willingly eat the half-bad one (except, perhaps the curate under the eagle eye of his bishop).
COBUILD CORPUS.

In the last analysis, the ILEA school system would, I suppose, pass the Advanced Curate Egg Test. Good in parts, depending on how you looked at it.
COBUILD CORPUS. The Times, 1990.

curry favour, to

to seek someone's approval through flattery, to ingratiate oneself with someone

The phrase is a corruption of Middle English *to curry favel* or *fauvel*, itself from the Old French *estriller fauvel*, meaning 'to rub down or groom a chestnut horse'. *Fauvel* derives from the French *fauve*, meaning 'fallow-coloured'. In a fourteenth-century French allegory, *Le Roman de Fauvel*, a fallow horse, representing hypocrisy and deceit, is carefully curried, or smoothed down, by other characters in order to gain his favour. The popularity of the work led people to accuse those intent upon furthering their own ends by flattery of *currying favel*. Through the closeness in pronunciation between 'favel' and 'favour' and the link in meaning, it is not surprising that the phrase became *to curry favour*.

In order to curry favour with the Grand Duke, who might at any moment become Tsar, the Schouvalovs encouraged him to bring to St Petersburg a detachment of his Holstein troops.
HAROLD NICOLSON. The Age of Reason, 1960.

Young Quintus was indeed thought to have gone to curry favour with Caesar by denouncing his uncle as one of Caesar's enemies. This was bad enough for Cicero; it was tragic for Cicero's brother.
F. R. COWELL. Cicero and the Roman Republic. c1960.

cut and run, to

to make a quick get-away, to quit

Formerly anchor cables on sailing vessels were made of hemp. If a naval warship at anchor were in danger of enemy attack and needed to make a speedy departure, the crew would not take the time to wind in the anchor but would simply *cut* through the cable and then let the ship *run* before the wind.

Thus spake Bavaria's scholar king,
Prepared to cut and run:
'I've lost my throne, lost everything,
Olola, I'm undone.'
EPIGRAM quoted in Quarterly Review, 1887.

I've not met the man. I've tried to, but he wouldn't see me. But if you do decide to cut and run, you'd best do it early before he and his mother have got into the way of you.
ANGUS WILSON. Anglo-Saxon Attitudes. 1956.

usage: informal

cut no ice with someone, to

to make no impression upon someone, to be powerless to influence someone

This expression originated in America towards the end of the nineteenth century and came into British usage in the 1920s.

It refers to ice skating. One can only move about with ease on ice skates if the blades are keen and cut into the ice. Blunt blades make no impression on the ice, just as a plan or a project, for instance, makes no metaphorical impression on someone – the skater makes no progress and neither does the plan.

Jeremy soon found out that Professor Tibbitts cut very little academic ice at the Sorbonne, but was too cautious to betray his surprise.
RICHARD ALDINGTON; Soft Answers, 'Stepping Heavenward', 1932.

We had him tied up in no time, just like you rope a calf to take to market. He yelled some, and kicked a great deal, but that didn't cut no ice with the boys and me.
ERSKINE CALDWELL, God's Little Acre, 1933.

The charge was hotly and repeatedly denied, not just by Ministers but by the hospital concerned. That cut no ice with Neil Kinnock.
DAILY EXPRESS, October 8, 1991.

usage: colloquial

cut to the quick, to

to cause someone deep emotional hurt

Quick comes from the Old English word *cwicu*, meaning 'living', and refers to the most sensitive flesh on the body, that protected by the fingernails and toenails. Someone who has been figuratively *cut to the quick* feels inner pain as intense as if the quick had been pierced.

The Authorised Version of the Bible uses *quick* in the sense of 'living'. New Testament passages which speak of God's judgement declare that he will come to judge 'the quick and the dead'. There is

no sense of speed of movement for *quick* here, although the evangelist Billy Graham neatly drew upon the potential ambiguity in suggesting that in New York there were only two types of pedestrian – the quick and the dead!

I am in trouble again with a regular reader of this column who has berated me 'for being far too gloomy'. By his count, at least half of what I write is 'riddled with defeatist pessimism'. This cuts me to the quick. Most of my colleagues in the environment movement are infinitely gloomier than I am, and deeply suspicious of any tendency to look on the bright side.
WEEKEND TELEGRAPH, May 9, 1992.

usage: literary

dampers: to put the dampers on something

to discourage; to hinder

A damper is a device in a piano which presses upon the strings to stop them vibrating. When the dampers are on, the effect is that of cutting the sound dead. The term is used figuratively to describe the stifling effect that an unhappy event, circumstance or person might exert upon the enjoyment of others.

Author Anne Edwards blames it on the undescended Royal testicles. They certainly put the dampers on the more steamy bits of this extraordinary story.
DAILY MAIL, August 22, 1991.

'Easter is normally such a joyous family gathering but this year the Duke is so sad it is putting the dampers on everyone.'
DAILY EXPRESS, April 20, 1992.

usage: colloquial

dark horse, a   ⚓

an unknown quantity, a person whose abilities are not yet known and tested

Benjamin Disraeli is credited with bringing this racing term to public attention. His novel *The Young Duke* (1831) contains a description of a horse race in which the two favourites cannot make the running while '*a dark horse which never had been thought of rushed past the grandstand in a sweeping triumph.*' In the competitive world of horseracing, owners sometimes like to conceal the potential of a promising young horse until it has been tried on the racecourse. A *dark horse* is one whose form has been withheld from public scrutiny in this way.

By extension the phrase might simply be used to describe someone who has not yet had the opportunity to show what he can do. It is also applied to candidates for an election or for a job who are not well known but who might well be appointed. This particular use owes a lot to the election of James Knox Polk to the Presidency in the USA in 1844. More likely candidates for the Democratic nomination could not muster the required number of votes, so the compromise candidate, the relatively unknown *dark horse* Polk, came through. A few years later, in 1860, Abraham Lincoln was a similar dark horse compromise candidate for the Republican Party.

I congratulate you on falling in love with Rose. It makes me feel that I understand you so very much better. You have always been a bit of a dark horse.
DAVID GARNETT, Aspects of Love, 1955.

Jerry Knowles. The dark horse of the family. Dad started up an Action Saver Account for her. She's ended up with gross interest *on her savings (Jerry's a non-taxpayer who's registered with us). Now her account has a very healthy balance.*
ABBEY NATIONAL ADVERTISEMENT, Good Housekeeping, September 1991.

usage: Used as a noun or adjectivally.

devil: between the devil and the deep blue sea

trapped between two equally difficult sets of circumstances

Despite first appearances, there is no satanic influence behind this phrase. All authorities are agreed that it is a nautical term but differ on the details. The *devil* was either a seam or a plank on a wooden sailing ship but opinions vary, even in sailing manuals, as to where it actually was. Some say it was an outboard plank on the upper deck, others that it was a seam in that same place and still others that it was a seam close to the water level. Whatever it was, seam or plank, it was an awkward place to reach and a precarious place to be. Pity the poor sailor, then, to whom it fell to caulk the *devil* and its difficult seams. Perched *between the devil and the deep sea* he ran a grave risk of plunging, unnoticed, into the waters below. The original form did not contain *blue*, which was added later for emphasis.

The expression *the devil to pay*, meaning that unpleasant consequences will surely follow a course of action, probably has the same nautical origin.

Newlyn's fishermen are caught between the ministry and the deep blue sea. With falling profits and growing foreign competition, they fear their livelihoods could soon be washed away.
THE TIMES, Saturday Review, August 31, 1991.

Friendly fire is a term familiar primarily to the military since at least the Vietnam War, and more widely since the Gulf War of 1991. However, being under fire from one's own side is as old as warfare itself. It certainly happened to Colonel Robert Munroe, a Scotsman in the middle of a battle in the 1620s. He was with a Scottish regiment that was serving under a Swedish commander. During one engagement he found himself exposed not only to the fire of the enemy in front of him, but also to Swedish guns at his back. The guns weren't sufficiently elevated. So the cannonballs from them were falling short, killing Scottish soldiers, not the enemy. No wonder Colonel Munroe wrote afterwards 'I with my party did lie on our post as **betwixt the devil and the deep sea.**'

Oh dear! And I thought I had been ever so even-handed in the 'political' part of my Reflections! The Labour Party was 'the Devil', and the Tories were 'the deep blue C', yet still Gill Gardner thought that I was urging people to vote Conservative.
MID SUSSEX TIMES, January 17, 1992.

usage: Blue is now an essential element of the idiom.

---

devil: the devil to pay

terrible consequences following a course of action

There are two convincing etymologies. The first concerns the obvious reference to Satan. Many have tried to make a Faustian bargain with him (hence *to sell*

one's soul to the devil), but for the favours or powers received there is always a price to pay later. Halliwell in about 1400 has:

Beit wer be at tome for ay,
Than her to serve the devil to pay.
(Reliquae Antiquae)

The second explanation is probably more persuasive. There is plenty of evidence that this idiom is part of a longer nautical expression, *the devil to pay and no pitch hot. The devil* here is a seam or a plank on a ship – for a full account see *between the devil and the deep blue sea.* 'Pay' is from the Old French *peier* meaning 'to caulk'. If the devil were not caulked because the pitch had not been heated through, the necessary maintenance could not be done and revenue would be lost through the vessel's not being seaworthy. The consequences would be severe – just the sense of the contemporary idiom.

If they hurt but one hair of Cleveland's head, there will be the devil to pay and no pitch hot.
WALTER SCOTT, The Pirate, 1821.

It was so obvious, too, that old Lilian was also quite gone on the fellow and making a fool of herself about him. Did she want to compete with her Aunt Lilian? There'd be the devil and all to pay if Mrs Aldwinkle discovered that Irene was trying to cut her out.
ALDOUS HUXLEY, Those Barren Leaves, 1925.

usage: Colloquial. The full form of the expression is no longer in use.

see also: between the devil and the deep blue sea

dickens, the

hell, the devil

Many suppose the phrase to have something to do with the Victorian novelist Charles Dickens. This is not the case. The word has been in use since the sixteenth century. It is a euphemism for 'devil' and may be a contracted form of 'devilkin'. See 'Every Tom, Dick and Harry' under **People**, page 104.

So wherever this wretched word [impractical] occurs I'm left wondering what the dickens the writer means.
G. V. CAREY, Mind the Stop, 1971.

usage: The phrase can be used in a variety of ways: *What the dickens, how the dickens, the dickens I will, a dickens of a . . .* It is as flexible as the word hell that it euphemistically replaces. It should not properly be written with an initial capital.

die is cast, the

an irrevocable step has been taken

The phrase is a translation of 'Jacta alea est', words attributed to Julius Caesar as he crossed the Rubicon and committed himself to war with Rome. Although it is his momentous use of the expression which we recognise, he was, in fact, quoting a well-known Greek proverb to be found in the writings of Meander as early as 300 BC.

The meaning of the phrase speaks for itself. All dice games carry an element of chance and, once the die has been thrown, the player must reconcile himself to the outcome, whether favourable or not. The die cannot be thrown again.

See *to cross the Rubicon*.

I have set my life upon a cast,
And I will stand the hazard of the die.
WILLIAM SHAKESPEARE, Richard III, 1592.

The die is cast – I cannot go back.
GEORGE MEREDITH, The Egoist, 1879.

usage: literary

dodo: as dead as a dodo

dead, extinct, obsolete, out of date

The dodo was a peculiar, comical-looking bird with a large, hooked bill, and short, curly tail-feathers. Heavy and clumsy, the dodo was flightless, its small wings being totally out of proportion to its bulky body. Its name comes from the Portuguese *doudo* meaning 'silly, stupid'. There were two known species, one unique to each of the islands of Mauritius and Réunion in the Indian Ocean. Sadly, the increase in exploration and trade in the sixteenth and seventeenth centuries brought about the extinction of the dodo. Seamen and colonists found the cumbersome creatures both tasty and easy to catch. The settlers introduced pigs to the islands, which destroyed their nests and young as they foraged. By the close of the seventeenth century the luckless bird was extinct.

There is a curious after-effect of the extinction of the dodo. The tambalacoque tree flourished in Mauritius and Réunion up to the time of the demise of the dodo. No new seeds would germinate. By the 1970s, only thirteen tambalacoque trees were left in the world. It is known that many seeds will only germinate if they pass through the digestive system of a certain animal. It seems the tree's seeds need the dodo! As an experiment, an American expert used turkeys as a replacement, with some success. So perhaps the tambalacoque tree will not in its turn become *as dead as a dodo*.

They coined the phrase as 'dead as a dodo' in Victorian times, but at the rate we're going we may soon be saying 'as elusive as an elephant' or 'as likely as a grunting gorilla'. They are just two of the endangered species we see on this round-the-world safari, showing animals whose future hangs in the balance.
DAILY MIRROR, May 27, 1992.

usage: An alternative form is *as dead as the dodo*. Colloquial.

see also: as dead as a doornail

dog days

the hottest days of the year

The 'dog days', or *dies caniculares* as the Romans called them, last approximately from the beginning of July until the middle of August. During this period the dog star Sirius rises with the sun. The Romans believed that the star gave off heat which, together with that of the sun, made this the hottest time of the year.

As teachers return, refreshed and ready to meet the new term, education journalists are heaving a sigh of relief. The dog days of August, when school's out and we scribblers have little or nothing to chew over, are thankfully behind us.
TIMES EDUCATIONAL SUPPLEMENT, September 1991.

Isn't it time we British learned to keep our cool, emotionally speaking, in hot weather? It takes only a few days of high temperatures to bring tempers to boiling

point. We start by welcoming the warm weather – and end up cursing it. And we aren't even in the dog days of summer yet.
DAILY MAIL, June 30, 1992.

dog in a manger

unwilling to let others benefit from things one cannot use oneself; spoiling

One of Aesop's fables tells of a dog which sat in a manger full of hay and snapped at a hungry ox to prevent it from eating. The dog had no use for the hay but begrudged the ox its fodder. The application is to someone who holds on to things he cannot use in order to deprive someone else of having use of them.

There you are; the dog in the manger! You won't let him discuss your affairs, and you are annoyed when he talks about his own.
WILLA CATHER, The Professor's House, 1925.

You told me the other day that you weren't going to write anything about him yourself. It would be rather like a dog in a manger to keep to yourself a whole lot of material that you have no intention of using.
W. SOMERSET MAUGHAM, Cakes and Ale, 1930.

usage: The phrase can be used as a noun but today is much more commonly found adjectivally e.g. *a dog-in-the-manger attitude*. It is then often hyphenated.

dog: to see a man about a dog

a phrase used to disguise the purpose of one's business

The expression is from a play, *Flying Scud* by Dion Boucicault. It was produced in London in 1866 and in New

York the following year. It has long since been forgotten, except for the phrase *to see a man about a dog*, which was used by a character as a ploy to get away from a tricky situation.

I've got to get back to London to see a man about a dog.
DOROTHY SAYERS, In the Teeth of the Evidence, 1939.

I've an appointment with a dog about a walk.
J. J. CONNINGTON, Four Defences, c1950.

usage: Informal, sometimes humorous. When the phrase is used, both parties in the conversation know it is a conventional way of refusing to be specific. A particular use is to signal in a humorous, socially acceptable way a trip to the toilet.

doldrums, in the

depressed, low in spirits

The origin of the form of the word *doldrum* is thought to lie in the Old English word *dol* meaning 'dull'. As for the meaning, there are two schools of thought.

Early in the nineteenth century, and probably before, *in the doldrums* was used as a synonym for 'in the dumps, depressed'. Later sailors borrowed the phrase to describe the region of sultry calms and baffling winds within a few degrees of the Equator where the north-east and south-east trade winds converge. Here the progress of sailing ships would be greatly delayed for many days, their crews becoming frustrated and demoralised through inactivity. Hence their feelings provided the name for the area.

Other authorities suggest that the reverse is true: the idiom is derived from

the name of the place, the doldrums. It is difficult to be sure, but the dating of the usages given in the *OED* gives support to the first version.

Rudyard Kipling was in the doldrums, partly because his politics were unpopular in the decade following the Boer War, and partly because his later work was inferior to the work by which he became famous.
F. SWINNERTON, The Georgian Literary Scene, 1934.

see also: down in the dumps

donkey's years: not for donkey's years

not for a very long time

The long characteristic of a donkey isn't his life, as this phrase might lead one to believe, but his ears. Formerly if you met a friend you hadn't seen for a long period of time you might say, 'I haven't seen you for *as long as a donkey's ears*', which was the original expression, but quite a mouthful. Economy of effort together with a certain play on words gave us the current form of the expression, *donkey's years*, which is neater if misleading.

Years ago – years and years and donkey's ears, as the saying is.
E. M. WRIGHT, Rustic Speech, 1913.

I haven't seen her for donkey's years. I'd like to see her again and have a chat about the old days.
W. SOMERSET MAUGHAM, Cakes and Ale, 1930.

I can at least vouch for Ian Botham being in good form with both bat and ball . . . He is still trying to win games single-handedly, and damn near succeeding. I

suppose I have to admit he got me out for the first time in donkey's years.
DAILY TELEGRAPH, June 4, 1992.

usage: informal

doornail: as dead as a doornail

unquestionably dead

It is to be expected that preoccupation with death will give rise to a number of euphemisms and similes. Over recent centuries people have been *as dead as mutton, a mackerel, a herring, a nit* and even *Queen Anne (the day after she dy'd)*. Strangely, the oldest expression of them all, *dead as a doornail*, used in *William of Palerne* around 1350, is the one which has best survived into modern usage.

Medieval doors were studded with large-headed nails, but it is not easy to understand why the comparison with a doornail should have arisen unless the nail in question were that which was struck by the knocker. Anything repeatedly pounded in this fashion would definitely be dead.

Whoever did it, the same person put a couple of poisoned aspirin tablets by Letty Blacklock's bed – thereby bumped off poor Dora Bunner. And that couldn't have been Rudi Scherz, because he's as dead as a doornail. It was someone who was in the room that night.
AGATHA CHRISTIE, A Murder Is Announced, 1950.

'You can't just leave him there like that.'
'He's dead, ain't he?' Floyd said dazedly.
'He's deader than a doornail,' Spence said. 'And you've got to do something about him. He can't stay here.'
ERSKINE CALDWELL, Tragic Ground, 1963.

usage: colloquial

see also: as dead as a dodo

down in the dumps

depressed, low, dejected

Such a very evocative phrase seems to call for a pleasing etymology. Instead, *dumps* is no more than a borrowing from Northern European languages. Swedish has *dumpin*, 'melancholy'; Dutch has *dompig*, 'damp or hazy'; and German has *dumpf*, meaning 'gloomy, damp' – all depressing stuff.

Nevertheless, the usage is old. People have certainly been in the dumps since the early sixteenth century and perhaps even earlier. A ballad thought to have been composed by Richard Sheale about 1475 has the line: 'I wail, As one in doleful dumps.' Singing the blues is not a twentieth-century malady.

What heapes of heauynesse, hathe of late fallen amonge vs alreadye, with whiche some of our poore familye bee fallen in suche dumpes.
SIR THOMAS MORE, A Dialoge of Comforte against Tribulation, 1534.

Mildred was in the dumps. She felt heavy and tired and she wasn't interested in anything.
JOHN STEINBECK, The Wayward Bus, 1942.

'It's an odd business. Spending the day in studio can be nice, but it can be pretty awful, too, and you go home feeling really down in the dumps.'
TV QUICK, September 18, 1991.

usage: The expression has standardised with the more emphatic form *down in the dumps*.

draw a blank, to

to fail in attempts to discover something; to be unsuccessful in efforts to remember something

The 'blank' in the expression refers to a blank lottery ticket in a draw where only numbered tickets win prizes.

First of all I tried to trace details of books, et cetera, sent in large consignments across the Tibetan frontier, but at all the likely places, such as Shanghai and Peking, I drew complete blanks.
JAMES HILTON, Lost Horizon, 1933.

Detectives, who had been unable to establish that any assault took place, immediately called off the investigation. An inquiry by club staff had also drawn a blank.
DAILY MAIL, October 2, 1991.

drive a coach and horses through something, to

to reveal the inadequacies of an argument or proposal, to rebut; to breach

Sir Stephen Rice, Chief Baron of the Irish Exchequer, is credited with coining this phrase around 1670 in his vigorous opposition to the Act of Settlement. According to Archbishop King, it was a term he employed often in this context:

He was (to give him his due) a man of the best sense among them, well enough versed in the law, but most signal for his inveteracy against the Protestant interest and settlement of Ireland, having been often heard to say, before he was a judge, that he would 'drive a coach and six horses through the act of settlement,' upon which both depended (State of the Protestants of Ireland).

The more familiar generalisation, '*I can drive a coach-and-six through any Act of Parliament*', arising from Rice's words is, however, attributed to Daniel O'Connel, another Irishman who defended the Catholic cause in the following century.

Councillor Edwards said: 'I see no evidence that there is no other suitable site and it would be foolish to breach our strategic gap policy.'
    Councillor Crane said: 'We have a planning policy to stick to but we are driving a coach and horses through it.'
CRAWLEY OBSERVER, January 15, 1992.

usage: To drive a coach and horses through something is the only current form.

duck: a lame duck

An ineffectual person, a failing business

The original allusion to a duck with clipped wings or injured webbed feet seems to have been applied to someone who could not pay his debts on the Stock Exchange: '*Frauds of which a lame duck on the stock exchange would be ashamed*' (Macaulay, *Mirabeau*, 1841). The great actor Garrick apparently coined the phrase in a play he wrote in 1771: '*Change Alley bankrupts waddle out [like] lame ducks.*' Stock Exchange slang then spread far wider, developing new senses. It reached America after the Civil War and became attached to politicians whose term of office was nearly over and whose power, therefore, was waning. This usage is now widespread in England.

We rarely hear of him now. In the early seventies there was Selsdon man, a prototype Thatcherite in the days when Mrs

Thatcher was ensconced in the Department of Education . . . The term derived from the Selsdon Park Hotel, where Edward Heath and his new Conservative Cabinet took various tough-minded decisions not to help lame ducks over stiles. But it only survives today in the form of the so-called Selsdon group which has run into trouble in Blackpool this week for failing to pick up the new Conservative message to soft-pedal on privatisation.
GUARDIAN, October 10, 1991.

usage: Can be used as a noun or adjectivally, particularly in phrases like *a lame duck presidency.*

Dutch courage

courage found by drinking alcohol, cowardice

Dutch courage is an expression of contempt implying, as it does, a bravery that is alcohol-induced. A magnificent, though short-lived, victory over the Dutch at the battle of Lowestoft during the Second Dutch War brought the following lines from the pen of Edmund Waller and show what the English thought of the courage their adversaries displayed:

The Dutch their wine and all their brandy lose,
Disarm'd of that from which their courage grows.
(Instructions to a Painter for a Picture of the Victory over the Dutch, 3 June, 1665).

For other anti-Dutch expressions dating from the seventeenth century, see National rivalries (page 76.)

Not the twentieth part of a drop. No Dutch courage for me.
WALTER SCOTT, Redgauntlet, 1824.

A dose of brandy, by stimulating the circulation, produces 'Dutch courage'.
HERBERT SPENCER, The Study of Sociology, 1873.

'Could I have a drink?'
I had no compunction in gaining the Dutch courage for assassination at his own expense. I had two whiskies very quickly.
GRAHAM GREENE, Loser Takes All, 1955.

Dutch courage or a French Connection. *Hurstpierpoint could do with a drop of Dutch courage when it comes to twinning with a town in Holland.*
MID SUSSEX TIMES, September 27, 1991.

usage: derogatory

Dutch: double Dutch

gibberish, incomprehensible speech

The contempt in which the English held the Dutch in the seventeenth century is evident in this phrase. It implies that the Dutch language is unintelligible, nothing more than gibberish.

See National rivalries (page 76).

'The symptoms can generally be controlled by deep inhalations of carbon dioxide and only if they persist would one consider the possibility of resorting to a course of chlorpromazine.'
'Hic!' said Hamlet, who thought the Chinese doctor was talking double Dutch.
GYLES BRANDRETH, The Hiccups at No. 13, 1988.

see also: to talk gibberish, mumbo jumbo

National rivalries

Most nations seem to have a love–hate relationship with their neighbours. The British tend to look with respect at French *cordon bleu* cooking and admire French style in clothing, for instance. The English language borrows many cooking terms from French and menus in expensive restaurants are commonly in French, too. An elegantly dressed lady may be described as looking very *chic* – a word we have adopted from the French.

But the British can be distinctly uncomplimentary about other nations. Let's just look at two cases, the Dutch and the French.

There are a number of expressions which speak of the Dutch in sneering and critical tones. These phrases have their origins in the seventeenth century when the Dutch were hated commercial and military rivals. The extensive trading empire they had built up and the control they had over the European carrying-trade were prejudicing the development of the English economy. A literary example of the relations between the two countries comes from John Dryden, who set out to fan the flames of chauvinism with his tragedy *Amboyna* (1673). Amboyna was the name of a place in the Moluccas, or Spice Islands, where some Englishmen had been massacred by the Dutch in 1623.

The antipathy was very strong. Finishing off a remark with **or I'm a Dutchman** implies the strongest possible confidence in the truth of the statement, since the acceptance of the name 'Dutchman' would be the ultimate disgrace. This example is from J. B. Priestley's *The Good Companions* (1929):

> *Now it's started, mark my words. Elsie's nobbut the first, more to follow, or I am a Dutchman.*

Less commonly, *a dutchman* is a contrivance of builders to hide faulty construction work. In *a Dutch auction*, everything is done the wrong way round: the auctioneer starts at a highly inflated price, then slowly drops the figure until someone indicates they accept it – quite the opposite of the approved British way of starting at a low figure and allowing subsequent bids to push up the price.

The consumption of alcohol is a frequent taunt (see **Dutch courage**). *A Dutch bargain* is a one-sided one, struck during a drinking session. *A Dutch feast* is when the host gets drunk before the guests and *a Dutch concert* is a drunken uproar.

Even animals do not escape: *a Dutch nightingale* is a frog. Family relationships, it seems, are the reverse of those in England, for *to talk to someone like a Dutch uncle*, 'to reprimand', implies a stern relative, not the amiable, indulgent British stereotype. **A Dutch treat** is when you pay for yourself, as you do when you **go Dutch**. Such was the Englishman's opinion of Dutch practices and customs. Equally low is his respect for the language: anything incomprehensible in English is described as **double Dutch**.

By no means all of these expressions are still in common use, although those chosen for entries in this book are well-attested in recent literature and speech.

Strangely, the negative linguistic heritage left by many centuries of rivalry between the British and the French seems smaller than that left from the intense dislike of the Dutch which only lasted about a hundred years.

There is that mock apology *Pardon my French*. Colloquially, it's used after some swearing or offensive language: the bad language isn't English, it's my French that needs pardoning. Another example is **to take French leave**, meaning 'to go absent without leave or permission', and it is a direct reflection on the bravery, or rather the supposed lack of it, of French soldiers. It is well-known that the French get their own back: the equivalent phrase in French translates as 'to sneak off in the way the English do'.

Other fixed phrases imply a moral censure but also a grudging envy. The French have traditionally had a reputation for sexual prowess, recorded in *a French kiss* (with the tongue in the partner's mouth), *the French way* (oral sex), *a French letter* (a condom) and *the French disease* (venereal disease). At the risk of extending the feuding, it is perhaps some small defence to note that these terms might be a riposte to that Latin lover Casanova's use of language. In the eighteenth century, he was one of the first to use prophylactic sheaths, calling them *redingotes d'Angleterre* ('English overcoats') and since then the French have called them *capotes anglaises* ('English cloaks').

If consolation were needed, blaming other people seems to be an international pastime. Just within the area of language, to an Englishman unintelligible speech is, as we have seen, *double Dutch* or *It's all Greek to me*. To a Spaniard it is *as if it were spoken in Greek*, and to a Frenchman it is *Hebrew* or even *Iroquoian*! To add insult to injury, anyone who speaks poor French is said to *talk like a Spanish cow*.

Dutch: to go Dutch

to share the costs of an outing instead of allowing one's companion to pay (especially if a man has invited a woman out)

See *Dutch courage*, and **National rivalries** (page 76).

Then she said, 'Aren't you going to say anything.' I couldn't. I was miles away. The business about going dutch had really got me.
COBUILD CORPUS.

Dutch treat, a

an outing where guests are expected to pay for their share and which is not a proper treat at all

See *Dutch courage*, and **National rivalries** (page 76).

A. – It is up to you if you feel you can afford it. If you cannot, explain to the other guests that it is a 'Dutch treat', so they know in advance that they'll be paying for themselves.
GOOD HOUSEKEEPING, September 1991.

see also: to go Dutch

Dutchman: or I'm a Dutchman

a phrase to show strong disbelief

See *Dutch courage*, and **National rivalries** (page 76).

You come along with me and I'll take you to a place where they have Japanese girls, and if you don't see something you like there I'm a Dutchman.
W. SOMERSET MAUGHAM, Ah King, 'Neil Macadam', 1933.

dyed in the wool

totally committed to one's opinions

In medieval times vegetable dye was added to raw wool rather than to the spun yarn or finished cloth. By this method the dye permeated all the fibres so the colour of the finished cloth was more even and longer lasting. This process gives us our expression *dyed in the wool*, meaning someone who is imbued with a certain characteristic or set of beliefs, as in *a dyed in the wool politician*; a politician through and through.

In half an hour (he can) come out an original democrat, dyed in the wool.
DANIEL WEBSTER, Speech, February 10, 1830.

. . . Ifor Lewis was puzzled yesterday. After 61 years of dyed-in-the-wool bachelorhood, what little he knows about matrimony has only confirmed his view that it is definitely not a state to be in. Yet . . . his council colleagues have picked him as their representative on the marriage counselling service Relate.
DAILY MAIL, August 8, 1991.

usage: There are overtones of the incorrigible, the intractable, the inflexible associated with the idiom. It is not usually complimentary. Sometimes hyphenated.

> **There's a whole class of adjectival** idioms that will only follow the verb: *up a gum tree, bright as a button*. And another class that can normally only precede a noun, such as **dyed in the wool** and *hard core*.

eager beaver, an

an overly zealous person, one who tries to impress others with enthusiasm and hard work

An American phrase which came into vogue about the time of the Second World War. Some authorities say it originated amongst the American forces to describe those keen recruits who volunteered for absolutely everything; other American sources say it was widely used in student circles from about 1940. Beavers are reputedly industrious animals as phrases such as *to beaver away* show and 'eager' conveys enthusiasm. Put together, these two words make a catchy little rhyming phrase but one which carries the critical overtones of trying rather too hard to please.

[Itami's film] proves as funny and sexy as his satire on eating as eager-beaver lady tax-inspector Nobuko Miyamoto tracks down every fiscal scam under the rising sun.
WEEKEND TELEGRAPH, September 7, 1991.

ears: my ears are burning

a remark made by someone who thinks they are being talked about

A tingling or burning sensation in the ears supposedly means that a person is being discussed by others. The origin of this belief goes back to Roman times when augurs (see *under the auspices of*) paid particular attention to such signs. Pliny wrote:

It is acknowledged that the absent feel a presentiment of remarks about themselves by the ringing of their ears. (*Naturalis Historia*, AD 77).

The ancient belief that the left signified 'evil' and the right 'good' (see *set off on the wrong foot*) applies here also. Both Plautus and Pliny hold that if a person's right ear burns then he is being praised, but a burning left ear indicates that he is the subject of evil intent. English literature, from Chaucer to Dickens, abounds with references to burning ears.

According to ancient belief, other unexpected bodily twitches and sensations also, warn of events to come, among them the eye and the thumb. A flickering right eye, for instance, indicates that a friend will visit or that something longed for will soon be seen and a pricking in one's left thumb warns of an evil event.

I suppose that daie hir eares might well glow,
For all the towne talkt of hir, hy and low.
JOHN HEYWOOD, Proverbs, 1546.

I dine with Dolby . . . and if your ears do not burn from six to nine this evening, then the Atlantic is a non-conductor.
CHARLES DICKENS, Letters, 1868.

eat humble pie, to

to admit one's fault, to humiliate oneself while admitting wrong

'*The Accomplisht Lady's Delight in Preserving, Physick, Beautifying, and Cookery*' (1683) gives its readers a '*Bill of Fayre upon an Extraordinary Occasion*'. There follows a great list of dishes beginning with the magnificent and ending with '*no. 18 – an umble pye*'. This pie would have been filled with 'umbles', the offal and entrails of a deer, and was definitely a dish to feed those of low estate at the second table, while the lord's family and guests enjoyed the venison. Because those who ate umble pie were of humble stock confusion arose between 'umble' and 'humble', so that the phrase we know today means 'to admit a wrong to the point of humiliation'. Yet, even though lowly folk have been tucking into their 'umbles' since the fifteenth century, the expression has only been in use since the first half of the nineteenth century.

If you've made a fool of yourself you must eat humble pie. Your wife doesn't strike me as the sort of woman to bear malice.
W. SOMERSET MAUGHAM, The Moon and Sixpence, 1919.

The more she tried to find excuses to get away, the more cleverly Constance contrived to keep her, having a very large portion of humble pie she was determined the girl should eat to the last crumb.
RICHARD ALDINGTON, Soft Answers, 1932.

It's time to sink the critical teeth into a large slice of humble pie. Having hated episode one, I was utterly hooked on A Fatal Inversion (BBC1, 9.05 p.m.) by episode two.
DAILY EXPRESS, May 25, 1992.

egg on one's face, to have

to look foolish having made a wrong choice

Brandreth gives an American origin in the 1960s and a British use in 1972. It has certainly spread rapidly in this country, mainly in journalism. Throwing eggs at an opponent is not uncommon, especially on the political hustings. The idea seems to be that a politician with egg on his face is made to look foolish. Metaphorically, a decision that backfires leaves those responsible *with egg on their faces*.

We aimed to grow up with our readers and in so doing hoped to be around to define the new decade. Now we have egg on our face and the Face and iD, who stuck with a tried and tested style formula, must be crowing.
GUARDIAN, September 2, 1991.

The campaign polls made a hash of forecasting the result, and few people are inclined to feel sorry for soothsayers who end up with egg-spattered faces.
INDEPENDENT, May 1, 1992.

usage: colloquial

egg: to be a bad/good egg

to be an untrustworthy/dependable person

It is impossible to tell from simply looking at the shell whether an egg is fresh or not. Once the egg is broken it may reveal an unpleasant surprise, but a good egg will be found to have been completely sound right through to its very centre. So it is with people; the outward appearance will not reveal the content of the character. This is only discovered when time is taken to get to know a person better. Someone who is a *good egg* is known to be dependable through and through. A *bad egg* is someone to avoid.

The first written reference is to a *bad egg*. It makes it clear that it was current in spoken English for some time before: '*In the language of his class, the Perfect Bird generally turns out to be "a bad egg".*' (Samuel A. Hammett, *Captain Priest*, 1855.)

Good egg did not come into use until the beginning of this century, when it was probably coined amongst the students at Oxford.

The remarks about the freshness of eggs apply to another common expression, *like the curate's egg – good in parts*, which refers to something which is mediocre but has its good points. The edition of *Punch* published on November 9, 1895 carried a cartoon showing a timid curate eating a bad egg at the home of his bishop and bravely assuring his host that 'parts of it are excellent'. The simile is sometimes halved so that *good in parts* and *like the curate's egg* may be heard independently.

'A bad egg' . . . a fellow who has not proved to be as good as his promise.
THE ATHENAEUM, 1864.

'She's always off slaloming or down a coal mine,' says Ned Sherrin. Good-egg stories about her abound. Once she was asked to blow into a windmill which turned out to be a soot-blowing machine.
EVENING STANDARD, December 2, 1991.

Morse and Sgt Lewis gradually uncover the truth about a murder victim – an artist, a drinker and therefore a reasonably all-round good egg in the inspector's book. But things are not what they seem.
WEEKEND TELEGRAPH, January 18, 1992.

Is Red Ken a good egg on Labour's new menu?
HEADLINE, OBSERVER, April 19, 1992.

eggs: as sure as eggs is eggs

absolutely certain, beyond doubt

It is widely agreed that this phrase has nothing to do with eggs but is a corruption of the logic statement 'as sure as *x* is *x*'. The frequent use of a singular verb even with plural *eggs* supports this explanation.

As sure as eggs is eggs, the bridegroom and she had a miff.
OLIVER GOLDSMITH, The Good-Natur'd Man, 1768.

As the bishop said, 'Sure as eggs is eggs, this here is the bold Turpin.'
CHARLES DICKENS, Pickwick Papers, 1837.

A penalty taker always steps up and if he scores makes no mistake from the spot. Nothing is merely 'to the left/right' but away to the left/right; and as sure as eggs is eggs (or spheres are balls) you will hear your radio commentator tell you that Liverpool are playing from left to right.
WEEKEND TELEGRAPH, May 9, 1992.

usage: A plural verb is common: *as sure as eggs are eggs.*

eggs: to teach one's grandmother to suck eggs

to offer unnecessary advice to someone who is older and more experienced

This phrase is used to reprimand someone who, though young in years and green in experience, takes it upon himself to lecture an older and wiser person. The first written record is in John Stevens' translation of *Quevedo's Visions* (1707). A more well-known reference is in Swift's *Polite Conversation* of 1738: 'Go, teach your grannam to suck eggs.'

A number of earlier expressions existed along the same lines. In the mid sixteenth century the young were exhorted not to *teach our dame to spinne* and from the beginning of the seventeenth century they were advised not to *teach your grandame to gropen her ducks* (that is, to feel a duck and decide whether it will lay or not).

Quite why anyone should wish to suck

eggs has not been explained, unless it was to decorate the empty shell. It has been pointed out that a toothless grandmother would naturally be more successful in this than a grandchild with a complete set of teeth. Neither is it apparent why this form of the expression rather than the other more obvious ones should have come down to the present day.

This said, the phrase is open to a certain amount of humorous embroidery. R. D. Blackmore alluded to it thus: '*A . . . twinkle, which might have been interpreted – "instruct your grandfather in the suction of gallinaceous products"*' (*Christowell*, 1882), and there is a little Victorian ditty of unknown origin:

Teach not a parent's mother to extract
The embryo juices of an egg by suction:
The good old lady can the feat enact
Quite irrespective of your kind instruction.

According to Partridge (1950), in later years 'egg' became an underworld slang term for a confidence trickster's victim, in other words for a 'sucker', a reference to the expression under consideration.

This revolutionary idea is called Self Evaluation. Fancy . . . Doesn't everybody do it? This is the 'teaching your grandmother to suck eggs' syndrome I meet on every course. Arthur tries to start a debate on why grandmothers would want to suck eggs, but Ken and Steve and Sir will not be sidetracked.
TIMES EDUCATIONAL SUPPLEMENT. September 6, 1991.

. . . but then let him get on with it: it may be your kitchen and you may be the expert. But if he's washing (or cooking or shopping or child-minding) he doesn't need you giving egg-sucking instructions while he's doing it.
DAILY TELEGRAPH. May 29, 1992.

It may be impossible to teach grandmothers to suck eggs, but Asda, the supermarket chain, reckons it can teach the Spanish a thing or two about picking oranges. What is more, it has persuaded the European Community to pay for the lesson.
THE TIMES. June 15, 1992.

usage: informal

fair game

someone or something which may be attacked or ridiculed with good reason

Over the centuries there has been much legislation to deter poachers and to uphold the rights of landowners. The reign of George III saw an abundance of legislation, thirty-two Game Laws in all, which were essentially introduced with the motive of keeping hunting rights for the aristocratic minority who justified the laws by voicing fears that, without them, game stocks would be severely depleted. At the beginning of the nineteenth century it was illegal for anyone except the squire or his eldest son to take game, even if they had been permitted to do so by the landowner. A law of 1816 stipulated that anyone taking so much as a rabbit unlawfully should be transported for seven years. Poachers became increasingly skilful and landowners fought back by setting man-traps, some of which inflicted great damage, not only upon the intended victim but upon innocent passers-by.

The expression *fair game* was first used in 1825 and, against this background of abundant restrictive legislation to give the ruling classes exclusive rights to the countryside and its creatures, refers to those animals and birds which could be lawfully hunted. As the quotation of 1852 shows, it wasn't long before the phrase was extended to very different contexts.

As to the unfortunate Jews, each party considered them fair game.
CHARLOTTE M. YONGE. Cameos. 1852.

The law says that public figures like film stars are fair game because in their line of work they have voluntarily exposed themselves to public interest.
DAILY MAIL. August 8, 1991.

A dazzling variety of organisations now carves off slices of the calendar in the competition to catch the public eye. The coming year will bring round Million Tree Week, Breast Feeding Week, No Smacking Week, Condom Week, Veggie Pledge Week and a host of others..Months, years and even decades are all treated as fair game. There will be as many days in 1992 as there will be weeks, ranging from Pancake Day to National Kevin Day.
THE TIMES. January 1992.

---

feather in one's cap, a

credit, acknowledgement for one's work, achievement

It has been the custom amongst the people of very different cultures to wear a feather on the head for every enemy killed. The American Indians with their head-dresses are perhaps most well known for this, but the custom existed closer to home, too. Richard Hansard in *A Description of Hungary* (1599) writes:

It hath been an ancient custom among them [the Hungarians] that none should wear a feather but he who had killed a

Turk, to whom only it was lawful to show the number of his slain enemies by the number of feathers in his cap.

In England, too, bravery in combat was rewarded by the wearing of a feather. Knights who had shown outstanding valour in battle wore feathers in their helmets. It is possible that the origin of the phrase may be traced to one particular early example, that of Edward, the Black Prince who, at the age of sixteen, showed such bravery in the Battle of Crecy (1346) that the crest of blind John of Bohemia, one of the mighty knights in the enemy forces, was bestowed upon him. The crest, three ostrich plumes, is the emblem of the Princes of Wales to this day.

There are modern-day versions of this practice – pilots, for example, in the Second World War and the Gulf War put a symbol on the fuselage of their planes for each kill.

He wore a feather in his cap, and wagg'd it too often.
THOMAS FULLER. Church-History of Britain. 1655.

Ford had heard that my mother was worrying about my education and wrote: 'Send him to me for a few years and I will teach him to write like Flaubert.' This offer was not considered seriously and I missed the opportunity of becoming a feather in Ford's cap.
DAVID GARNETT. The Golden Echo. 1953.

Economic reform, political stability and close ties with Washington are the biggest feathers in Mr Menem's cap.
FINANCIAL TIMES. November 13, 1991.

Out of the considerable body of work he has produced, he has never had a flop. Most playwrights would be delighted by this. Bennett, forever wary, isn't so sure. He says: 'I don't think that it's necessarily

a feather in my cap. Perhaps you learn more from a real flop. Perhaps it's because I'm timid and tend to play safe.'
GOOD HOUSEKEEPING, December 1991.

feather: to show the white feather

to show cowardice

This is a phrase from the cock-pit. The plumage of a pure-bred cock had no white feathers in it. A cock with a white feather. in its tail was underbred and unlikely to perform as well as the best of the breed. Thus showing a white feather was equated with cowardice. This was, of course, a great defect as high stakes were wagered on fighting cocks.

During the First World War it was the practice of some women to give white feathers to able-bodied men in civilian clothes who they thought should have been away fighting in the trenches.

All the rejected men talked like that. War was the one thing they wanted, now they couldn't have it. All of them had a side-long eye for the women they talked with, a guarded resentment which said, 'Don't pin a white feather on me, you blood-thirsty female. I've offered my meat to the crows and they won't have it.'
K. A. PORTER, Pale Horse, Pale Rider, 1939.

The early attacks from the air were notice-able enough for a naval officer to be heard saying playfully to another, 'What! Going to sea, are you? So you're showing the white feather!'
W. PLOMER, At Home, 1958.

usage: dated

feet of clay

a weakness perceived in someone held in high regard

This is a biblical expression and comes from a story to be found in the Book of Daniel. Daniel, after spending the night in prayer, is the only wise man in Nebuch-adnezzar's kingdom who is able to tell the king what his troublesome dream means.

In his dream Nebuchadnezzar sees a huge and awesome statue made of differ-ent metals starting with gold at the head down to iron on the legs. The statue's feet are part iron and part clay. In the interpretation Daniel tells the king that by God's will he is the golden head but that other inferior kingdoms will succeed him, ending with a divided kingdom rep-resented by the feet of iron and clay:

As the toes were partly iron and partly clay, so this kingdom will be partly strong and partly brittle. And just as you saw the iron mixed with baked clay, so the people will be a mixture and will not remain united, any more than iron mixes with clay. (Daniel 2:42, New International Version.)

The mighty, awe-inspiring statue was not as strong as it first appeared, its great-est weakness being its *feet of clay*. Even the greatest – and superficially perfect – have hidden flaws.

Mr Carlyle made an inimitable bust of the poet's head of gold; may I not be forgiven if my business should have more to do with the feet of clay?
R. L. STEVENSON, Some Aspects of Robert Burns, 1880.

I look for clay feet before I even glance at an idol's head.
RUFUS KING, A Variety of Weapons, 1943.

usage: A literary cliché.

see also: Achilles' heel

fiddle: as fit as a fiddle

on top form, in excellent health

The earliest reference to the expression has been traced to William Haughton's *Englishmen for My Money* (1597): '*This is excellent, i'faith; as fit as a fiddle.*' In the sixteenth century the word *fiddle* was applicable not only to the instrument but also to the fiddler and, by extension, to an entertainer or mirth-maker. It is possible, therefore, that the phrase describes the fiddler, a vivacious character who made the company merry and played his instrument with vigour.

Supporters of the theory that the phrase is really about the instrument, not its player, point out that in past centuries 'fit' did not mean 'healthy' but 'suitable for a purpose'. So the phrase meant 'as suitable for its purpose as a fiddle is for music-making'. They argue that the phrase changed in meaning, and subsequently became nonsensical, when 'fit' gradually came to be synonymous with bodily well-being.

In the sixteenth century *fine as a fiddle* was also found. Possibly people were excited by the appearance of this new instrument, for it was not until that century that the fiddle in the form we know it today came over from Italy. Certainly the fiddle was admired, for an expression *a face made of a fiddle* was used, from the seventeenth to the nineteenth centuries, to describe someone with fine features. By contrast, the only comparison that survives nowadays between the face and the fiddle is a relatively recent one from the turn of the century, *to have a face as long as a fiddle*, and that means 'to look miserable'.

The epidural provided instant relief. I feel that if women have children they should have anything to stop the pain, provided it doesn't damage the baby. I had no problems afterwards, I felt tired, but fit as a fiddle.
DAILY TELEGRAPH, May 19, 1992.

usage: Another phrase with a long history that remains colloquial.

fiddle while Rome burns, to

to be occupied with trivialities while a crisis is taking place

An old story alleges that in AD 64 the Emperor Nero, in order to gain an impression of what Troy had looked like while ablaze, set fire to Rome, then sang and played his lyre while he watched the flames. It is said that the city burned for six days and seven nights. Nero himself denied the charge and put the blame upon the Christians, whom he then persecuted ruthlessly – first locally, then further afield. His claim to innocence is supported by contemporary historians who say he was far from the city at the time.

Tragedy has been stalking through this house: doctors have been telephoned for, sick rooms made ready, cool compresses prepared: and here are you two young men carelessly playing billiards. Fiddling while Rome burns is about what it amounts to.
P. G. WODEHOUSE, Uncle Fred in the Springtime, 1939.

filthy lucre

money, dishonourable profit

The middle English word *lucre* comes from the Latin *lucrum*, 'gain'. This in turn has the root *leu*, 'to win, to capture as booty' which lends the meaning of 'profit', 'booty', 'loot', 'value' to different words in a number of languages. The word stands by itself to mean 'dishonourable gain' but is usually found with the reinforcement of *filthy*. The phrase is used three times in the Authorised Version of the New Testament, in Titus 1:7 and in 1 Timothy 3:3 and 8. Indicative of the rather dated air of the phrase is that all the modern versions of the Bible replace it by 'money' or 'gain'.

If a Jew wants to be a rich man, he is apt to be keener about his business than a Gentile; but if he has no ambition to make money, and chooses to be a philosopher, or a musician, he will often show a noble indifference to filthy lucre, like Spinoza.
W. R. INGE, Lay Thoughts of a Dean, 1926.

Some farmers in their desperation to squeeze extra cash from alternative use of their land are turning green fields into rubbish tips . . . Nowhere is the pursuit of this filthy lucre more in evidence than among the downs of Wiltshire, where it is said they have the sort of clay that makes seepage from decaying waste easier to control.
WEEKEND TELEGRAPH, May 9, 1992.

Filthy lucre? Seems pretty clean-cut to me. The rule is that the higher you get up the tree the less you want the money to be mentioned. White-collar types, creative souls, even field-marshals of industry tend to prefer the vocabulary of vocation, challenge and service.
THE TIMES, June 15, 1992.

usage: The expression can still be used with negative connotations but is much more frequent today as a jocular term for money.

finger: to have a finger in the/ every pie

to play a part in doing something; to interfere in a matter

There is an ellipsis in this expression. It is better understood if read 'to have a finger in *making* the pie', when the sense of involvement becomes clear. There is nearly always an implication of meddling in other people's business. This universal human tendency has been reflected in this phrase for at least four hundred years.

No man's pie is freed From his ambitious finger.
WILLIAM SHAKESPEARE, Henry VIII, 1612.

You would have a finger in every bodies pie.
THOMAS SOUTHERNE, The Fatal Marriage, 1694.

Instead of every man airing his self-consequence thinking it bliss to talk at random about things, and to put his finger in every pie, you should seriously understand that there is a right way of doing things.
MATTHEW ARNOLD, Literature and Dogma, 1873.

Mike Castelton is as local as they come, a King's Lynn man through and through with a finger in numerous pies. Erstwhile trawler owner, market trader, expert on shellfish and a plasterer by trade, he's the kind of chap who gets up at five in the morning and is still going strong at 11 at night, preferably in the pub.
COUNTRY LIVING, September 1991.

usage: The use of *every* stresses the wide-ranging interest, even meddling, in matters.

flash in the pan, a

a brilliant initiative which amounts to nothing

The expression comes from a misfunction in the old flintlock gun. When the musket was fired, a flint striking against the hammer produced a spark which fired the priming, a small quantity of gunpowder held in the *pan*. This explosion ignited the main charge, forcing the ball to fly from the barrel. Sometimes the priming caught but failed to ignite the main charge, resulting in nothing more than *a flash in the pan*. When this happened the gun was said to be 'hanging fire', giving rise to another idiomatic phrase meaning 'slow to act'.

See also *to hang fire.*

There was little or no surprise that a play of mine should be so appallingly bad, for, in their minds at least, I had never been anything but a flash in the pan, a playboy whose meteoric rise could only result in an equally meteoric fall into swift oblivion.
NOËL COWARD, Present Indicative, 1937.

Engineers are flushed with pride at the success of a new scheme to wipe out a nagging problem and help reduce passenger inconvenience.

Passengers drying their hands on paper handtowels sometimes throw them into aircraft toilets instead of rubbish bins — resulting in frequent blockages which drove engineers round the bend.

On newer aircraft with vacuum toilets, like 747-400s, passengers were often badly inconvenienced . . . and complaints flooded in.

Now special new handtowels which disintegrate in water will be used on all fleets, after trials on Boeing 747s and 767s

proved that their early success was no flash in the pan.
BRITISH AIRWAYS NEWS, October 4, 1991.

flavour of the month, the

something temporarily in fashion

American ice cream parlours, certainly by the 1950s, encouraged their customers to eat more (by lowering the price in a promotion) and try new flavours (by featuring a less known one) with a *flavour of the month*. This has been a widespread marketing ploy in recent decades in many fields.

Flavour of the month is undoubtedly actor Sean Bean, cropping up here, there and everywhere on our screens this autumn.
GOOD HOUSEKEEPING, November 1991.

There is so much sensitivity (quite rightly) over male-dominated committees and organisations that as a woman you could find yourself flavour of the month.
GOOD HOUSEKEEPING, July 1992.

usage: Applied widely now to any fad or person. The implication is that the fame is very transitory and therefore not worth having. There is a hint that the speaker feels superior and scornful, even condescending.

see also: to climb on the bandwagon

flog a dead horse, to

to waste one's time pursuing a matter that has already been settled

This telling metaphor was first used in Parliament in the mid nineteenth century by John Bright MP, to castigate the apathy of his fellow parliamentarians towards a reform bill introduced by Lord John Russell. It was such an arresting phrase that he used it again when a measure proposed by Richard Cobden similarly found little parliamentary support.

One would have thought the etymological fallacy – that word sense is determined by original meaning – was a sufficiently dead horse in educated theological circles to spare it the humiliation of further flogging. However, Barr was able to provide a long chapter of examples to demonstrate that the horse in question, far from being dead, was actually enjoying rude health in even some of the most learned pastures.
COTTERELL AND TURNER, Linguistics and Biblical Interpretation, 1989.

usage: colloquial

fly in the ointment, a

something trifling that spoils or mars the whole

Funk (1950) suggests that an earlier version of the phrase was 'a fly in (the) amber' and it is indeed true that insects fossilised in amber were the subject of wonderment. Francis Bacon is one writer who remarked on it:

We see spiders, flies, or ants entombed and preserved forever in amber, a more than royal tomb. (Historia Vitae et Mortis, Sylva Sylvarum, 1623.)

There were many other similar comments, from Martial in his *Epigrams* to Herrick's poem *On a Fly buried in Amber*. Sydney Smith, in typical fashion, wrote of Canning:

He is a fly in amber; nobody cares about the fly; the only question is, How the devil did it get there?

The connection of amber with ointment is that, at one time, amber was the word commonly used for 'ambergris', which is an ingredient in some sweet-smelling ointments. However, the senses of wonderment, surprise and curiosity of *a fly in amber* are not close to the meaning of *a fly in the ointment*. In the Old Testament, in Ecclesiastes 10:1 we find: '*Dead flies cause the ointment of the apothecary to send forth a stinking savour.*' This is very much the sense of the contemporary phrase. So, in all probability, here is the source of our modern expression.

The only fly in the ointment of my peaceful days was Mrs Cavendish's extraordinary and, for my part, unaccountable preference for the society of Dr Bauerstein.
AGATHA CHRISTIE, The Mysterious Affair at Styles, 1920.

Do these explicit suppressions really serve the interests of the highest morality? Dr Toynbee reminds one of the man who . . . But enough: for, after all, it is not the fly but the ointment that claims our attention.
LYTTON STRACHEY, Biographical Essays, 'The Eighteenth Century', 1948.

usage: informal

fly off the handle, to

to fly into a fit of rage

This expression was current amongst American frontiersmen about 150 years ago. The reference is to an axe-head which, having worked loose on its home-made handle, finally flies off at the next hefty blow. For an axe to break in this way was not only dangerous but also meant that work had to stop until a new handle had been made. It was not surprising, therefore, that the event was invariably accompanied by a furious outburst of temper, so that angry behaviour came to be associated with the loss of an axe-head and a person was said to have *flown off the handle*.

Capricorn. Now is the moment to take a firm grip of yourself and not allow too many distractions to have you on edge. You can fly off the handle too easily if you feel pressured.
DAILY EXPRESS, September 24, 1991.

usage: informal

foot: to put one's foot in it

to make a blunder, a *faux pas*

Authorities usually refer to the common-sense explanation which immediately springs to mind when this expression is considered; that is, the embarrassment of putting one's foot in some mess on the pavement.

A more interesting and reasonably plausible suggestion is that the present-day idiom comes from a much earlier phrase *the bishop hath set his foot in it*, which was a common cry when broth or milk was burnt. Bishops, it seems, were not popular in the Middle Ages. According to William Tyndale:

If the podech [soup] be burned to, or the meat over-roasted, we say the Bishop hath put his foot in the pot, or the Bishop hath played the cook. Because the Bishops burn who they lust and whosoever displeases them (The Obedyence of a Chrysten Man, 1528).

Francis Grose, in his *Provincial Glossary* (1790), suggests a different origin for the phrase, claiming that many a pan of milk burned while cottagers, on hearing that a bishop was passing through their village, dashed out into the street to implore a blessing.

John Milton used the expression in *Animadversions* (1641): '*It will be the bishop's foot in the broth.*'

Swift employed it almost a century later in *Polite Conversation* (1738): '*This cream is burnt too – Why madam, the bishop hath set his foot in it.*'

Interestingly, the French had a phrase of similar origin, *pas de clerc* ('priest's footstep'), which was used when someone had committed an indiscretion through ignorance or lack of good sense.

Those who support the theory that the expression has an ecclesiastical origin point out that the roots of many idiomatic phrases wither with the passage of time and that this is no exception; all connection with the clergy has long since been forgotten.

'*I find a little of my family goes a very long way,*' said Maxim. '*Beatrice is one of the best people in the world but she invariably puts her foot in it.*'
I was not sure where Beatrice had blundered, and thought it better not to ask.
DAPHNE DU MAURIER, Rebecca, 1938.

She lies low till she's found out all the weak points in your alibi, and then suddenly, when you've put your foot in it by some careless remark, she starts on you.
GEORGE ORWELL, Coming Up for Air, 1939.

usage: informal

foot: to put one's foot in one's mouth

to say something accidentally that could cause offence

This is a vivid extension of *to put one's foot in it*. It singles out the verbal nature of the mistake. Very many people have been accused of putting their foot in it every time they open their mouths. Church people seem to have a habit of it:

'Vicar,' beamed the old lady appreciatively, 'we didn't know what sin was until you came to this parish.'

A bishop visited a church in his diocese. Only three people turned up to hear him preach. He asked the rector,
'Did you give notice of my visit?'
'No,' replied the rector, 'but the word seems to have got round.'
(Murray Watts, Rolling in the Aisles, 1987)

Brandreth claims the expression was first used of Sir Boyle Roche, an Irish politician, in the 1770s.

Opening my mouth and putting my foot in it is almost a hobby of mine. I try not to but it just keeps popping up there like some esoteric form of aerobics.
GOOD HOUSEKEEPING, May 1992.

usage: familiar, humorous

foot: to set off on the right/wrong foot

to begin something well/badly

The left foot is the wrong foot. The Romans held that anything to do with the left had evil consequences. The gods guarded your right but evil spirits hovered on your left. The Latin for 'left' is 'sinis-

ter', a word that has lost its 'leftness' in English but retains the ancient meaning of foreboding. Petronius exhorted his fellow Romans to 'enter a house right foot foremost'. They were to leave it in the same way. The Romans lived in such intense dread of the powers of evil that guards were appointed to stand at the doorway to all public places to make sure that the right-foot rule was obeyed. Augustus is said to have been particularly superstitious in this respect.

The tradition of the bride being carried over the threshold is thought to have originated in this superstition. It would not do for her to start the marriage off on the wrong foot.

After beginning on the wrong foot with a lot of heavy handed comedy ... it changes step to become ... a social piece with a message.
MID SUSSEX TIMES, September 6, 1991.

We are asked to believe that they are the greatest hoaxers since the perpetrators of Piltdown Man. That puts them on the wrong foot with me for a start because the Piltdown Man is another thing I happen to believe in.
MID SUSSEX TIMES, September 27, 1991.

see also: to get out of bed on the wrong side

footloose and fancy free

free from care and responsibility

Footloose describes someone who, without responsibilities to restrain him, can wander wherever he wishes. If that person is also *fancy free* he has a free heart, having no sweetheart to tie him down. The word 'fancy' originally meant 'fantasy' or 'imagination' before coming to mean 'whim' and finally 'love'. The phrase is appealing because of the alliteration and the balance of the two words.

Because of your age, it develops into a serious thing and then you can't get involved with other people. You want the closeness, but because you've only got three years at university, you also want to be footloose and fancy free.
DAILY EXPRESS, October 8, 1991.

French leave: to take French leave

to leave one's duties without permission, to steal away secretly without notice

Although the expression was current amongst the armed forces during the First World War (see **National rivalries**, page 76) it is, in fact, considerably older and originated not in the trenches but in polite French society towards the end of the seventeenth century. In these circles it was not considered impolite to leave a social gathering without first making a formal farewell to one's host and hostess. English society was stricter and was not amused by the lax ways of its French counterparts, so it seized upon the custom to express the idea of 'sneaking off without permission'. The French, however, have coined a phrase of their own which carries the same meaning. *Filer* (or *s'en aller*) *à l'anglaise* means 'to leave in the English fashion', but, before we criticise our neighbours for lack of originality, it is worth pointing out that in the sixteenth century *un anglais* was a French term for a creditor.

You must take French leave and run away from Newly and your charming wife for six months.
AUSTEN PREMBER.

But as I was certain I should not be allowed to leave the enclosure, my only plan was to take French leave, and slip out when nobody was watching.
R. L. STEVENSON, c1886.

usage: This original connotation of opprobrium has weakened, though there is still disapproval, for example, of someone leaving a social event where he ought to be present. Rather dated.

see also: go AWOL

gauntlet: to run the gauntlet

to suffer or risk abuse, criticism or danger

Gauntlet, here, has nothing to do with gloves. The word comes from the Swedish *gatulopp* (*gata* 'a lane' and *lopp* 'a chase, running'). The early English forms were *to run the gantlope* and *to run the gantlet*. *Running the gauntlet* was a fearful military punishment of Swedish invention in which the offender, stripped to his waist, was forced to run between two lines of soldiers who beat him with clubs or ropes. This torture came to the fore during the Thirty Years War of 1618–1648. The well-disciplined army of King Gustavus Adolphus clearly impressed the British military commanders. The navy implemented the punishment in 1661, for example, to deter theft from on board ship. It was abolished in 1813 but its use had caught on in public schools where it remained as a form of schoolboy bullying until well into this century. Hammond Innes tells of one particular experience of his from the 1920s:

When the dormitory leader came back, I poured out the whole incident. The leader then told the school prefect – he didn't go to the masters – and together they lined up the whole school so that the bully had to run the gauntlet, being hit with a sockful of earth. (Telegraph Magazine, September 7, 1991.)

We went to the jetty to see the 'usband's boat come in, and formed part of the long row of spectators, three deep, who had assembled to watch the unfortunate passengers land and run the gauntlet of unscrupulous comment and personal remarks all down the line.
T. H. BAYLY, The Mistletoe Bough, 1885.

These children are running the traffic gauntlet every schoolday of their lives.
MID SUSSEX TIMES, November 15, 1991.

usage: Today running the gauntlet is usually a verbal scourging and an occupational hazard of politicians and others in the public eye. In a more physical sense, it could be used appropriately of, say, canoeists going through the dangers of rapids.

see also: to throw down the gauntlet, to take up the gauntlet

gauntlet: to take up the gauntlet

to accept a challenge

See to throw down the gauntlet

He had taken up the gauntlet that Europe had flung at the feet of America, as he had seen it in his youth, he had accepted his handicap, as he also saw it, and striven with faith and force.
V. W. BROOKS, New England: Indian Summer, 1940.

usage: literary

gauntlet: to throw down the gauntlet

to challenge someone

In medieval times a knight challenging another to combat would throw his gauntlet. his mailed glove, on the ground. If his opponent picked it up, then the challenge had been accepted. The custom persisted through the years, the gauntlet being replaced by a gentleman's glove when a challenge to a duel was made.

The expression to take up the gauntlet means 'to accept a challenge'.

It was due to those English merchant adventurers, who, trying vainly to find a passage to China round the icy coasts of North Europe and North America, flung down the gauntlet to Spain, and drove their cockle boats into the heart of the Spanish Main.
SIR ARTHUR BRYANT. The National Character, 1934.

[She] had thrown down her gauntlet to him, and he had not been slow in picking it up.
ANTHONY TROLLOPE, The Last Chronicle of Barset, 1867.

But how many of you managed to solve the mystery? When The Archers Editor Vanessa Whitburn threw down the gauntlet and challenged Addicts to name the character she would be bringing back, she found herself overwhelmed by the response.
AMBRIDGE VILLAGE VOICE. Spring 1992.

usage: literary

see also: to take up the gauntlet

gibberish: to talk gibberish

to talk unintelligibly or in an obscure and meaningless way

Hammer horror stories

Disregarding cartoons, Count Dracula has appeared in 133 feature films and Frankenstein in ninety-one, according to a recent filmography. The living dead, mummies, werewolves, aliens – all are themes prominent in the cinema. Many of the plots and characters are drawn from literature, where there is a long tradition of the macabre. In the nineteenth century alone, within the conventions of the Gothic novel Mary Shelley published *Frankenstein* in 1818; Edgar Allan Poe followed her in mid-century with his *Tales of the Grotesque and Arabesque, the Pit and the Pendulum* and *Murders in the Rue Morgue*; Bram Stoker gave the world vampires and werewolves in *Dracula* (1897). The side of human nature that likes to be frightened by horror stories in film and print is doubtless the one that has seized on the macabre in human actions and preserved it in idioms.

Superstitions have an element of the spooky about them. But why are the spirits of the Druids relevant? Where do graves come into shivering? What evil intent is associated with the left ear? For answers, see **to touch wood, someone's just walked over my grave, my ears are burning**.

Body-snatching from graves has a long tradition behind it. Dissection of human corpses became legal in 1832. Soon afterwards, in 1845, Thackeray was referring to **a skeleton in the cupboard** and everyone knows Robert Louis Stevenson's 1886 novel *The Strange Case of Dr Jekyll and Mr Hyde*, since the inspiration for many films.

Many other expressions record man's inhumanity to man. In some instances, there is doubt about the grisly etymology: perhaps it is not slitting people's noses or hastening their death from hanging (see **to pay through the nose, to pull someone's leg**) but a (slightly) less distasteful origin. In other cases, there is no doubt about the rigours of military punishments (**to run the gauntlet**) or the viciousness of American gang warfare (**a hatchet job**). It is hardly surprising that the pursuit of heresy by fanatical religious adherents made such an impact on popular consciousness that we have idioms today that stem from it (**to haul somebody over the coals, a baptism of fire**). See **Rights for animals!** (page 205) for the gruesome role animals sometimes play in idioms.

The taste for the macabre has always been with us. The image of a sword hanging by a hair above its victim in **the sword of Damocles** finds an echo in *The Pit and the Pendulum* and modern-day chillers from Hollywood. Even dictionaries might frighten – try reading the entries referred to in this trailer, all alone, late one wild winter's night.

A theory that convinces several etymologists says that *gibberish* comes from Geber, the name of an Arabian alchemist who lived in the eleventh century. He invented a strange terminology of his own so that his notes would not be understood if found, and in this way he avoided any accusation of heresy, which was punishable by death.

Other scholars feel that this is an unlikely root since the word is not spelt *geberish*. Instead they advance a plausible, if much less entertaining, origin which says that *gibberish* comes from 'gibber', a verb allied to 'jabber', meaning to speak rapidly and unintelligibly. The problem here is that *gibberish* came into use before 'gibber'. This forces an investigation into the origins of 'gibber' which might be traced to 'gabber' and 'gabble', but do these bear any resemblance to *gibberish*? . . . and so the debate continues.

He repeated some gibberish, which by the sound seemed to be Irish.
SMOLLEY.

usage: Still familiar, despite its long history.

see also: mumbo jumbo, a load of codswallop

---

goalposts: to move the goalposts

to change the rules

A recent expression borrowed from the sports field. Changing the rules, as by moving the goalposts during play and so reducing the possibility of success, seized the public imagination and it is now widely applied to any situation: a government bill, a marriage, etc.

Julia moves the goalposts of her partnership slightly, Kate abandons them entirely. For both the effects are far reaching.
GOOD HOUSEKEEPING, May 1992.

usage: So frequently used in recent years that it is bordering on a cliché.

---

goat: to get someone's goat

to irritate, annoy someone

The phrase came into use early this century in America where it was common for a highly strung racehorse to have a goat as a stable companion. Goats were thought to have a calming influence on nervy thoroughbreds. It seems that attempts were sometimes made to sabotage a horse's chance of success by stealing the goat the night before a big race, thus reducing the would-be champion to a state of agitation. This, at least, is the theory and, although it may be unconvincing, no better one has been advanced.

[He] stopped at third with a mocking smile on his face which would have gotten the late Job's goat.
CHRISTY MATHEWSON, Pitching, 1912.

Are you deaf, or are you tryin' to get my goat?
J. C. LINCOLN, Shavings, 1918.

Why does nanny get their goat?
HEADLINE, GUARDIAN, July 22, 1992.

---

goose: to cook one's/someone's goose

to ruin one's/someone's plans or chances of success

A favourite story connected with this phrase attributes it to King Eric XIV of Sweden whose reign began in 1560. According to an old chronicle:

The Kyng of Swedland coming to a towne of his enemyes with very little company, his enemyes, to slyghte his forces, did hang out a goose for him to shoote, but perceiving before nyghte that these fewe soldiers had invaded and sette their chiefe houlds on fire, they demanded of him what his intent was, to whom he replyed, 'To cook your goose!'

Unfortunately, no copy remains of the old chronicle to testify to the antiquity of the legend and the expression does not seem to have been current before the middle of the nineteenth century, when it was used in a street ballad objecting to the attempts of Pope Pius IX to revive the influence of the Catholic church in England by the appointment of Cardinal Wiseman:

*If they come here we'll cook their goose
The Pope and Cardinal Wiseman.*

Funk (1950) is not convinced by this explanation. He prefers the story recorded in *to kill the goose that lays the golden eggs*, where the aspirations of the greedy peasants are frustrated.

'I'm quite sure,' he cried, 'that I could turn out something better than most of the stuff that gets published.'
That remark would have cooked Oswald's literary goose with anybody who had experienced young literary genius, but Aunt Ursula was struck by it.
RICHARD ALDINGTON, Soft Answers, 'Yes, Aunt', 1932.

They say Max de Winter murdered his first wife. I always did think there was something peculiar about him. I warned that

fool of a girl she was making a mistake, but she wouldn't listen to me. Well, she's cooked her goose now all right.
DAPHNE DU MAURIER, Rebecca, 1938.

usage: Colloquial. Used either of thwarting another's plans by design, or of suffering the unintentional results of one's own ill-judged actions.

goose: to kill the goose which lays the golden eggs

to destroy a source of profit through greed

In 1484 William Caxton translated into English a fable by Aesop which tells the tale of a peasant who had the good fortune to own a goose that laid golden eggs. In his hurry to become rich he cut the goose open to have all the eggs at once, thus butchering his source of future wealth. The moral Aesop intended was that of being content with one's fortune and guarding against greed. It entered English as the expression *to kill the goose which lays the golden eggs*, meaning 'to make excessive demands on a source of profit, such that it is ruined'.

An altered form of the expression, *the goose that lays the golden eggs*, is also sometimes found to refer to a valuable source of income.

We're all respectable householders – that's to say Tories, yes-men, and bumsuckers. Daren't kill the goose that lays the gilded eggs.
GEORGE ORWELL, Coming Up for Air, 1939.

These northern manufacturers were making money hand over fist to spend and invest. Pitt is scarcely to be blamed that he refused to kill the men that laid the golden

eggs. *For he saw in the swelling industrial wealth of the country his trump card against the Jacobin.*
SIR ARTHUR BRYANT, The Years of Endurance, 1942.

He went there without any particular object in view, impelled by the belief that somewhere in that large organisation was a goose who would lay eggs for him.
EVELYN WAUGH, Put Out More Flags, 'Spring', 1942.

For the communist city government, which owns a half share, McDonald's will be like the goose which laid golden eggs. No wonder then that the Chinese side has given its blessing to a McDonald's logo which shows McDonald's golden arches rising above the Tiananmen rostrum, where Mao Tse-Tung declared the founding of the communist republic.
THE TIMES, April 24, 1992.

usage: There are quite a lot of minor variations possible in the form and connotation: a promising business proposition might approvingly be referred to as *a goose that lays a golden egg.*

grapevine: on the grapevine

through gossip, rumour; through an informal network of contacts

'What God hath wrought' was the first telegraph message from Washington to Baltimore, sent by Samuel Morse on May 24, 1844, in a demonstration of his new invention to Congress. The invention was welcomed with great excitement and companies rushed to erect telegraph lines. Hasty work often leaves a lot to be desired. An account of 1899 tells of a certain Colonel Bee who in 1859 had put a line up between Placerville and Virginia City. He used trees as poles but their movement stretched the wires until they fell in tangles to the ground. People referred to it jokingly as the 'grape-vine telegraph' because it looked like the wild vines found in California.

During the American Civil War military commanders used the telegraph for messages from the front, but the telegraph system was also used to relay false information about battles and victories so that people were always unsure about the veracity of the news. Reports heard *by the grapevine telegraph* were rumours that may or may not have been true.

Heard it through the grapevine.
HEADLINE, TODAY, May 12, 1992.

'*In the end I found Emma Caulkin, who had heard about the job at a nanny group meeting,*' she says. '*I pay Emma £130 a week, but if I was to do it all again, I'd just sign on with a few of the larger agencies. The nanny grapevine is very effective!*'
TODAY, May 12, 1992.

usage: By the grapevine is American; British English has both *through* and *on the grapevine.*

grave: someone's just walked over my grave

a remark on feeling an uninvoluntary shiver

A sudden shivering sensation is often accompanied by the person declaring, 'Someone's just walked over my grave.' An old wives' belief holds that the shivering is felt when the spot where one will eventually be buried is being trampled on – a reminder of mortality.

Sometimes somebody would walk over my grave, and give me a creeping in the back.
CHARLES KINGSLEY, Geoffrey Hamlyn, 1859.

Joan shuddered – that . . . convulsive shudder which old wives say is caused by a footstep walking over the place of our grave that shall be.
HOLME LEE, Basil Godfrey's Caprice, 1868.

groggy: to feel groggy

to feel dizzy, unsteady, shaky

Until 1971 the officers and men of the Royal Navy were entitled to a daily ration of rum. In 1740 Admiral Vernon, dubbed 'Old Grog' because of the grogram cloak he always wore, started to issue rum diluted with water which the sailors called *grog* after him. Men who could not take their drink or perhaps drank others' rations as well as their own would end up *feeling groggy* or 'drunk'. Today the term could be used to describe someone suffering the after-effects of a party the night before but is more likely to be used of someone who was generally unwell.

The pheasants would be up in the trees by then, roosting, and they'd be starting to feel groggy, and they'd be wobbling and trying to keep their balance and soon every pheasant that had eaten one single raisin would be a sitting target.
COBUILD CORPUS.

halcyon days

times of peace and tranquillity

The word halcyon comes from the Greek for kingfisher and is made up of *hals* (the sea) and *kuo* (to brood). It reflects the ancient Greek belief that kingfishers built nests for rearing their young which floated on the sea. Greek mythology tells of the goddess Halcyone who, beside herself with grief when her husband was drowned in a shipwreck, cast herself into the sea. The gods, moved by her devotion, brought him back to life, changing both Halcyone and her husband into kingfishers. Further, the gods said that from that time whenever kingfishers were brooding on their nests in the sea, the water would be kept calm and no storm would arise. According to legend, kingfishers bred on the seven days before and the seven days after the winter solstice. These were *halcyon days*, guaranteed to be calm and fair.

And wars have that respect for his repose
As winds for halcyons when they breed at sea.
JOHN DRYDEN, Stanzas on Oliver Cromwell, 1658.

It is always a test of character to be baffled and 'up against it', but the test is particularly severe when the adversity comes suddenly at the noon of a halcyon day which one has fatuously expected to endure to eternity.
A. J. TOYNBEE, Trial on Civilization, 'The Present Point in History', 1948.

They were halcyon days unaffected by the war, and a group of us evacuees spent our time after school hours enjoying the lovely Devon countryside.
WOMAN AND HOME, June 1991.

But the resorts reached their peak in the Sixties in a boom period that saw the birth of modern Newquay and its tourist monoculture, a time still fondly remembered by the older hoteliers as the 'halcyon days' before the birth of cheap foreign package holidays with guaranteed sunshine.
OBSERVER, July 5, 1992.

usage: Usually plural. A cliché.

ham actor, a

a poor actor with an exaggerated, unnatural style

Speculation, all of it quite plausible, abounds over this little phrase. A favourite theory is that the term is an abbreviation of *hamfatter*, an American word dating from about 1875, which described seedy, second-rate actors who, through lack of money, were forced to use ham fat to clean off their make-up. A variation of this is that the ham fat was used as a base for burnt cork by touring minstrels wishing to black-up their faces. There was also a well-known song from the George Christie Minstrels days called 'Ham Fat', which was all about an amateurish actor: possibly the phrase came from this.

Another theory refers to Hamish McCullough, nicknamed Ham and leader of a troupe known as Ham's Actors, who toured Illinois around the 1880s giving performances that were less than wonderful.

If in doubt, try Shakespeare! *Troilus and Cressida* (1601) has in Act 1, scene iii:

Like a strutting player, whose conceit
Lies in his hamstring, and doth think it
rich
To hear the wooden dialogue and sound
'Twixt his stretch'd footing and the scaffoldage.

The unnatural, exaggerated gait that is typical of a poor actor, Shakespeare suggests, involves the excessive, peculiar exercising of the hamstring, a tendon forming part of the ham.

Maclean plays a Spanish inquisitor trying to detect Jewish infiltrators with a plate of ham sandwiches. The 48-year-old veg-
etarian said: 'I've always been something of a ham actor.'
TODAY, May 12. 1992.

usage: The phrase can be reduced to the simple *ham*, with two different senses. One continues the derogatory meaning of *ham actor* but applies it to a third-rate performer of any kind. The other has no negative associations, in phrases like *radio ham*, a short-wave radio enthusiast.

hang fire, to

to be pending, delayed

This is an expression from the use of fire arms. When the main charge in a gun was slow to ignite, the gun was said to be *hanging fire*. Now the term is used of someone slow to take decisive action on a matter to the frustration of all concerned.

Leyden's Indian journey . . . seems to hang fire.
WALTER SCOTT. Letter to G. Ellis. December 7, 1801.

usage: Usually used of a decision or event that is delayed, but may be found referring to a person who is indecisive.

see also: a flash in the pan

hangdog look, a

a shamefaced, guilty expression

In medieval times animals which had caused harm or death were put on trial and, if found guilty, sentenced to death. The practice was common throughout Europe. In Savoy, in eastern France, in 1487, beetles were formally charged with the destruction of a vineyard and in Switzerland in the same century it was claimed that a cock had laid an egg and should therefore answer charges of sorcery. In an age when unhygienic conditions were widespread, it was only to be expected that dog bites would quite often prove fatal, thus bringing about a charge of murder.

A *hangdog look* originally described the expression of someone considered fit to hang, like a dog, for his crimes, but has weakened to mean little more than 'shamefaced'.

'He, he!' tittered his friend, 'you are so – so very funny!'
'I need be,' remarked Ralph dryly, 'for this is rather dull and chilling. Look a little brisker, man, and not so hang-dog like.'
CHARLES DICKENS. Nicholas Nickleby. 1838–9.

usage: Hang-dog was frequent as a noun (Thackeray has: *'Paws off. You young hang-dog'*), but it is now more commonly used adjectivally and without a hyphen.

hanky-panky

mild trickery; something improper; minor sexual impropriety

The phrase is thought to come from *hocus pocus*, although the path is not entirely clear. See that entry.

We've heard the tales of holiday hanky-panky. Your average male ski instructor is a preening, mirror-shaded hunk with a professional status one step up from a gigolo. Yet whatever their reputation, there is no doubt that many skiers are happy to entertain the possibility of a holiday fling with their instructor.
WEEKEND TELEGRAPH. November 2, 1991.

usage: The general sense of mild impropriety can be applied to a range of fields: naughtiness in a child, fiddling expenses, etc. Most commonly, with a humorous tone, it is applied to sexual misdemeanours of a minor kind.

see also: hocus pocus

hat: at the drop of a hat

immediately, without hesitation or need for persuasion

In the American frontier country dropping a hat was a signal that an event, especially a fighting bout, should begin.

He lies. The typical American lies at the drop of a hat, as a way of life, about almost anything!
RADIO BIBLE CLASS EUROPEAN NEWS. March 1992.

Gemini Unfortunately there is a chance that you can take your natural ability to communicate to extremes and exaggerate wildly at the drop of a hat. A little flowery detail never hurt anyone, but keep it within the bounds of reality, Gemini.
AMBRIDGE VILLAGE VOICE. Spring 1992.

hatchet job, a

an attempt to kill or discredit a prominent person

Hatchet jobs are carried out by *hatchet men*, agents hired for the sole purpose of performing some brutal, unpleasant or unethical task. The origins are said to lie in US gang warfare where large-city Chinese gangs would sometimes hire an assassin to hack a prominent member of a rival gang to death with a hatchet. By 1925 the term *hatchet man* was applied to any professional gunman and its use was later extended to refer to any journalist or politician's aide who by vicious use of words and information succeeded in ruining the reputation of a public, and usually political, figure.

Joan Crawford's daughter published her vitriolic biography Mommie Dearest. *Bing Crosby met a similar fate at the pen of one of his sons . . . More recently Nancy Reagan has been accused of brutality by her daughter Patti . . . And I now read that Marlene Dietrich's daughter Maria Riva is to rush into print with what is said to be a hatchet job on her mother.*
DAILY MAIL, May 8, 1992.

Inspection as a business, rather than a profession, will lead to operators providing a service which they think the customer wants and which they hope will get them further recommendations. Does the chairman of the governors want a hatchet job on the head teacher, or a whitewash?
OBSERVER, September 15, 1991.

usage: informal

haul someone over the coals, to

to give someone a severe reprimand

This is a reference to the ordeal by fire. In the fifteenth and sixteenth centuries, heresy was regarded as a crime against society and punishable by death. One way of deciding the guilt of a heretic was to haul the suspect over a bed of glowing coals. A person who survived the ordeal escaped with severe burns but was declared innocent. Death meant that the person had been guilty of the charge.

If this strike's not brought to an end before the General Meeting, the shareholders will certainly haul us over the coals.
JOHN GALSWORTHY, Strife, 1909.

Poor man, he really looked like death. I suppose he was mortally afraid that he'd get hauled over the coals for carelessness in leaving dangerous chemicals about.
AGATHA CHRISTIE, Murder in Mesopotamia, 1936.

usage: A variety of verbs are found: *to haul, rake, bring, fetch over the coals.* Informal.

havoc: to play/wreak havoc

to devastate, destroy, spoil

Havoc was borrowed from the Old French *havot*, meaning plunder. A shout of *havoc* was an order, a war cry, a signal for pillage and the seizure of spoil to begin. The phrase *cry havoc* from the Anglo-French *crier havok* is especially common in fifteenth- and sixteenth-century texts, from its first use in 1419, recorded in *Excerpta Historica*.

There are several references to *havoc* and *cry havoc* in Shakespeare's plays. In *Henry IV Part I* (Act V, scene i) we hear of '*pellmell, havoc and confusion*', and in *Julius Caesar* (Act III, scene i) come the lines:

. . . Caesar's spirit, ranging for revenge, With Ate by his side come hot from hell, Shall in these confines with a monarch's voice Cry, 'Havoc!' and let slip the dogs of war.

The other part of the contemporary phrase, *to wreak*, also dates back to the fifteenth century with the sense of 'to give vent to, to carry out by way of punishment or revenge'. One could wreak resentment, vengeance, punishment, wrath or havoc. Over the centuries, *to cry havoc* died out, whereas *to wreak* tended to collocate more and more with *havoc*, hence the principal form of the contemporary expression.

Foreign medical experts in the region say Aids could devastate the Pacific Island nations. 'In the past, a procession of whalers, slavers, traders and soldiers sowed havoc in these islands with measles, smallpox and sexually transmitted diseases,' said a foreign specialist.
THE TIMES, September 4, 1991.

I don't like them taking their crayons to my white walls. I don't like them for not thinking about anybody but themselves. There are all sorts of attributes that we wouldn't tolerate for a moment in adults, yet children have carte blanche to wreak havoc.
GOOD HOUSEKEEPING, July 1992.

usage: To play havoc is a less formal alternative to *to wreak havoc.*

haywire: to go haywire

to go wrong, to be out of order; to go completely out of control

The phrase originated early this century in America where haywire, it seems, is used to mend anything from tools to fences. One American authority claims that the properties of lazy farmers who cannot be bothered with permanent repairs are virtually held together with the stuff. Haywire rusts quickly and the result is an untidy and chaotic mess. Such places would be referred to as having *gone haywire*. It should be pointed out,

though, that this view is based on a meaning of *to go haywire* which has not permeated into British English, that of something being in general disorder, just cobbled together.

Another American authority bases his interpretation on the real purpose of haywire, which is to bind up bales of hay. Haywire is thin and easily bendable but it is also very strong, requiring cutters to break it. Once the tight wires wound around a bale have been snipped, however, they spring apart and writhe wildly and dangerously in the air, totally out of control.

A third American source says the notion of general disorder and confusion alludes to the tangled mass of wire that is heaped in a corner of the yard once it has been cut off the bales.

Whatever the final make-up of the England side, Botham's medium pace will be a vital component. If that goes haywire then the first outright risk this management have taken could leave them with egg on their faces.
DAILY MAIL, August 8, 1991.

usage: informal

high and dry: to be left high and dry

to be stranded; to be left out of things

This is a nautical phrase from the early nineteenth century and is used to describe a ship that is left grounded when the tide goes out.

He couldn't understand why people were impatient with him for saying very much the same sort of thing as he had been

saying for the last thirty years. The river has flowed on and left him high and dry on the bank. The writer has his little hour, but an hour is soon past.
W. SOMERSET MAUGHAM. A Writer's Notebook. 1949.

'. . . the bus fare is 69p which is a very big addition to a pensioner's shopping bill. We have been left high and dry. Surely Sainsbury's could provide a free minibus shuttle service between their old site and the new store?
MID SUSSEX TIMES. September 27. 1991.

Ruination-on-Sea left high and dry.
Cornish Riviera reels as tourists stay away.
HEADLINE, OBSERVER, July 5, 1992.

for by swallowing an additional bumper, or by paying a small sum toward the reckoning (Guy Mannering, 1815).

They have no common language save sex, love, drink, and, of course, their art. He [the playwright] has high jinks with all this – at one point, in a magnificently comic coup de théâtre, staging a dinner party where no two guests speak in the same native tongue.
DAILY MAIL. August 7, 1991.

usage: The earlier connotations of drunkenness and gambling have largely been lost. Today the idea is that of high-spirited fun – which may, however, be irresponsible and insensitive to those around.

high jinks

excited, high-spirited behaviour

The phrase, of Scottish origin, goes back to around the turn of the century and refers to pranks and frolics indulged in at drinking parties. One game was to throw dice to see who amongst the assembled company should drink a large bowl of liquor and who should then pay for it. A passage from Walter Scott suggests that *high jinks* was a game of forfeits:

The frolicsome company had begun to practise the ancient and now forgotten pastime of high jinks. This game was played in several different ways. Most frequently the dice were thrown by the company, and those upon whom the lot fell were obliged to assume and maintain for a certain time, a certain fictitious character, or to repeat a certain number of fescennine verses in a particular order. If they departed from the characters assigned, or if their memory proved treacherous in the repetition, they incurred forfeits, which were compounded

Hobson's choice

no alternative, no choice at all

Thomas Hobson (1544–1631) ran a livery stable in Cambridge. Customers were never permitted to choose their own mount but were obliged to take *Hobson's choice*, which was always the horse nearest the stable door. As Hobson moved his horses round in rotation, he was thus able to ensure that every horse was worked fairly and that no animal was ridden too often.

Hobson's name survives not only in this expression but in two epitaphs – by Milton, a student at Christ's College, Cambridge, at the time of Hobson's death, and in the street named after him in old Cambridge.

Can any woman think herself happy, that's obliged to marry only with Hobson's choice?
COLLEY CIBBER, The Non-Juror, 1718.

hocus pocus

something said, or done, to confuse or deceive; funny business; nonsense

Hocus pocus are the first words of a sham Latin phrase (*Hocus pocus, tontus talontus, vade cleriter jubes*) that conjurors have murmured over their tricks since the early seventeenth century. It has been suggested that they might be a Puritan parody of the words of consecration in the Latin Mass (*Hoc est corpus meum*). According to Thomas Ady, in the time of King James I there was one particular man who called himself 'The Kings Majesties most excellent Hocus Pocus' (*A Candle in the Dark; or, A Treatise Concerning the Nature of Witches and Witchcraft*, 1656). He is generally thought to have been the author of the Latin phrase, taking his name from it.

An alternative etymology, which has some merit, is proposed by Todd in his late eighteenth-century edition of Dr Johnson's monumental *Dictionary of the English Language* (1755). A famous Italian juggler, Ochus Bochus, gained such a reputation that other jugglers, and then conjurors, repeated his name over their tricks – perhaps for luck or to impress a gullible public. Early uses of the phrase are, indeed, often in the context of jugglers rather than conjurors, as here:

One of the greatest pieces of legerdemain, with which jugglers hocus the vulgar (Nalson).

It could be, however, that the conjurors were invoking a much older power. A note to the Dragon King in James Fitzgerald Pennie's *Britain's Historical Drama* of 1832 tells us that Ochus Bochus was in fact a magician and demon among the Saxons, dwelling in forests and caves (the name still extant, according to one etymology, in the Somerset place name Wookey Hole, near Wells). Who, then, knows what dark powers are being called upon?

The reduced form of the phrase, *hocus*, used as a verb, shows the origin of our contemporary *hoax*. It is thought that *hanky-panky* may also come from this root.

The phrase has had various interesting developments in America. *Hokum*, 'nonsense', is apparently a blend of *hocus* and *bunkum*. It dates from 1917. A *hokey-pokey man* is a salesman of cheap ice cream or confectionery that masquerades as something better than it is. This sweet delight crossed the Atlantic and was known in Victorian England.

On Hocas Pocas
Here Hocas lyes with his tricks and his knocks,
Whom death hath made sure as a juglers box;
Who many hath cozen'd by his leigerdemain,
Is presto convey'd and here underlain.
Thus Hocas he's here, and here he is not,
While death plaid the Hocas, and brought him to th' pot.
WITTS RECREATIONS, 1654.

Our author is playing hocus-pocus (hoodwinking his readers) in the very similitude he takes from that juggler.
RICHARD BENTLEY, A Dissertation on the Epistles of Phalaris, 1699.

The hostess was too adroit at that hocus-pocus of the table which often is practised in cheap boarding-houses. No one could conjure a single joint through a greater variety of forms.
WASHINGTON IRVING, c1820.

People

There are quite a few people immortalised in English idioms. The stories behind **Hobson's choice** and **Keeping up with the Joneses** are dealt with in detail under the appropriate entry. *As queer, tight* or *fine as Dick's hatband* were originally taunts or insults referring to Richard Cromwell, son of Oliver and Lord Protector from 1658–59, who never wore a crown.

We do not have such precise information on the origins of other expressions. Who is Jack Robinson? *Before you can say Jack Robinson* was first used in print by Fanny Burney in *Evelina* in 1778, in a way that suggests the expression was well-known. A few years later, in 1811, Grose in his *Dictionary of the Vulgar Tongue* claims it originated from *'a very volatile gentleman of that appellation, who would call on his neighbours, and be gone before his name could be announced'*. There are other ideas that it might come from an old play, or have been made popular, at least, by a poem of Thomas Hudson's called *Jack Robinson*. But for all this speculation, we are really none the wiser about who precisely Jack Robinson was – he's just been a very popular character for over two hundred years.

every Tom, Dick and Harry: This trio dates back to at least 1815 in America, but alternative forms of the phrase, with variations on the names used, are earlier. The obvious explanation is the best one: the commonest names denote the man in the street, or that archetype of normality, the man on the Clapham omnibus.

More fancifully, there might be a rather sinister explanation. Harry, as in Old Harry, has for centuries referred to the devil. Similarly, so has Dick – Heywood uses it thus in his *Edward IV* of 1599. It has been relatively interchangeable over four hundred years with **dickens**, which is still as familiar to us today as it was to Shakespeare in *The Merry Wives of Windsor* in 1601: *I cannot tell what the dickens his name is.* Tom, however, has no known diabolical links, which tends to make this theory fall apart. What a shame we do not have a trio of idiomatic euphemisms for Old Nick himself!

It's always nice to have the support of a famous person for our own views. So it's not surprising that we use the name of authorities and experts in certain set phrases and associate them with our own opinions.

according to Cocker: A certain Mr Cocker wrote a mathematics textbook that was popular in British schools for many years. So if anything was described as *according to Cocker* it must be right and correct in all areas, not simply mathematics. But as Cocker's textbook hasn't been used for years now, this phrase is restricted primarily to older people.

according to Gunter: In America there is a parallel phrase *according to Gunter*. Mr Gunter was another mathematician who in the early seventeenth century invented the standard measure for surveyors. This is twenty-two yards long, divided into a hundred links, and called Gunter's Chain. From this grew the American phrase meaning 'correctly, accurately'.

Authorities in other fields have made their idiomatic mark. Edmond Hoyle's definitive statement of the rules of whist (1742) provided us with *according to Hoyle*, which now has the wider sense of 'according to the rules'.

Conversely, some people commemorated in idioms have an unsavoury reputation that it is not pleasant to be associated with. Who wants to be described as a *nosey parker*? It is likely that this expression refers back to a specific person – Matthew Parker, the Archbishop of Canterbury under Elizabeth I, is the prime candidate. However, it could be connected with a dialectal verb *to pauk*, meaning 'to be inquisitive', or (as one eminent etymologist suggests) with a park-keeper (a *parker*) officiously spying on everything going on in his domain. Other characters are inventions of fiction or age-old figures made known to us through the Bible.

a Mrs Grundy: Quite a lot of these phrases come from literature. Mrs Grundy, for instance, is mentioned repeatedly in Thomas Morton's play *Speed the Plough*, first produced in 1800, but she never appears on stage. The other characters constantly wonder what she will think or say, as she is the type of lady who takes a rather narrow, very moral view of things. She is somebody to be feared. As a poet once said: '*And many are afraid of God, and more of Mrs Grundy.*'

a Jeremiah: The Bible provides us with similar sorts of expressions. Jeremiah, the Old Testament prophet, is popularly considered to be a foreteller of doom and disaster. Although his reputation for laments and mournfulness is not really justified, that is the way we look at him today and, by association, how we view anyone we call a *Jeremiah*.

From the Greek tradition, Cassandra is renowned as a similar prophet of doom.

usage: The phrase is often hyphenated. Usually used disapprovingly, because of the connotations of trickery.

see also: hanky-panky

hog: to go the whole hog

to do something thoroughly

A number of theories have been advanced for this phrase and there is also some uncertainty as to whether it was coined in America or England. Although written use occurred first in the US in 1828 and in England soon after, there is no way of knowing on which side of the Atlantic it first gained spoken currency.

Speculation over the country of origin is not clarified by the fact that, in the last century, a hog was a slang term for a ten cent piece in America but also for an Irish shilling, so that, according to one theory, to go the whole hog meant to be willing to spend the whole amount on something. As Brandreth aptly comments, this would make the phrase a close relation of in for a penny, in for a pound.

The poet Cowper apparently enjoyed popularity on both sides of the Atlantic and Funk (1950) suggests that a likely origin is to be found in one of his poems, The Love of the World Reproved: or Hypocrisy Detected (1779), in which he discusses the strictures Muslims placed upon the eating of pork. Mohammed prohibited his followers from eating certain parts of a pig but was singularly unclear about what these were. Muslims were wont to interpret his decree according to their own personal taste so that, between them, the whole hog was devoured:

Had he the sinful part express'd,
They might with safety eat the rest;
But for one piece they thought it hard
From the whole hog to be debar'd;
And set their wit at work to find
What joint the prophet had in mind.
Much controversy straight arose,
These choose the back, the belly those;
By some 'tis confidently said
He meant not to forbid the head;
While others at that doctrine rail,
And piously prefer the tail.
Thus, conscience freed from every clog,
Mahometans eat up the hog.
Each thinks his neighbour makes too free,
Yet likes a slice as well as he:
With sophistry their sauce they sweeten,
Till quite from tail to snout 'tis eaten.

A final theory – in Men and Manners in America, dating from the first half of the nineteenth century – is sure of the American origin. It claims that it was a term used by butchers in Virginia who would ask their customers whether they wanted to go the whole hog or buy only parts of the animal. The phrase was popularly used in the wider context of thoroughness in radical reform or democratic principle.

Don't you think it would be more interesting if you went the whole hog and drew him warts and all?
W. SOMERSET MAUGHAM. Cakes and Ale. 1930.

He was rich, but he had refrained from going the whole hog and becoming a millionaire, and he showed the same spirit of restraint in his style of living.
JOHN WAIN. Hurry on Down. 1953.

usage: informal

hold the fort, to

to take care of things, take over briefly

'Hold the fort, for I am coming,' is popularly believed to be the message that General William Tecumseh Sherman signalled to fellow Union General John Murray Corse as he faced a Confederate attack at Allatoona Pass on October 5, 1864, during the American Civil War. What the signal from the top of Kenesaw Mountain really read was 'Hold out, relief is coming', but the misquote caught popular imagination and soon appeared in the spoken and written word. Philip Paul Bliss wrote the words into the chorus of a well-loved gospel hymn:

Ho my comrades! See the signal,
Waving in the sky!
Reinforcements now appearing,
Victory is nigh!

'Hold the fort, for I am coming,'
Jesus signals still.
Wave the answer back to heaven,
'By thy grace we will.'

It was widely used in evangelistic meetings in England in the 1870s.

Daniel went to Cambridge to open the new business, Alexander held the fort in London, and on the tenth of November the British Museum acknowledged the receipt of their first publication.
C. MORGAN, The House of Macmillan, 1943.

I began to search the flat to see if I could find a key, but I did this without much hope of success. I was of course perfectly certain that Sadie had done this on purpose. She wanted me, for reasons of her own, to hold the fort all day, and her method of making sure that I did so was to keep me a prisoner.
IRIS MURDOCH, Under the Net, 1954.

hole: to be in a hole

to find oneself in difficulty; to have financial problems

An American source quotes evidence from John P. Quinn's book *Fools of Fortune* (1892) to support his theory that this is a nineteenth-century American phrase and comes from the poker tables in a gambling den. The owners of the joint, it seems, had the right to a percentage of the money put down in stakes. For this purpose, each table had a 'hole' or slot in its centre. The proprietor's due was posted through this and collected in a locked drawer beneath.

Although the expression can be used to describe being in difficulty of any kind, it is especially used in the context of financial problems. This theory would fit in with this meaning, the allusion being to a gambler who eventually finds he has put more money in the hidden drawer than he has left to his name.

Lawyers, even the most respectable, have been known to embezzle their clients' money when they themselves are in a hole.
AGATHA CHRISTIE, Murder in the Mews, 'Dead Man's Mirror', 1925.

We were in an awful hole, you know. We'd made all sorts of preparations for his coming of age, and I'd issued hundreds of invitations. Suddenly George said he wouldn't come. I was simply frantic.
W. SOMERSET MAUGHAM, First Person Singular, 'The Alien Corn', 1931.

usage: familiar

hook: by hook or by crook

using every possible means, honest or dishonest, to achieve something

The Old Curiosity Shop of Linguistics

Preserving old words

Delving into the etymology of words, and particularly idioms, has been aptly described by the chairman of Harvard's Department of Linguistics as the Old Curiosity Shop branch of linguistic research. One French etymologist entitled his book *The Museum of French Expressions*. In that shop or museum, there are some antiques that can no longer be found in normal life (or language). Here are three examples:

To leave in the lurch: The old French *lourche* is the probable origin of a medieval card game, *lourche* in French and *lurcio* in Italian, which was somewhat similar to backgammon. On its arrival in England, some of the vocabulary associated with it was translated into English: *il demoura lourche* became 'he was left in the lurch, he was so far behind that he had no hope of winning'. This type of anglicisation is a common linguistic process; see **bandy about** for the international travels and shifts of meaning of the early French tennis term *bander*.

The original context of use was extended slightly when the phrase was employed to describe the player of cribbage (a newly invented game) whose opponent had reached sixty-one when he had not yet reached thirty-one: he was *left in the lurch* – a hopeless situation. In time, the usage widened much further and any sense of the origin in card games was lost. The meaning, too, generalised to the contemporary 'to be abandoned in difficulty'.

To be on one's mettle: The word 'mettle' originally meant 'temperament, character, spirit' or even 'courage'. It is widely used in Shakespeare: he describes one of his characters as a Corinthian, a lad of *mettle*: in other words a man of some character. *To be on one's mettle* today has a related sense of 'to be in a position where one must do one's best, do one's utmost, make every effort'. In other words, in a position where one can show one's character, one's *mettle*.

The words *mettle* and *metal* were used indiscriminately in spelling and meaning in early editions of Shakespeare's plays. The common core of sense is that *metal* (or *mettle*) refers to the steel of the sword blade: *mettle* (or *metal*) refers to its temper. A tempered character is as strong as tempered steel. Today, *mettle* is an antique exhibit only on display in **to be on one's mettle**; *metal* is very common, but only with the narrower sense of iron, copper, etc.

the Blue Riband of the Atlantic: The Blue Ribbon usually forms part of a larger phrase, such as *the Blue Ribbon of the Turf*. In *the Blue Ribbon of the Atlantic* only, it has an alternative form, *the Blue Riband of the Atlantic*. This became popular in the first half of this century when great liners such as the *Queen Mary* and the *United States* vied with each other to be quickest across the Atlantic. With the decline of the great passenger ships of those earlier years, not surprisingly the expression itself is rarely heard and used today. There is no difference in meaning or connotation between *ribbon* and *riband* in the phrase.

Lurch and *mettle* are like **loggerheads** and **scot-free** (and still others in this dictionary): they are only used in common idioms. *Riband* is rather different, in that the very idiom in which it finds its unique use is now dying out.

Alliteration

We are very fond in English of alliterative expressions, that is, words which repeat the same letter. **Spick and span** is one example in this book. There are plenty more like that, where antiques are left over from a previous generation.

might and main: *With might and main* or *by might and main* are the usual forms. The word *main* is a synonym of *might*, with the sense of 'strength and force'. It is preserved only in this fixed phrase, thanks to the power of alliteration.

rack and ruin: Similarly with this expression. *Ruin* we use today, *rack* we don't. It comes in fact from the word *wreck* – of a ship, for example. Again, it is a synonym of the other word in its doublet. So for emphasis and added effect we have *rack and ruin*, with the current idiomatic phrase containing an old word unused elsewhere.

kith and kin: Here the phrase is probably more frequent than either noun in it taken individually, although *kin* still has some currency in its own right. *Kith* means one's friends and neighbours, rather than one's blood relations, one's *kin*. Interestingly, the contemporary meaning of *kith and kin* has narrowed to mean only one's relatives. John Galsworthy was using it in this way in 1920 when *In Chancery* was published: *Its depleted bins preserved the record of family festivity: all the marriages, births, deaths of his kith and kin*.

110

The Old Curiosity Shop of Linguistics continued

In the cases above and some below, the idioms owe their preservation to alliteration. In several of the following instances, rhyme and emphasis preserve little-used words in fixed phrases:

chop and change	humming and hawing
part and parcel	**by hook or by crook**
scot and lot	jot or tittle
neck or nothing	ever and anon
hither and thither	to and fro
beck and call	**cut and run**
hammer and tongs	hard and fast
hole and corner	hue and cry
sackcloth and ashes	stuff and nonsense

Preserving old meanings

So far the examples have been of words that are used mainly or exclusively in idioms. The two instances that follow are words very commonly employed on their own. However, in certain idioms they preserve an old sense that has been lost in wider usage.

mind: The word *mind*, for instance, used to mean 'memory', so when we say to *keep in mind* or *to call to mind*, we are saying we are 'keeping it in memory, we are calling it to our memory'. And *time out of mind* means 'so long ago that no one can remember it'.

Mind didn't only mean 'memory', it also meant 'intention' or 'purpose', so when we use the phrases *to know one's own mind*, or *to change one's mind, to be in two minds, to have a mind to do something*, we are referring to this earlier meaning.

pain: Similarly, the word *pain*. Today it means 'physical suffering', such as the hurt you experience when you cut yourself with a knife, but it does have earlier senses. For instance, it meant 'punishment'. So when we use the phrases *under pain of death* or *on pain of death*, we are actually saying 'on the punishment of death'.

Pain had a second sense in earlier years of 'trouble' or 'effort'. So the expressions *to take great pains to do something*, or *to be at pains to do something* or *for one's pains*, all refer to the trouble or effort that it costs us.

The hook is thought to be a bill-hook and the crook a shepherd's crook. A law from feudal times permitted the poor to gather firewood from nearby forests, but in order to prevent the indiscriminate felling and lopping of trees and branches, peasants were only allowed to take dead wood and what they could cut using their hooks and crooks. The Bodmin Register for 1525 says that 'Dynmure Wood was open to the inhabitants of Bodmin . . . to bear away upon their backs a burden of lop, hook, crook, and bag wood.'

So what with hoke and what with croke
They make her maister ofte winne.
JOHN GOWER, Confessio Amantis Bk V,1 c1390.

Nor will suffer this book
By hook ne by crook
Printed for to be.
JOHN SKELTON, Colin Clout c1523.

Up the stone steps to the Hall he bounded, and only on the Hall's threshold was he brought to pause. The doorway was blocked by the backs of youths who had by hook and crook secured standing-room.
MAX BEERBOHM, Zuleika Dobson, 1912.

If she could not have her way, and get Jon for good and all, she felt like dying of privation. By hook or crook she must and could get him!
JOHN GALSWORTHY, To Let, 1921.

---

hook, line and sinker

completely, totally

This phrase is often, though not always, prefixed by 'to swallow' and refers to a person's extreme gullibility. The allusion is to the fish who, not crafty enough to recognise the bait on the hook for what it is, swallows it trustingly, and then goes on blindly to take in the line and sinker (weight) at the same time. Len Deighton appropriately chose Hook, Line and Sinker as the title for a trilogy of novels exploring the treachery and deceit of the world of the spy.

Another phrase meaning 'completely' and using a string of connected nouns to the same effect is lock, stock and barrel. Its sense is different, however, as it does not refer to a person's easy credulity but means 'everything in its entirety'.

A couple of private dicks that you don't know anything about show up with a cock-and-bull story, and you swallow it hook, line, and sinker.
ERLE STANLEY GARDNER, The Case of the Stuttering Bishop, 1936.

You, my dear Charles, whether you realise it or not, have gone straight, hook, line and sinker, into the very worst set in the University. You may think that, living in digs, I don't know what goes on in College; but I hear things.
EVELYN WAUGH, Brideshead Revisited, 1945.

America, they tell us, was there all along, complete with happily innocent North American Indians, South American Indians and, in the far north, the Eskimo. But you are no longer allowed to call them that. Native North Americans and South Americans, if you please. And Eskimo is no longer P[olitically] C[orrect] either . . . We must henceforth say Inuit, a word meaning simply 'person' in the Eskimo – sorry Inuit – language; and I am sorry to report that respected speakers on the BBC are swallowing it. Raw. Hook, line and sinker.
FRITZ SPIEGL, Weekend Telegraph, March 28, 1992.

see also: lock, stock and barrel

horse: from the horse's mouth

from an original or reputable source, on good authority

Before the 1930s when it came to refer to any kind of evidence given on the best authority, this expression was a piece of racing slang meaning 'a hot tip'. It alludes to the fact that a horse's age can be discovered just by inspecting its teeth. A dealer may twist the truth but the evidence in the horse's mouth is absolutely reliable.

Each of them carried a note-book, in which, whenever the great man spoke, he desperately scribbled. Straight from the horse's mouth. It was a rare privilege.
ALDOUS HUXLEY, Brave New World, 1932.

The friends expressed anger at the portrayal of the prince in the book, which they say is one-sided. 'Most of the book is completely true; it comes from the horse's mouth,' said one. 'But it paints the Princess of Wales as perfect and gives a distorted picture of the prince.'
THE SUNDAY TIMES, June 28, 1992.

usage: Regularly strengthened to *straight from the horse's mouth.*

see also: long in the tooth

hour: at the eleventh hour

at the very last moment

The Gospel of Matthew records the parable of the labourers (Matthew 20:1–16). It tells of a householder who went out one morning to hire men to work in his vineyard. He took men on at different times throughout the day right up until the eleventh hour. When the men were paid, however, the householder gave them all the same wage even though those hired at the eleventh hour had done only one hour's work. By this illustration Jesus was saying that God accepts everyone who comes to him on equal terms, whether they have spent a lifetime obeying him or approach him just before death, *at the eleventh hour*, at the last possible moment.

Sandybay had discovered, at the eleventh hour, that The Good Companions were offering it an unusually good show. Ten minutes before the performance began all the unreserved seats were filled and there were numbers of people standing at each side and at the back.
J. B. PRIESTLEY, The Good Companions, 1929.

From the abstract the theories looked identical. Darwin ran the risk of being beaten at the eleventh hour.
BBC 1, Timewatch, 'Charles Darwin – Devil's Chaplain', October 2, 1991.

hunch: to have a hunch

to have an intuitive feeling about something

This is an American gamester's term from the turn of the century. According to a gambling superstition, touching a hunchback's hump brought good luck. But recognition of the hunchback's powers did not originate then. Belief that these people were inspired by the devil to see into the future had been circulating for hundreds of years.

'Too bad I loaded the gun with blanks.' I grinned nastily. 'I had a hunch about what she would do – if she got the chance.'
RAYMOND CHANDLER, The Big Sleep, 1939.

'On a hunch he bought a Polish horse, Rumak, which was untried. Last December Rumak won the world championships in Paris and it proved Paolo was right.'
DAILY MAIL, September, 1991.

looked at each other in amazement. When the bloke stopped jumping he turned round to us and said: 'Right, now that that's broken the ice between us – would you two care to join us for a drink?' How could we refuse?
CHAT, October 1991.

ice: to break the ice

to break down social awkwardness and formality

This idiom is at least five hundred years old. It is not unique to English, but is found in other European languages also. The allusion is thought to be to the hard ice that formed on European rivers in severe winters centuries ago. In years gone by it was indeed possible to skate on the Thames. But ice was not enjoyed by those whose livelihood depended on plying a small boat up and down the river. Their first task was that of breaking it up so that work could begin.

Originally the expression was used to mean just that, making a start on a project. Gradually it came to mean embarking upon a relationship and breaking down the natural reserve one feels in the presence of strangers.

On things that are tender and unpleasing, it is good to break the ice, by some whose words are of less weight, and to reserve the more weighty voice, to come in, as by chance.
FRANCIS BACON, Essays: Of Cunning, 1597.

Recently my friend and I were standing at the bar in a club, when two blokes came up and stood beside us. Suddenly one of them snatched the ice bucket off the end of the bar, tipped all the ice cubes on to the floor and started vigorously jumping up and down on them. My friend and I

irons in the fire: to have too many/other irons in the fire

to have too many/other projects in hand, undertakings to be attended to

Someone with *other irons in the fire* has a choice of projects he can turn his attention to. If he has *too many irons in the fire* he has too many plans and cannot pay sufficient attention to any of them.

Some authorities say the phrase is from the smithy where the efficient blacksmith has several irons in the fire ready for when he needs them. Others say it alludes to the industrious laundress who would keep two or three flat irons heating in the fire for when the one she was using cooled. If she had *too many irons in the fire* she might find that some had become too hot and scorched the clothes instead of smoothing them. The second of the two allusions is generally preferred and seems to fit the different shades of meaning well.

He was always busy, always had twenty different irons in the fire at once, was always fresh, clear-headed, never tired. He was also always unpunctual, always untidy.
ALDOUS HUXLEY, Antic Hay, 1923.

I have other things to do, Paula, other irons in the fire, and I really should be getting back.
ERLE STANLEY GARDNER, The DA Takes a Chance, 1956.

ivory tower, an

a sheltered existence away from the problems and realities of life

The French romantic poet, playwright and novelist Alfred de Vigny led a life of disappointment and frustration. In his later years he withdrew from society and became very solitary, although he continued to write. In a poem, *Pensées d'Août* (1837), the critic Sainte-Beuve called Vigny's isolated existence his *tour d'ivoire* (ivory tower).

The phrase is regularly used of academics who have a reputation of living in a world separate from the harsh realities of life.

There is no denying his ability to turn a moribund establishment upside down, inflicting the demands of commerce upon the inhabitants of an ivory tower.
OBSERVER REVIEW, July 28, 1991.

Experience has taught her not to trust in or confide in members of the royal family. She realises that blood ties matter most. As a result she has kept a deliberate distance from her in-laws, skirting round issues, avoiding confrontations and locking herself away in her ivory tower. It has been a double-edged sword as she has failed to build any bridges, so essential in a closed world infected by family and office politics.
ANDREW MORTON, Diana: Her True Story, 1992.

usage: Often used adjectivally: *an ivory tower existence* or *approach*. Also commonly *to live in an ivory tower*.

see also: to live in cloud cuckoo land

Janus-faced

hypocritical

Janus was a Roman deity and guardian of the gate of heaven (hence, god of gates and doors). Having two faces, he was able to look ahead and behind at the same time. People who are hypocritical have long been described as having two faces. In his *Sermons* (1550), Thomas Lever writes: '*These flatterers be wonders perilous fellowes, hauynge two faces under one hoode.*' It is easy to see how the deity depicted with two faces came to be linked with the idea of hypocrisy.

See *two-faced*.

Labour had a 'Janus-faced attitude' and there was no scope for even a 'fraction of Labour's reckless spending promises'.
THE SUNDAY TIMES, November 10, 1991.

usage: literary

Joneses: to keep up with the Joneses

to endeavour to keep up financially and socially with one's friends and neighbours

February 1913 saw the first publication of a comic strip called *Keeping up with the Joneses* which was to run for twenty-eight years and find publication in a number of newspapers throughout the US. The subject of the strip was its writer, Arthur R. Momand, who based it on his own family's struggles to manage on a limited income whilst maintaining a show of material affluence in keeping with the neighbourhood. Momand explains in a personal letter to C. E. Funk, quoted in Funk (1955):

We had been living far beyond our means in our endeavour to keep up with the well-to-do class which then lived in Cedarhurst. I also noted that most of our friends were doing the same; the $10,000-a-year chap was trying to keep up with the $20,000-a-year man.

I decided it would make good comic-strip material, so sat down and drew up six strips. At first I thought of calling it Keeping up with the Smiths, but finally decided on Keeping up with the Joneses as being more euphonious.

My father might have cared more than I did what the Joneses thought, but at least he was far from worrying himself sick trying to 'keep up with the Joneses'.
J. B. PRIESTLEY, 'The Bradford Schoolmaster' in The Listener, July 23, 1959.

In their early Republican commonwealth the Romans would not tolerate private ambitions thirsting for unusual social distinction. Energies now spent on 'keeping up with the Joneses' in clothes, furnishings and accessories had to find other outlets in ancient Rome.
F. R. COWELL, Cicero and the Roman Republic, c1960.

jump the gun, to

to be hasty in embarking upon a course of action

Running races are started by a pistol being fired into the air. An athlete who, in anticipation, starts to run before the gun sounds is guilty of jumping the gun.

'I am certainly not engaged. The divorce isn't going to be very nice at all. Marriage is not on the cards – that would be jumping the gun. We haven't talked about it.'
DAILY MAIL, September 12, 1991.

usage: familiar

keep something/someone at bay, to

to keep someone/something out or at a safe distance

One source finds the origin of the term in the significance the ancients attached to the bay tree, which has been perceived over millennia as warding off harm or keeping it at bay. The Romans and Greeks singled this plant out for its protective qualities. Noting that lightning never seemed to strike the bay laurel, the ancients took to wearing its leaves on their heads during thunderstorms. Some of the Roman emperors wore wreaths of bay as a protective charm. In later centuries bay trees were planted near houses to offer the household their protection.

The same source claims that the hysterical population of London turned to the bay laurel when the Great Plague swept through the city in 1665. It is certainly true that herbs were relied upon for remedy by the desperate populace. In A Compendyous Regyment (1567) Borde recommends herbs to disinfect the air should a plague strike: '. . . in such infeccyous tyme it is good for every man . . . to use dayly, specyally in ye mornyng and evenyng to burne Juneper, or Rosemary, or Baye leves, or Majerome or frankensence.' But other herbs are also thought to be efficacious and there is no real evidence to suppose that the bay was looked upon as being especially so. It is unlikely, then, that this is the origin of the expression to keep at bay.

A totally supportable alternative is that the phrase is connected to an Old French word abai, meaning 'barking of hounds in a pack'. The English word 'baying', as of hunting hounds, shares this root. There are a number of Old French idioms connected with stag hunting which come from this same source, for example *rendre les abois* and *être aux abois*. They are used when a hunted stag tires in the chase and turns to face the pursuing hounds. At this point the stag is both at bay itself and also holds the dogs at bay – precisely the senses of the English phrase.

The English expression has had several conventional forms under the influence of translations from the French: *at abay, at a bay* and today *at bay*.

If, on the other hand, she reported unenthusiastically to keep the packaged hordes at bay, the travel company would not be too pleased.
OBSERVER. July 28, 1991.

Skin problems, hitherto merely kept at bay by cortisone creams, can clear up completely with Acupuncture.
CRAWLEY OBSERVER. September 11, 1991.

From the opening chapter in the blazing summer of 1939, when Helena Cuthbertson reveals that the weather is too hot for wearing knickers, to a funeral service 45 years later when the older generation keep thoughts of death at bay by remembering their wartime promiscuities, hardly anyone gives convention even a nod of recognition.
TELEGRAPH MAGAZINE. January 25, 1992.

The AA recommends an electronic alarm system for all-round protection, which costs about the same as a car radio. It's a simple and relatively cheap means of keeping scavengers at bay.
AA MAGAZINE. Issue 1, 1992.

kettle of fish, a

a mess, a problem, a predicament; another matter

Some authorities agree that 'kettle' is a corruption of 'kiddle', a type of grille put across a stream to catch fish, but differ in their subsequent accounts. One suggests that poachers damaged them while helping themselves to the catch. When the keeper returned to empty the kiddle, he might describe rather ruefully the resulting mess as *a pretty* or *fine kettle of fish*. Alternatively, but still ironically, when the kiddle had been in place for some time it would have collected not only fish but also weed and assorted debris from the river – in other words, a collection of rubbish or *a pretty kettle of fish*.

But most etymologists agree that the source lies in a type of picnic. A common arrangement for an outing or social get-together amongst the gentry in the Scottish border country was to arrange a feast on the banks of a river. The main course would be salmon, straight from the river and cooked outdoors in a 'kettle'. Outings of this kind were known as *a kettle of fish*. Quite how the expression came to mean a mess or confusion is a matter for speculation; anything that could have gone wrong with such an entertainment has been suggested, from spilling the kettle to being unable to catch or land the fish.

My God, this is a pretty kettle of fish. For goodness' sake, explain yourself, Charlie. A man doesn't commit suicide for fun.
W. SOMERSET MAUGHAM. The Bread-Winner, 1930.

Giving it to them hot and strong

Intensifying the force of one's word is a very common device of language. 'It's nonsense' becomes 'It's absolute/complete/perfect/proper/pure/sheer/thorough/total/utter nonsense.' It is a characteristic that works with idioms, too, especially where the word *blue* is involved:

To the old *between the devil and the deep sea* we add the adjective *blue*, to produce the emphatic **between the devil and the deep blue sea**.

You can *get away with murder* or, if you do something absolutely outrageous and still aren't punished for it, you can *get away with blue murder*.

To scream blue murder implies you scream louder even than if you were being murdered. *To drive like blue murder* is to drive ridiculously fast.

In a funk becomes *in a blue funk*.

To throw a fit is on occasion *to throw a blue fit*.

The sulphurous blue flames (blazes) of hell strengthen the euphemistic *What* or *where the blazes . . .* to *What* or *where the blue blazes . . .*

There are other similar instances:

To play hell becomes *to play merry hell*.

In a pickle is often *in a pretty pickle*.

To come to a pass is commonly *to come to a pretty pass*.

An alternative for *a fine* **kettle of fish** is *a pretty kettle of fish*.

Until now the word 'Colonel' for Basil had connoted an elderly rock-gardener on Barbara's GPO list. This formidable man of his own age was another kettle of fish.
EVELYN WAUGH, Put Out More Flags, 'Spring', 1942.

Do we, then, prefer foxes to children? I suspect not. Or rather, I imagine that most people prefer their own children to foxes. Other people's children, however, are a different kettle of fish altogether and it may well be that they are generally held in lower esteem than the farmer-baiting fox.
THE TIMES, February 27, 1992.

usage: There are two distinct senses: *a fine, pretty, nice kettle of fish* means 'a mess'; *another, a different kettle of fish* means 'another matter'. The above quotations show the different senses clearly. Both are colloquial, and the first is often ironical.

kick the bucket, to

to die

Three grim etymologies are suggested for this expression.

The first concerns the slaughter of pigs. Once killed, the animals would be suspended by the back legs from a wooden frame known as a bucket. Any muscular twitch or spasm after death caused the pig to kick against the bucket. Another common country practice was to suspend a living pig from a beam by its heels and cut its throat. The blood from the struggling animal then drained into a strategically placed basin beneath.

Opinions vary as to how the bucket got its quaint name. One view is that it comes from the Old French word *buquet*, meaning 'balance', which suggests that the

The absurd

There is a whimsical and absurd side to many people. It finds its reflection in the writings of Lewis Carroll and Ogden Nash, amongst many others. Children (and the child in all of us) seem especially to enjoy the superficially senseless:

> *Hey diddle diddle, the cat and the fiddle,*
> *the cow jumped over the moon.*
> *The little dog laughed to see such sport*
> *and the dish ran away with the spoon.*

This is one of the best known nursery rhymes in the English language. Its appeal and popularity stem largely from the fact that it doesn't make very much sense at all. In general, we like the illogical and we enjoy the humour of the ridiculous. Indeed the nursery rhyme tells us that the little boy laughed at the absurdity and fun of the cow jumping over the moon. This is exactly what Sir Henry Reed meant when, in discussing the origin of the rhyme, he rather neatly commented:

> *I prefer to think that it commemorates the athletic lunacy to which the strange conspiracy of the cat and the fiddle incited the cow.*

There are a good number of instances of obvious illogic. The colloquial *you can't have your cake and eat it* would make so much better sense if it were commonly said *you can't eat your cake and have it*. An American novel first published in 1950 was entitled *Have your cake and eat it*, but few are so precise. Idioms in general can appear totally illogical, because there is this gap (as **What is an idiom?**, page 6, tries to show) between the literal meaning of the individual words and the meaning of the idiomatic whole. It is unclear at first sight why **to knock spots off someone** as separate words ('to remove dots of colour') should have any logical connection with *to knock spots off someone* ('to defeat someone easily'). Readers of this dictionary and professional etymologists might know the connection (though the logical nature of the link is often obscure), but it is unknown and apparently nonsensical to the great majority. That, international experts agree, is part of the appeal of the idiom. Guiraud put it, about French idioms, that '*oddity, nonsense indeed, are a source of success and survival for many idioms*'. An English expert, Smith, summarises the attraction beautifully:

> *There is a certain irrelevance in the human mind, a certain love for the illogical and absurd, a reluctance to submit itself to reason, which breaks loose now and then and finds expression for itself in idiomatic speech.*

bucket was a beam rather than a frame. Another theory is that the carcase was first bound to a wooden block before being hoisted on to the frame by means of a pulley. This action brought to mind the drawing of water from a well and so the block, and not the frame, was called a bucket.

Suicide is suggested for the second etymology. An article by De Quincy in the *London Magazine* of 1823 talks of a tradition among the 'slang fraternity' that *'one Bolsover having hung himself to a beam while standing on the bottom of a pail, or bucket, kicked the vessel away in order to pry into futurity, and it was all up with him from that moment – finis!'*

Across the Atlantic there is the suggestion that a lynch mob would stand the hapless victim on a bucket, with the rope going up over a tree branch; the bucket would then be knocked away from beneath him.

The strongest case is the first, especially considering the early uses of the phrase that are recorded.

'You see, one of the boys has gone up the flume –'

'Gone where?'

'Up the flume, – throwed up the sponge, you understand.'

'Thrown up the sponge?'

'Yes; kicked the bucket.'

'Ah, – has departed to that mysterious country from whose bourn no traveller returns.'

'Return! I reckon not. Why, pard, he's dead!'
MARK TWAIN, Roughing It, 1872.

usage: colloquial

see also: to throw in the sponge

Kingdom: till/to Kingdom come

forever; to death

'He's gone to Kingdom come, he's dead' is the rather blunt way the expression is defined in Grose's *Dictionary of the Vulgar Tongue* (1785). It refers to the next life when every man will have to give account of himself before God. The words themselves may come from the Lord's Prayer as recorded in Matthew 6:10. The phrase was obviously much used in the spoken language long before it was considered suitable for the written word. The first reference in writing was in Peter Pindar's *Subjects for Painters* (1789):

And forty pounds be theirs, a pretty sum, For sending such a rogue to Kingdom-come.

Used with the conjunction *until/till*, the sense is rather different. The idea here is that the Second Coming of the Bible, when the Kingdom will be installed here on earth, is a very long way off – so long that the action can be continued almost forever, with impunity.

'There,' he said when they had finished. 'You can wet the bed till Kingdom come.'
MICHELLE MAGORIAN, Goodnight Mr Tom, 1981.

'The gun ... where is the gun?' she demanded, before seizing her trusty blunderbuss and dispatching a rogue male in her citadel to kingdom come.
DAILY EXPRESS, April 20, 1992.

'We don't have any problem about contraception. It is wrong that the wife should bear the burden of lots of children. A woman can go on producing until kingdom come. Charles Wesley was child number 23!'
DAILY TELEGRAPH, May 18, 1992.

usage: Colloquial. The contemporary tendency is to write *kingdom* without an initial capital letter.

knock into a cocked hat, to

to beat roundly, to show someone/something to be inferior to the opposition

There are several theories about this American phrase. One of them claims that it refers to the three-cornered, or tricorne, hats worn by army field officers in the eighteenth and early nineteenth centuries. Apparently much fun was made of them because of their strange shape and their brims which curled up on three sides. So *knocked into a cocked hat* became synonymous with 'pushed out of shape', 'good for nothing'.

An alternative theory concerning hats suggests that the cocked hat of the eighteenth century was simply the Puritan headgear of the 1600s with the brim 'cocked', or turned up, on three sides, giving a triangular shape. *To knock into a cocked hat*, therefore, meant to make dramatic changes to something, and from there to defeat roundly.

A final suggestion is that the expression alludes to an American skittle game where only three pins were set up, like the three corners of a cocked hat, as the points of a triangle. This would seem to be a much more plausible explanation; however, Funk (1950) points out that the first use of the expression in print was in 1833, but that there is no mention of the bowling game before 1858.

Would that we could do something at once dignified and effective to knock Mr Bryan once for all into a cocked hat.
WOODROW WILSON, Letter to Adrian H. Joline, January 1912).

You make your plans, then all the things you hadn't figured on kick them into a cocked hat.
FRANK YERBY, A Woman Called Fancy, 1952.

usage: informal

lap: it is in the lap of the gods

the unknown outcome will be revealed in the future, Providence will decide

One very obvious suggestion that has been made about this idiom is the practice, common in many cultures since ancient times, of placing gifts on the knees of statues depicting seated gods in the hope that, in return, a prayer would be answered.

Most authorities agree, however, that the phrase originated in Homer's *Iliad*. Patroclos, friend of Achilles, had been killed and the Trojans, having first stripped his corpse, were intending to sever the head and march with it through the city to help them gain the upper hand in the battle. It was at this point that Automedon, aware that the outcome was in the balance, said, '*These things lie on the knees of the gods.*' In fact, the impending humiliation brought the sulking Achilles back into the battle and led to the rout of the Trojans and the death of Hector. The gods, it seemed, were on the side of Achilles. As for why he was invincible, look up *Achilles' heel*.

The future may not be as unalterably determined by the past as we used to think; in part at least it may rest on the knees of whatever gods there be.
J. JEANS, The Mysterious Universe, 1930.

An attractive foreigner will set your heart fluttering, but whether or not he'll become part of your future is in the lap of the gods.
WOMAN'S OWN, September 14, 1991.

Yet if the weather does not hold – at present it is gloriously sunny and warm – it may be that the images of the most chaotic road conditions imaginable will linger in the memory far longer than the pursuit of excellence which is the birthright of the Olympic Games. Albertville's fate remains in the lap of the gods.
DAILY TELEGRAPH, February 3, 1992.

leaf: to turn over a new leaf

to begin again, to resolve to behave better

The need to turn over a new leaf or embark upon a programme of self-improvement and character-building occurs to everyone at one time or another. New leaves here have nothing to do with budding leaves on trees but rather the leaves of a book. The expression originated in the first half of the sixteenth century and it has been suggested that the book might therefore be one of precepts to be learnt and mastered for self-edification. This fits with the improving tone of the expression but does not satisfy the present-day notion of making a totally new beginning. The image is more likely to be that of turning over a page of blots and crossed out words and beginning again on clean, white paper.

He intended to take an opportunity this afternoon of speaking to Irene. A word in time saved nine; and now that she was going to live in the country there was a chance for her to turn over a new leaf! He could see that Soames wouldn't stand very much more of her goings on!
JOHN GALSWORTHY, The Man of Property, 1906.

A little while ago he started on whisky again. He said he was too old to turn over any new leaves. He would rather be happy for six months and die at the end of it than linger on for five years.
W. SOMERSET MAUGHAM, Of Human Bondage, 1915.

leap in the dark, a

a step of faith, a venture whose outcome cannot be predicted

'Now I am about to take my last voyage, a great leap in the dark.' These are said to have been the words with which English philosopher, Thomas Hobbes (1588–1679), quit this world. It was not long before Hobbes' striking words were being borrowed by others. In 1697, just eighteen years after Hobbes' death, Sir John Vanbrugh published his play The Provok'd Wife in which one of the characters exclaims, 'Now I am for Hob's voyage – a great leap in the dark.'

Defoe, Byron and Disraeli are amongst those who have quoted Hobbes when writing about death. Over the years, however, the original reference of the words has been forgotten and the term is now loosely applied to any venture whose outcome is full of uncertainty.

Who'd marry if he was afraid he'd regret it later? What is life, old boy, but a leap in the dark?
W. SOMERSET MAUGHAM, The Bread-Winner, 1930.

One of these mental healers was Dr Quimby, who cured Mrs Eddy at Portland and died of an 'erroneous' tumor shortly after. Partly because the people were sickly and partly for want of other experiments, they amused themselves with leaps in the dark.
V. W. BROOKS, New England: Indian Summer, 1940.

leg: to pull someone's leg

to make someone the target of a good-humoured joke or deception

A Scottish rhyme using 'draw' rather than 'pull' shows us the expression's country of origin:

He preached, an' at last drew the auld body's leg,
Sae the kirk got the gatherins o' our Aunty Meg.
(Alexander Anderson, *Rhymes*, 1867)

Aunty Meg, it seems, was the subject of a certain amount of trickery and deception, a sense which American usage of the idiom retains but which has been weakened to mean a bit of good-humoured, harmless fun in English.

There is speculation as to why the leg needed to be pulled. It is difficult to make the connection between the sense of the expression and the macabre suggestion that it refers to the right of a criminal sentenced to hanging to have his relatives pull on his legs, so hastening his death. More likely is the proposal that pulling a person's leg meant pulling it from under him, so tripping him up in public and making him a subject of ridicule.

It even occurred to me that he had been pulling my leg, and that the conversation had been an elaborate and humorous disguise for his real purpose.
GRAHAM GREENE, The Quiet American, 1955.

My friend Sarah went one worse than that many years ago, when, as a bright-eyed young student nurse, she found herself working on the men's surgical ward. Among her charges was one especially foul-tempered old chap, and Sarah put much time and effort into cheering him up, to absolutely no avail. Finally she told

him she was having him thrown out of the hospital. When a fresh spurt of abuse came her way, she said: 'Don't be silly, Mr Jones. I was only pulling your leg.' Poor Mr Jones had no legs to pull.
GOOD HOUSEKEEPING, May 1992.

lick into shape, to

to give form to something, to make something or someone presentable

The ancients believed that bears gave birth to nothing more than formless lumps of flesh which they then literally licked into cub-shape. Pliny the Elder describes this in his *Naturalis Historia* (AD 77) and Plutarch takes up the theme in *Moralia: On Affection for Offspring* (cAD 95). This ancient belief seems to have prevailed until at least the mid sixteenth century, for Rabelais writes about it in *Pantagruel* (1545).

The belief took on a figurative dimension quite early. Around AD 150 Aulus Gellius described how Virgil, close to death, begged his friends to destroy the *Aeneid* because he had not had time to perfect it:

For he said that as the bear brought forth her young formless and misshapen, and afterwards by licking gave it form and shape, just so the fresh products of his mind were rude in form, but afterwards by working over them he gave them definite form and expression (Noctes Atticae).

Which is the exact meaning of our modern idiom: putting something in order and making it presentable, or getting someone to behave or work as expected.

One can see he's been very badly brought up. He wants licking into shape.
W. SOMERSET MAUGHAM, Of Human Bondage, 1915.

usage: informal

limelight, in the

in the public eye, the centre of public attention

When calcium oxide, or lime, is heated it gives off a glaring white light. Thomas Drummond, a British army engineer, used this discovery to help his map-making in dismal weather conditions. The very visible limelight (the Drummond light of 1826) was used as a marker for measuring distances accurately. Scientists took up this invention, adapting it to produce powerful lights that were then used in film-projection, lighthouses and later in the theatre, rather like spotlights, to draw attention to the principal artiste on the stage. Someone standing in the limelight was very much the focus of public attention. So powerful was the light that there were cases of people going blind through too great exposure to it.

To steal the limelight suggests deliberately seizing the public attention, to the detriment usually of a rival, as may be the case in one of the quotations.

'It's difficult to grow up in the limelight and come out your own person, people don't allow you to.'
EVENING STANDARD, December 2, 1991.

Plant lilies in the garden, or in pots that can be moved into the limelight when buds appear. White lilies are the most stunning – try the fragrant Easter Lily, Madonna Lily or L. regale with its yellow throat.
GOOD HOUSEKEEPING, January 1992.

Regular as clockwork, the mighty prune steps forward once a year for its brief moment in the limelight. All the year round it works wonders behind the scenes: National Prune Week, which begins on Monday, gives the nation its chance to say thank you.
THE TIMES, January 1992.

Karen, who was Boris's lover for more than two years until last summer, stole the limelight from Babs when she turned up to watch Becker playing in the Open.
DAILY MAIL, May 8, 1992.

lion's den: to enter the lion's den

to undergo an extreme test, to face overwhelming opposition

The lion is legendary for ferocity and bravery, so to enter its very lair is a most challenging test, requiring the same virtues in even greater measure.

The modern use implies choice and willingness to take on the daunting task. This contrasts with the practice of the ancient world where being thrown to the lions was a mode of carrying out the death sentence. This is exactly the case in the incident that popularised the phrase. In the Old Testament story, political plotters trapped King Darius into throwing one of his three senior ministers, Daniel, to the lions for praying publicly to his God. Because he had signed an irrevocable law (a law of the Medes and Persians – the origin of that phrase), Darius had to carry out the prescribed punishment:

So at last the king gave the order for Daniel's arrest, and he was taken to the den of lions. The king said to him, 'May your God, whom you worship continu-

ally, deliver you.' And then they threw him in. (Daniel 6:16.)

It is hard to imagine a more daunting arena for the South Africans to play . . . A Test at Kensington is akin to entering the lion's den, West Indies having a remarkable record here.
DAILY TELEGRAPH, April 18, 1992.

lion's share, the

the larger part

In a fable by Aesop, a lion and three other animals go hunting together and kill a stag which is then divided into equal pieces. Just as the animals are about to eat, the lion stops them. The first portion is his, he says, by right of his kingship over them, a second share is his due because he is the strongest among them and a third part must be made over to him because of his courage. The lion allows that the fourth portion belongs to the others but warns them to touch it if they dare!

He wants the lion's share for himself and his client. He'll condescend to let my client have twenty-five per cent.
ERLE STANLEY GARDNER, The DA Calls a Turn, 1954.

Its budget is derived, not from UN's general funds, but from contributions paid by individual member states (the US pays the lion's share, and Britain the next largest share, as is just).
A. J. TOYNBEE, East to West, 'The Gaza Strip' 1958.

The building work added a further £2000 to the bill – with the new side wall accounting for the lion's share of the cost.
HOUSE BEAUTIFUL, June 1992.

lock, stock and barrel

completely, in its entirety

Although these sound like the contents of a hardware shop, the lock, stock and barrel referred to are the main parts of a gun. The lock is the device which sparks the charge; the stock is the handle and framework holding the other parts in place; the barrel is the metal tube through which the shot is propelled. *Lock, stock and barrel* means the complete weapon, with nothing omitted or changed in any way, hence the emphatic sense of the idiom.

Like the highlandman's gun, she wants stock, lock, and barrel, to put her into repair.
WALTER SCOTT, Lockhart, 1817.

When a woman is a trump there is nothing like her; but when she goes to the bad, she goes altogether, 'stock, lock and barrel.'
GEORGE WHYTE-MELVILLE, Digby Grand, 1853.

'Yes, we are a valuable swarm,' said the Queen, proudly. 'We will honour you with our company. We will take the Rose and Crown – lock, stock and barrel, wine, mead and barley-brew.'
ALISON UTTLEY, Tales of Little Brown Mouse, 1984.

usage: The only accepted order of the words today is *lock, stock and barrel.*

see also: hook, line and sinker

loggerheads: to be at loggerheads over something

to have a bitter argument with someone

A loggerhead was a long-handled device with a spherical cup at one end, which was filled with pitch for heating over a fire. Such implements were used in medieval naval battles where the hot pitch was slung at enemy sailors. In an exchange of this kind, the opposing forces were truly *at loggerheads.*

They almost reached an agreement, then their lawyers intervened. Suddenly they found themselves at loggerheads again and the bitter case continued.
DAILY MAIL, September 12, 1991.

'I found it odd that we had that massive publicity campaign about Aids but I haven't seen another like that about the environment. Why is that? Is it because the Government might find itself at loggerheads with its own philosophy on the economy?'

long in the tooth

old

Authorities are divided as to whether the teeth in question are human or equine. Advertisements claim that more teeth are lost through gum disease than through decay. Diseased gums recede over the years and this makes teeth look longer. Our ancestors had none of the benefits of modern dentistry and a mouthful of 'long teeth' meant that the wearer of the smile was past the first flush of youth. The French playwright Molière was well aware of the problem. In *Le Médicin Malgré Lui* (1666) he writes: '*The teeth have time to grow long while we wait for the death of someone.*'

Alternatively, a horse's front teeth appear to protrude more as it gets older, so a look at the length of them will help a dealer decide upon the age of the animal.

When trying to be funny the play is corny . . . There is a lot of patronising talk about wrinklies and geriatrics but really it is the writing that is long in the tooth.
MID SUSSEX TIMES, September 6, 1991.

usage: informal, derogatory

see also: from the horse's mouth

loose end, at a

having nothing in particular to do

There are two suggested etymologies. The first is that the expression goes back to the time of sailing ships when the vast number of ropes on the rigging needed to be kept in good order. The ends of the ropes were tightly bound to prevent them unravelling. When there was little else to do on board ship, the captain would order the crew to check them and bind any loose ends to keep his men occupied.

Alternatively the phrase may refer to an untethered working horse turned out into its field at the end of the day to kick up its heels.

Although John Heywood in his *Proverbs* (1546) writes that '*some loose or od ende will come man, some one daie*' it may not be our modern phrase which is intended, for the expression is not picked up again until the mid nineteenth century.

My brother Eric, then aged twenty-three, was rather at a loose end. He had had two or three jobs, in none of which he had been particularly happy.
NOËL COWARD, Present Indicative, 1937.

However he may well be right in suggesting that this quiz could be useful at the end of term when examinations are over

and both teachers and students are at a loose end.
TIMES EDUCATIONAL SUPPLEMENT, November 1974.

Nor has the law been adequate to deal with the situation that arose over the Bank Holiday weekend when 20,000 hippies, travellers and teenagers at a loose end took over a corner of the Malvern Hills.
DAILY TELEGRAPH, May 27, 1992.

make (both) ends meet, to

to live within one's means

People have been lamenting their inability *to make both ends meet* and live within their income since the seventeenth century, though some people are content with just enough to satisfy their needs. Thomas Fuller, writing in 1662, describes the saintly Cumberland thus: *'Worldly wealth he cared not for, desiring onely to make both ends meet'*. (*Worthies*, 'Cumberland').

In all probability the expression comes from accountancy. *Meet* as an adjective meant 'equal' or 'balanced', so the accounting practice of balancing profits and losses was described as *making both ends meet*. Also, *ends* refers to ends of the accounting year – hence the fuller version used by Smollett: *'He made shift to make the two ends of the year meet'* (*Roderick Random*, 1748).

This story, set in the 1920s, is about two sisters coping with life after father and struggling to make ends meet.
WEEKEND TELEGRAPH, September 7, 1991.

Even if you think that one stately home looks very much like another, you have to admire all those owner-occupiers strug-

gling to make ends meet behind the grand, well-known façades.
DAILY MAIL, March 5, 1992.

usage: The original descriptive sense of balancing the year's accounts has been superseded by an emphasis on the struggle necessary to make ends meet. To reflect this, *both* tends to be omitted today.

mark, learn and inwardly digest

ponder and thoroughly assimilate something

The expression comes from the Church of England's Prayer Book. *'Grant that we may in such wise hear them, read, mark, learn, and inwardly digest them'* are words from a prayer for the second Sunday in Advent.

Well, having bought his cats, nothing remains for the would-be novelist but to watch them living from day to day; to mark, learn and inwardly digest the lessons about human nature which they teach; and finally write his book about Mayfair, Passy, or Park Avenue, whichever the case may be.
ALDOUS HUXLEY, Music at Night, 'Sermons in Cats', 1931.

McCoy: the real McCoy

the authentic, genuine article; the real thing

There are various possibilities for the derivation of this phrase, from both sides of the Atlantic.

Many authorities subscribe to the theory that it refers to Kid McCoy, an American boxer famous early this century. On one occasion he was being provoked by a drunk who would not accept that this was really the lightweight champion. Eventually the boxer, goaded beyond endurance, punched the drunk and knocked him out. The man's first words as he came to were, '*You're the real McCoy.*'

A second American, Bill McCoy, may be another source. This infamous smuggler in the Prohibition period brought in hard liquor down the Atlantic coast of America from Canada. Hence, anything described as 'the real McCoy' was the genuine article, not a home-brewed or distilled substitute.

Scotland provides two slightly earlier derivations. In the late 1800s a man named Mackay advertised his particular brand of whisky as 'the real Mackay', to distinguish it from another product of the same name. Yet another story tells of family feuds. There were two branches of the MacKay clan in dispute over which was the senior. Eventually it was established that the MacKays of Reay, *the Reay MacKays*, held this honour.

The evidence points to a British origin. Then the phrase spread far and wide: there is a mention of it in an Irish ballad of the 1880s and it was recorded in Australia in 1903. It would surely have reached the New World also, where one or both of the colourful McCoys at least influenced the spelling of the phrase.

Is this a remake, or the original colourised, or a 'restored' version inflated with newly found footage that Orson Welles never wished included? Fear not; this Citizen Kane *is the real McCoy, released on the occasion of its fiftieth anniversary in a new print taken from the original negative.*
COBUILD CORPUS: The Times. June 6, 1991.

usage: There are a lot of variant spellings. The preferred form in America and now in the UK is *McCoy*, but formerly in the UK *MacKay*.

middle of the road

a position midway between two extremes, a safe position

The middle of the road is a dangerous place for pedestrians. It is strange, therefore, that this position should have become synonymous with safety, with steering a middle course uninfluenced by extremes. It has been suggested that the phrase originated in times when there were no pavements and gutters ran with all sorts of foul rubbish and effluent, so that the middle of the road was a cleaner and easier place to walk than the edge. It was also a safer place. There was little traffic and a pedestrian ran less risk of being run over by a horse-drawn vehicle than of being dragged into some dark alleyway and robbed. The suggestion is just about plausible. There is, however, no evidence to support it.

The Democratic faithful have confessed their liberal sins of the past, pledged themselves to a new life of middle-of-the-road righteousness and the church doors at Madison Square Garden are swinging shut.
INDEPENDENT, July 18, 1992.

usage: Hypens are optional, though common immediately before a following noun. A useful phrase for any contexts with clear extremes and a spectrum of opinion between them.

mince: not to mince matters/one's words

to speak frankly, to be brutally honest

This expression is always used with the negative 'not' in modern speech although it was used in the positive in the seventeenth and eighteenth centuries as in: '[They] would either excuse or mince the matter' (Joseph Hall, Cases of Conscience, 1649). The allusion is to mincing cheaper, stringier cuts of meat in order to make them easier to chew and digest. Someone who does not mince his words, therefore, makes no attempt to soften his tough message.

On the phone, Paul doesn't mince his words to the grower. 'You are basically giving us a load of rubbish in the North,' he says, sitting at his desk in shirt sleeves, dark spotty tie and flashy watch.
GOOD HOUSEKEEPING, December 1991.

see also: to call a spade a spade, to beat about the bush

mind one's p's and q's, to

to take great care how one speaks and behaves

Speculation abounds on the origin of this phrase, which has been with us since the beginning of the seventeenth century. One explanation is that the expression used to be 'mind your toupees and your queues', the 'toupee' being false hair and the 'queue' being the pigtail popular in days gone by. A popular riddle connected these hairstyles to the alphabet:

Who is the best person to keep the alphabet in order? Answer – A barber, because he ties up the queue, and puts toupees in irons.

Hairpieces are never very secure and would certainly prohibit the wearer from anything but the most decorous behaviour.

Another suggestion is that it comes from the dancing school where wigs remained a problem. Students were constantly being reminded to perfect their 'pieds' (footwork) and to have care for their 'queues' (wigs).

Alternatively the phrase may have arisen from the old custom in alehouses of hanging a slate behind the door on which 'p' or 'q' (pint or quart) was written against the name of each customer according to how much he had drunk. The accounts would be settled on payday. The landlord had to keep a careful record of his p's and q's and the customer had to ensure that only the ale he had consumed was marked up.

There are also stories arising from the similarity of 'p' and 'q'. Children often have difficulty in distinguishing between these two letters. 'Mind your p's and q's' must have been on the lips of governesses and tutors throughout the land. A final thought in this regard is that typesetters had problems in keeping their p's and q's from getting mixed up.

He had not penetrated into the upper domestic strata of Bursley society. He had never been invited to any house where, as he put it, he would have had to mind his p's and q's.
ARNOLD BENNETT, The Card, 1911.

Minding your P's and Q's: Beyfus believes that roughest instincts should be tempered. 'Not only does self-control inflict less pain, it is a far better self-defence.'
PHOTOGRAPH CAPTION, DAILY TELEGRAPH, May 27, 1992.

usage: A difficult one to punctuate some prefer to mind one's Ps and Qs.

moon: over the moon

highly delighted

Someone who is *over the moon* is elated. This phrase was frequently used in the 1970s by footballers and their managers to express their delight at victory. This overuse was seized upon by the satirical magazine *Private Eye*, which proceeded to ridicule televised post-match interviews with the result that both *over the moon* and its counterpart *sick as a parrot* have become football cliches.

The allusion to feeling so high with excitement that one imagines one could jump or fly over the moon is easily understood – see **Moonshine** (page 130). A definite origin for the phrase is obscure. Rees (1990) mentions that the family of William Gladstone's wife invented idiomatic phrases which they used in private and *over the moon* is said, by some, to be one of these. Perhaps she was inspired by the well-known nursery rhyme 'Hey Diddle Diddle' – see **The Absurd** (page 117).

He went to the ground on his own and his soccer hero, Steve Bull, handed the football over. Simon was absolutely over the moon about it, especially when he was invited to watch Wolves train.
DAILY MAIL, September 12, 1991.

Over the Moon of Tunbridge Wells *Here's the score. We invest your savings on the stockmarket. Free of tax. We guarantee a return. Free of tax. And every year we add what we've made to your Bond. Free of tax. On average that's been 16.3% pa. A very nice net result.*
ADVERTISEMENT, DAILY MAIL, October 2, 1991.

Duncan Harris is over the moon. He's just bought the house of his dreams and, because he was ready to take on a larger

mortgage, Abbey National had just the right deal for him.
ADVERTISEMENT, SUNDAY TIMES MAGAZINE, October 1991.

Not that Mr Smith would be over the moon at an endorsement from Mr Kinnock. The last colleague to receive such blessing was a Mr Kaufman, who has since become invisible.
DAILY EXPRESS, April 20, 1992.

A flow of other Bond Street traders kept popping in to have a look at the place, he said. 'Everyone seems over the moon that we've come. They see us as a sign that things are looking up.'
DAILY TELEGRAPH, May 28, 1992.

usage: A colloquial cliché.

see also: sick as a parrot

moot point, a

an issue which is open to various interpretations or viewpoints but to which no satisfactory answer is ever found

The word 'moot' can be traced back to the old Anglo-Saxon words *mot* and *gemot*, meaning 'meeting'. The political structure of Saxon society took the form of different assemblies where public matters could be debated; the *wardmote* was a ward meeting, the *burgmote* a town meeting and the *witenagemote* a meeting of prominent wise men.

The sixteenth century saw the establishment of mootings, or moot courts at the Inns of Court in London. Here young law students were given the opportunity to sharpen their powers of argument and debate by participating in hypothetical trials. The practice continues today:

Moonshine

For centuries the moon has appeared to man to be distant and remote, quite untouchable and unreachable. So the moon has come to have the extended metaphorical sense of the impossible, that which it is futile to pursue. Shakespeare in *Julius Caesar*, Act IV, Scene iii (1599) captures this sense:

> *I had rather be a dog, and bay the moon,*
> *Than such a Roman.*

Since then the sense of being engaged in some fruitless enterprise has become common in good literary style. C. P. Snow in *Strangers and Brothers* (1940) writes:

> *I have never been in so many troubles. I am baying at the moon. Sometimes the group itself seems like a futile little invention of my own. I am thoroughly despondent.*

The moon's inaccessibility is perhaps the very reason it has been passionately desired and sought after. One example of this is *to ask for the moon* or, slightly less commonly, *to cry for the moon*, meaning 'to want what is difficult or nearly impossible to obtain'. The suggested origin for the phrase is children who *cry for the moon* in order to be able to play with it. A nice example of its use comes from J. B. Priestley's *Angel Pavement* (1930):

> *To have a little place of his own with a garden and a bit of music whenever he wanted it, that wasn't asking too much. And yet for all the firm's increased turnover and its rises, he couldn't help thinking it was really like asking for the moon.*

A related expression is *to promise somebody the moon*, that is, 'to promise somebody so much that it will be impossible to carry it out'. Here is an example of its use:

> *Their marriage was never very secure. During their courtship he promised her the moon and she, being a rather immature and naive girl, believed him. She soon found out the truth.*

A further extension of the same basic meaning comes in *to pay* or *offer somebody the moon for something*. That is, 'to offer a seemingly impossibly large amount of money'. The person is so desperate he will go to the very limit of his resources to get what he wants. In football today, transfer fees are so high that clubs find they have to *pay the moon* to get the players they want.

What could be more romantic than two lovers hand in hand in the moonlight? It is a universal scene, depicted in countless paintings and sung of in numerous popular songs. But things aren't always so perfect and idyllic. The hours of darkness can be the perfect cover for illegal deeds, with the moon providing just enough light to carry out the task, but not enough to make detection easy. There are strong connotations here of illegality – a far cry from the sugary sentimentality of romance in the moonlight.

Moonlighting is an American term, progressively more common in Britain, which means doing a second job in addition to one's regular work. In these days of the thirty-five- or forty-hour working week, many people are able to take on a second job and indeed many are forced to do so in order to maintain their standard of living in the face of recession, inflation and rising prices. There is nothing particularly wrong in that, but *moonlighting* implies that this second job is not declared to the authorities, in order to avoid paying taxes.

to do a moonlight flit: A clearly illegal activity comes up in this colloquial phrase. *To do a moonlight flit* is another instance of using the cover of darkness and the dim light provided by the moon, this time to disappear quickly and secretly from where one is living, to avoid paying the bills.

An alternative form of the expression had a certain vogue in the first half of this century, and it equally concerned the moon. The quotation is from George Orwell's *Down and Out in Paris and London* (1933): *I remember how surprised she was at my asking her instead of removing the clothes on the sly*, shooting the moon *being a common trick in our quarter*.

Moonshine is an American term. One sense of it – 'airy, empty nonsense' captures the ethereal and ephemeral quality of moonlight. More commonly in England, it is taken to mean 'illegally made liquor'. In the early years of this century, particularly during Prohibition, there was considerable distillation of spirits without the knowledge of the authorities, with the dim light of the moon as the best cloak for these illegal activities. Interestingly, there is a related eighteenth-century British use that refers to the illegality of the distribution of spirits, rather than to its production: *moonshine* was brandy smuggled from France to England.

Judge Anthony Nicholl was adjudicating the final of the Observer Mace Mooting Competition *organised by Coventry University's Department of Legal Studies. The moot (which simulates a Court of Appeal hearing) was the culmination of a competition entered last October by sixty-one law schools* (Observer, *July 5, 1992).*

'Moot' is also found as a verb. Matters are sometimes 'mooted' (brought up for general discussion) in meetings.

In the idiom, the sense shifts away from simple debate (often with a clear-cut verdict or decision in legal contexts) to a contentious issue, with many valid viewpoints and no obvious or easy outcome.

Despite the disorder that reigns in international currency markets, says the paper, it is a moot point whether this is really the moment for grandiose monetary visions in Europe.
COBUILD CORPUS.

There has been nothing like it since the long hot summer of '76. Whether this will spoil the insect's glowing image is a moot point. So far its voracious appetite for greenfly has made it an ally of all mankind.
COBUILD CORPUS.

usage: To reply to someone, '*It's a moot point*' means roughly, 'That may be your view, it's certainly not mine.'

mud: his name is mud

On April 14, 1865 Abraham Lincoln, President of the United States of America, was shot in a Washington theatre. The man responsible, John Wilkes Booth, broke his leg while jumping from the President's box to the stage below to make his escape. Booth had a horse waiting behind the theatre and galloped out into the countryside where he sought medical attention from a country doctor ignorant of events in the capital. The next day news of the President's death reached Dr Samuel Mudd, who remembered the man he had treated the previous day and hastened to inform the police. But in spite of his prompt and dutiful action, the doctor himself was arrested and charged with being a conspirator. Although innocent, he was convicted and sentenced to life imprisonment.

In 1869 Dr Mudd was pardoned and released by President Andrew Johnson in recognition of his help during an outbreak of yellow fever at the prison, but public hatred of Booth and anyone connected with him was so intense that Dr Mudd was never forgiven and his name came to be used to refer to any scoundrel or wrongdoer. Later generations suffered for bearing the name of Mudd and it was not until the 1970s that Dr Mudd's innocence was finally declared and the family name cleared.

Take pity on me Before my name is mud.
J. C. GOODWIN. Wang: The Elephant Song. 1891.

Your name'll be mud.
PATRICIA WENTWORTH. Dead or Alive. 1936.

usage: In the popular mind, all associations with Dr Mudd are lost and so is the spelling *Mudd.* The only form used today is *mud* – quite appropriately, given its meaning of 'dirty, wet earth'.

mumbo jumbo

nonsense, something that has no meaning

Explorers of the African interior brought back tales of *Mumbo Jumbo*. The earliest is in Francis Moore's *Travel into the Inland Parts of Africa* (1738): *'A dreadful Bugbear to the Women, call'd Mumbo-Jumbo, which is what keeps the Women in awe.'*

Mungo Park, writing about his travels in the African interior at the end of the eighteenth century, says that *Mumbo Jumbo* was a spirit invented by the men of the villages to keep their womenfolk in order. Polygamy was the tribal custom and bickering and backbiting was common amongst wives. When life became intolerable, the husband would disguise himself as Mumbo Jumbo and then visit the culprits at night, shrieking and moaning until they were frightened into submission. The main troublemaker was then bound to a tree and whipped.

The word has come into English to mean a superstitious ritual or gibberish, from the meaningless rantings of Mumbo Jumbo's nocturnal visitations.

Both her grandchildren are religious freaks. One is a Hare Krishna who lives in an ashram and spouts mystic mumbo-jumbo.
DAILY MAIL, August 22, 1991.

usage: As in English there is no sense of a deity, capital letters are not used. The phrase is sometimes hyphenated.

see also: a load of codswallop, to talk gibberish

nail: to pay on the nail

to make a prompt cash payment

In the medieval marketplace honest dealing was encouraged by the setting up of pillar-like counters known as 'nails'. Money was literally placed *on the nail* in full public view as bargains were struck. If proof were needed, four bronze 'nails' still stand on the pavement outside the Exchange in Bristol and there is another in Limerick, as well as a copper plate at the Liverpool Stock Exchange.

But the truth is that this old phrase was in use before the nails were put there and the market pillars probably took their name from the expression, not the other way round. Nor is the term unique to England; German and Dutch share the same expression. This is another of the language's mysteries – the origin has been lost in time.

The cost of the materials the gunners used up in a single day was prodigious. If they had had to pay on the nail, out of their wages, for the cannons they wore out and the shells they fired, there would have been no war.
G. B. SHAW, The Intelligent Woman's Guide to Socialism, 1928.

What d'you say to having this little drop o' sunshine in the old 'ome? What d'you think of that? Good company and a good payer, right on the nail every Friday night.
J. B. PRIESTLEY, The Good Companions, 1929.

'What I love about being archbishop/ admiral of the fleet/warden of All Souls is that they do pay bang on the nail!'
THE TIMES, June 15, 1992.

namby-pamby

sentimental and insipid

Namby pamby was a nickname for Ambrose Philips, who penned dainty pastoral verse in the first half of the eighteenth century. Pope, who had written some poems in a similar vein, was a harsh critic of Philips' verse, maintaining that his own was far superior, so that literary society of the day was divided in its allegiance. When Philips produced a poem written for the infant daughter of Lord Carteret which was especially cloying in its sentimentality, therefore, its publication sent dramatist and critic Henry Carey – a supporter of Pope – scurrying for his pen. He it was who coined *Namby Pamby*, though Pope was swift to join the attack and make use of the nickname.

Dr Johnson is gentler in his assessment of Philips' poetry, however. In his *Life of Philips*, he writes: '*The pieces that please best are those which, from Pope and Pope's adherents, procured him the name of Namby Pamby*.'

It is an advance: for decades, the prevailing official and social attitude was that therapy was a namby-pamby luxury, and more than these monsters deserved.
GOOD HOUSEKEEPING, September 1991.

usage: informal

needle: like looking for a needle in a haystack

a near-impossible search for something

An old alternative for 'haystack', which was current in this expression from the sixteenth to the eighteenth centuries, was 'bottle of hay'. 'Bottle' was an old word for a bundle of hay or straw, from the Old French *botel*, a diminutive form of *botte*, meaning 'a bundle'. The expression is very evocative of the total impossibility of a search – the thin needle in amongst the long slim stalks of the haystack or bundle.

Radio 5's needles in a haystack *The diversity of the Radio 5 schedules means that it hasn't a natural, day-long audience to target. But it does mean that there should be at least one small treasure there for everybody; if we can find it.*
GUARDIAN, September 2, 1991.

nest egg, a

part of one's savings put aside as a reserve for the future

Until the advent of factory farming, a common country trick to encourage hens to lay more eggs was to put a porcelain egg in the nest. In the same way, a small sum of money set aside for future use is an inducement to the saver to add to it and watch it grow.

Home, for most of us, is as much a nest egg as a place to hang our hat, and with the property market now in the doldrums, many people are delaying plans to move, opting instead to stay put and add to their existing homes, with a view to selling when things pick up.
GOOD HOUSEKEEPING, May 1991.

Living in a nest-egg *Once again a home will be the best investment, says Anatole Kaletsky.*
HEADLINE, THE TIMES, May 6, 1992.

nest: to feather one's (own) nest

to provide, probably by dishonest means, for one's future financial security

The allusion is to those breeds of bird who, having made their nests, line them with the softest feathers, plucked from their own breasts or found on the ground, to provide comfort for themselves while incubating their eggs and later for their young. The phrase is often used in a critical tone to suggest that those who are *feathering their nests* are doing so dishonestly. John Bunyan used it in this sense in *Pilgrim's Progress* (1680): *'Mr Badman had well feathered his Nest with other men's goods and money.'*

Neither party had any strong basis of support in the country, which tended to distrust them both, the Tories because they were supposed to oppose all change and the Whigs because they were popularly suspected of using office to feather their own nests.
SIR ARTHUR BRYANT, English Saga, 1942–50.

Rarely has the feeling been so strong that the US system of government has broken down, that the Washington establishment is beholden to lobbies and special interest groups, more concerned to feather its own nest than tend to the country's future.
INDEPENDENT, May 5, 1992.

nest: to foul one's own nest

to prejudice one's interests

A proverb which moralises *'It is a foul bird that defiles its own nest'* has been in existence for almost a thousand years and alludes to the observation that birds do not excrete in their nests and remove the waste of their young, so keeping the nest clean for the brood.

They said at first that he was a monster against life, that he had fouled his own nest. Then they said he had turned against the South, his mother, and spat upon her and defiled her. Then they levelled against him the most withering charge they could think of, and said he was 'not Southern'.
THOMAS WOLFE, You Can't Go Home Again, 1940.

The narrow streets of Menerbes are now full of 'Les Britiches', *both tourists and prospective house owners, who want to eat what Mayle ate, drink a muscat on his café terrace, meet the appealingly dotty tradespeople who appear in* A Year In Provence *and* Toujours Provence *and buy up every barn in sight. This has got the author into trouble with discreet, long-established British residents of the Luberon who accuse him of fouling the nest.*
OBSERVER, September 15, 1991.

nettle: to grasp the nettle

to face a problem with determination

The nettle, which causes so much discomfort when lightly touched, has been used for centuries for its medicinal and nutritious properties. In one of his poems (1745), John Gay advises *'Nettle's tender shoots, to cleanse the blood'* and John Wesley in his *Primitive Physick* (1747) urges *'Take an ounce of nettle juice'*. But how did intrepid cottagers gather this stinging plant? Aaron Hill's poem, *The Nettle's Lesson* (1743), tells the secret:

Tender-handed stroke a nettle,
And it stings you for your pains;
Grasp it like a man of mettle,
And it soft as silk remains.

Through the centuries, idioms have nearly always been looked down on. In the eighteenth century, Addison warned against their use in poetry and in the seventeenth Dr Johnson had laboured in his dictionary 'to refine our language to grammatical purity and to clear it from colloquial barbarisms, licentious idioms and irregular combinations'. There is not much charity for the humble idiom there.

Many writers, Henry James for instance, have tried to steer clear of them. Students in a 1960s textbook were warned against even slightly colloquial idioms as 'phrases which should not be used in the drawing room'.

At last courage was found to grasp the nettle firmly, and in February 1778 the almost moribund Congress sent an invitation to the several States to elect delegates to a convention to meet at Philadelphia in May for the sole purpose of revising the Articles of Confederation.
J. T. ADAMS, The Epic of America, 1931.

We couldn't resource both libraries ... The first nettle to grasp, therefore, was to close one library and concentrate on the other.
TIMES EDUCATIONAL SUPPLEMENT, June 28, 1991.

nick of time, in the

at the very last minute, only just in time (said of a desired outcome)

A tally, or nick-stick, was used to keep track of time, of points in sporting events, of commercial transactions and (till as late as 1826) of official government bookkeeping records. With the widespread use of the tally it is not surprising that reference to it should enter popular parlance. *To nick it down*, for instance, meant 'to record something' and *to nick the nick* 'to hit the right time' for something.

In the nick of time is the only extant expression. It probably has sporting origins. Team scores were notched up on nick-sticks and when a winning point or goal was scored just before the end of the contest it was 'in the nick of time'.

The patient's hand suddenly swooped down on the sterile field and was grabbed in the nick of time. 'Don't they restrain the patients here?' I asked. No, they did not.
THOMAS HALE, On the Far Side of Liglig Mountain, 1989.

usage: informal

nine days' wonder, a

something which arouses great interest that quickly fades

A fourteenth-century author, possibly Chaucer, reminds us that '*A wonder last but nyne night never in toune.*' What this wonder is, however, is open to speculation. One theory is that the phrase originates from the Catholic 'Novena', festivals of nine days' duration, in which the statue of the saint being honoured is carried through the streets, accompanied by relics and votive offerings. According to Hargrave, the Latin root is *novenus*, 'nine each', which not uncommonly was confused with *novus*, 'new, wonderful', thus perhaps reinforcing the *wonder* element of the English phrase. A more down-to-earth interpretation is that the festival focuses attention for nine days but is soon forgotten in the anticipation of and preparation for the next.

Or the phrase may refer to kittens and puppies, whose eyes remain shut for about nine days after birth, during which time they experience a wondrous existence before coming into the world of reality.

Some of the elder men, returning through the dewy darkness, would be seen showing the catch to a friend and provide a nine days' wonder.
EDMUND BLUNDEN, The Face of England, 'The Hop Leaf', 1932.

nip something in the bud, to

to prevent a problem growing by dealing with it at an early stage

Good gardeners are not afraid of pinching out new shoots or buds before they develop fully in order to encourage sturdier growth on the main stems and a better show of fruit or flowers. The emphasis of the idiom is not so much on early excision of a healthy shoot in order to develop better growth later, but on stopping an unhealthy development in its initial stages.

From at least the fifteenth-century anyone abandoned to his difficulties was said to be *left in the briers,* a brier being a thorny bush. Briers, therefore, meant 'troubles' or 'vexations'. A seventeenth-century proverb speaks of nipping briers in the bud. James Kelly includes it in *Scottish Proverbs* (1721) and Thomas Fuller records it together with this useful definition: '*It is good to prevent by wholesome correction, the vicious inclinations of children.*' Nip the Briar in the Bud (*Gnomologia*, 1732). It is better to deal with a problem in its infancy than allow it to come into full flower.

The tragedy is, this sort of anti-social behaviour can be nipped in the bud provided that appropriate action is taken at an early stage.
DAILY MAIL, August 22, 1991.

no holds barred

without restriction, with no regard to fairness, by any means possible

This is a wrestling term and refers to a no-holds-barred contest, that is one where the usual rules and restrictions are lifted and competitors are permitted to use any means they can to throw their opponents or keep their shoulders pinned to the floor.

A hard hitting TV commercial . . . will spearhead the Government's £1 million Christmas anti drink-drive campaign.
The no-holds-barred commercial follows the equally uncompromising Christmas 1990 advert which showed a six-year-old girl in tears as her distraught mother shouted at her father who killed a child when he was driving while drunk.
EVENING STANDARD, December 2, 1991.

nose: to pay through the nose

to pay an exorbitant price for something

A rather grizzly explanation is that following their successful invasion of Ireland in the ninth century the Danes imposed a hefty tax upon the people. Those who refused or omitted to pay it suffered the penalty of having their noses slit. It should be said, however, that no historical evidence has ever been found to support the theory.

A life on the ocean waves

Each kind and area of human activity has its own vocabulary of words, metaphors and idioms. Sportsmen, musicians, agricultural workers, managers, lawyers, sailors, all have terms peculiar to themselves to describe their own domain of interest. Some of their expressions find a wider use in analogous but non-specialist situations: the farmer talks of life in terms of farming; the sportsman describes business as training, racing and winning; the seaman uses his nautical vocabulary to describe the problems he meets on land. The most striking or useful of these images and phrases from the subgroups are often taken up by the majority, and so new fixed expressions join the standard language. **It's not cricket** (page 201) looks at how one sport has enriched the general language stock of idioms. Sailors, not surprisingly, have contributed over centuries far more vivid metaphors and idioms, to what has been traditionally a seafaring nation. Some of the terms in the following list are clearly nautical metaphors; others' maritime origins are genuine but not superficially obvious; still others may originate elsewhere, though at the very least some authorities attribute them to naval life.

to bear down upon
to be in the same boat
to make way
to throw over
to cut adrift from
to weather the storm
to take the wind out of someone's sails
to see how the land lies
to cut and run
to go ahead
to overhaul
to turn in
to touch bottom
to have in tow

to find one's bearings
to hold aloof
to be first rate
to skylark
to clear the decks
to take the helm
to swim against the stream

to pour oil on troubled waters
to forge ahead
to know the ropes
to sink or swim
to go by the board
to stem the tide
to have leeway to make up

to leave the sinking ship
to have no shot left in the locker
to fall foul of
to keep abreast of
to pull together
to trim one's sails
to steer clear of
to put one's oar in
to keep in watertight compartments
to give someone a wide berth
to be on one's beam ends
to sail under false colours
when one's ship comes in
on the crest of a wave
on the lookout
all told
three sheets to the wind
the lie of the land
lump sum
all hands on deck
on the wrong tack
on the stocks
hard and fast
taken aback
cross currents
tell that to the marines
at close quarters
by and large
high and dry
up the pole
the cut of one's jib

plain sailing
to keep one's head above water
to nail one's colours to the mast
to give way
to make headway
to take it easy
to launch into
to tide someone over
to sail close to the wind
to keep a weather eye open
to show one's true colours
to be broad in the beam
the coast is clear
in deep water
in the offing
out of one's depth
all at sea
left stranded
hard lines
there's the hitch
in the wake of
hand over hand
shipshape and Bristol fashion
the man at the helm
round robin
on the rocks
at a low ebb
in the doldrums
underway
to show a leg
distress signals

Extensive though this list is, it is by no means comprehensive. Clearly, the influence on the national culture and language from this source is very pervasive. It is a **moot point** if military or rural life has surpassed it, or whether **The Bible and Shakespeare** (see page 180) come near.

There is a less gruesome, though still messy, alternative. *Rhino* has been slang for 'money' since the seventeenth century. The word is very similar to the Greek *rhinos*, meaning 'nose', which is the root of 'rhinoceros'. The animal is so called because of the prominent horns on its nose. The suggestion is that the phrase connects the idea of being bled for money with a nosebleed. The fact that the expression came into written English no earlier than the end of the seventeenth century makes this theory the more convincing of the two.

Made them pay for it most unconscionably and through the nose.
ANDREW MARVELL, The Rehearsal Transpos'd, 1672.

Greer says that by developing policies and the means of implementing them, pooling knowledge and finding a means to pass it on, big companies can save smaller ones from having to reinvent the wheel or pay through the nose for advice.
FINANCIAL TIMES, November 13, 1991.

Restaurant wine-drinkers pay through the nose. It is an impertinent little wine: drink it at Le Gavroche in Mayfair and a bottle of Chateau Lafite 1970 will cost you £560. Drink it at Ard-na-Coille hotel, near Inverness, and it will cost a quarter the price. If you flew to Scotland and hired a taxi to the hotel you would still have change in your pocket.
THE SUNDAY TIMES, June 28, 1992.

oil: to pour oil on troubled waters

to soothe a quarrel, to calm a heated argument

That stormy waters could be quelled by pouring oil on to them was known at least as far back as the first century AD. Pliny knew the fact and Plutarch wrestles with the science:

Why does pouring oil on the sea make it still and calm? Is it because the winds, slipping over the smooth oil, have no force, nor cause any waves? (Moralia: Quaestiones Naturales, cAD 95).

But the phrase might owe its origin to the Venerable Bede who, in his *Ecclesiastical History* (completed in 731), recounts a miracle performed by Bishop Aidan. A priest by the name of Utta was charged with escorting King Oswy's bride across the sea. Before he left he was approached by the bishop, who gave him a phial of holy oil. The bishop prophesied that there would be a fierce storm at sea but promised Utta that, if he were to cast the oil upon the water, the storm would immediately cease and the journey home would be safe and calm. The storm arose as Bishop Aidan foretold, the waves began to fill the vessel and the sailors were in despair, but Utta remembered the oil and the sea was calmed.

Strangely, however, the phrase was not widely used until the nineteenth century, the suggested explanation for this being that, until then, oil was not available in the great quantities needed to still rough seas.

Today we use the oil of soothing words or deeds to calm stormy disputes.

It was, Curry judged, her sense of importance that was hurt. He hastened to pour oil on the troubled waters. 'I'm very sorry, Mrs Strete. Perhaps you don't quite know how we set about these things. We start, you know, with the less important evidence.'
AGATHA CHRISTIE, They Do It With Mirrors, 1952.

*Pearson pours oil on troubled interim
newspaper profits.*
HEADLINE, THE TIMES, August 13, 1991.

over-egg the pudding, to

to exaggerate, to spoil something by
going too far

To add too many eggs to a pudding, or
even to add any at all to the instant cake
mixes that claim none is necessary, is to
go too far, to be excessive. Hence the
current meaning of 'to exaggerate'.

This has become a common journalistic
idiom in recent years.

*On TV news yesterday lunchtime, BBC
Political Editor John Cole claimed that the
chances of a November election had
always been 'greatly over-egged'.*
DAILY MAIL, October 2, 1991.

usage: informal

paddle one's own canoe, to

to take total responsibility for one's own
direction in life, to do one's own thing

This is an American phrase which originated in the West and was used to describe
any young man who intended to be the
'architect of his own fortune'. The expression was brought to popular attention
as a recurring line in an inspirational
poem which was published in *Harper's
Monthly* in May 1854.

*Voyager upon life's sea,
To yourself be true;
And, whate'er your lot may be,
Paddle your own canoe.*

*Leave to Heaven, in humble trust,
All you will to do;
But if you would succeed, you must
Paddle your own canoe.*

This extract gives a fair idea of the subject
and tone of the rest.

*Now is your chance, Europe. Now let Hell
loose and get your own back, and paddle
your own canoe on a new sea, while clever
America lies on her muck-heaps of gold,
strangled in her own barbed wire of shalt-
not ideals and shalt-not moralisms.*
D. H. LAWRENCE, Selected Essays, 'Benjamin
Franklin', 1917–18.

*Even if I can't quite achieve such – such
splendour, there are other lessons for me.
There's the lesson of paddling my own
canoe, for instance – not just weighing
down somebody else's and imagining I'm
steering it!*
NOEL COWARD, Design for Living, 1932.

usage: A strong flavour of the independent individualist of the North American
wilds.

paint the town red, to

to go out on a spree, to indulge in excessive revelry

The phrase is American in origin and
dates from around 1880, coming into
British English in the 1890s. One American authority says that 'to paint' was once
a slang term for to drink, and hazards the
suggestion that the term is a reference to
the red nose and flushed cheeks caused
by excessive alcohol.

More likely is the theory advanced by
other US authorities that the phrase
alludes to revelling cowboys having a

good time by shooting up a town and issuing a defiant warning that they would *paint it red* if anyone tried to stop them.

They had reached the cow town after sixty or ninety days of hard work, from daybreak to dark on the trail, eighteen long hours of tenseness and strain every day. No wonder they painted the town red.
L. HUBERMAN, We, the People, 1932.

I was getting awfully fed up with London. It's so damn slow. I came back meaning to have a good time, you know, paint the place a bit red, and all that.
EVELYN WAUGH, Vile Bodies, 1930.

usage: informal

pale: beyond the pale

outside civilised society or limits, beyond acceptable conduct

Pale comes from the Latin *palum* meaning 'stake'. In English it came to mean a fence around a territory which was under a particular authority, such as a cathedral pale. By extension this came to apply to the limit of political jurisdiction. For example, there was an English pale around the part of Ireland under English rule in the fourteenth century and around Calais from 1347–1558. Life within the pale was civilised; beyond, barbaric. Nowadays the phrase is more generally applied to any behaviour or statement that the speaker disapproves of.

Socially he was almost beyond the pale. His mother, a gaunt little widow of a drunken loafer, supported herself and her son by scrubbing out sundry shops.
A. J. CRONIN, Adventures in Two Worlds, 1952.

The boiler was thought to be quite beyond the pale. Boilers with the same heat output are now half the size.
GOOD HOUSEKEEPING, March 1991.

A lost job pushes them close to the welfare underclass, only recently considered reserved for those beyond the pale of mainstream society. Class mixes uncomfortably with race, and some already talk of 'caste'.
DAILY TELEGRAPH, May 18, 1992.

usage: *Outside the pale* is an alternative, though less common.

Pandora's box

a seemingly harmless situation fraught with hidden difficulties

Prometheus offended the gods. In revenge Jupiter ordered Pandora, the first woman, to be made. Jupiter gave Pandora a box which she was to offer to the man she married. Prometheus was wary of Pandora, but his brother, Epimethius, married her and, though warned against it, accepted the box. The moment he opened it, all the problems and wickedness which afflict mankind were loosed to do their worst and have done so ever since. All that was left in the bottom of the box was Hope.

The Eighteenth was a Sceptical Century; in which little word there is a whole Pandora's Box of miseries.
THOMAS CARLYLE, On Heroes and Hero Worship, 1840.

Pandora's box was opened for him, and all the pains and griefs his imagination had ever figured were abroad.
MRS E. LYNN LINTON, Paston Carew, 1886.

In France those passions could not be reabsorbed: Pandora's box had been opened, and the only hope remaining seemed to be Napoleon . . .
OBSERVER REVIEW, July 28, 1991.

'When we allow doctors to take over the area of communal life that is concerned with how we communicate and how we morally judge, we open a Pandora's box. I'm not suggesting that there is a conscious conspiracy, it's rather a collective urge, a sort of Puritan desire to be smacked with one of Mummy State's hands, while being stroked with the other.'
THE TIMES, June 15, 1992.

usage: literary

parrot: as sick as a parrot

extremely disappointed

See *over the moon*. Rees (1990) provides two possible explanations for *sick as a parrot*. Aphra Benn amongst others in the seventeenth and eighteenth centuries used 'melancholy as a (sick) parrot'. In the early 1970s several people fell seriously ill with a disease known as psittacosis or parrot fever which was common amongst cage birds and can be caught by man. Given the widespread use of the phrase in sporting contexts, could it be that it was coined then by an imaginative footballer called upon to describe his disappointment after losing a vital game?

It was about fifty years too early to be as sick as a parrot, but Chapman did manage to communicate his disgust so effectively that two of his players never again kicked a ball for the club.
COBUILD CORPUS.

The average footballer faced with the stock inquiry: 'How did you feel when you had an open goal and missed?' mumbles the stock reply: 'I felt sick as a parrot.' The caricature hasn't always been that far from the truth, but Lineker is refreshingly different: modest and articulate.
COBUILD CORPUS, BBC World Service, 1989.

usage: colloquial

see also: over the moon

parting shot, a

a final, pithy or wounding remark, to which the listener has no chance of replying

Originally *a Parthian shot*, the expression refers to the war tactics of the Parthians, an ancient people of southwest Asia. These skilled mounted archers would feign retreat, then, twisting round in their saddles, fire backwards with deadly accuracy on to the enemy in pursuit.

Parthian military strategies were known to Ovid:

Flee: by flight the Parthian is still safe from his foe.
(Remediorum Amoris, c1BC)

References to Parthian wars are found throughout seventeenth-century English literature. *A Parthian shot* was used in the nineteenth century and was still in use in the first quarter of this century until *parting shot* gained currency. This was through the similarity in pronunciation between *Parthian* and *parting*, together with an association of ideas: the *Parthian shot* was indeed a *parting shot*.

Clenching his fist on the paper, George crammed it into his pocket. He could not resist a parting shot.

'H'mm! All flourishing at home? Any little Soameses yet?'
JOHN GALSWORTHY, The Man of Property, 1906.

usage: *A Parthian shot* is still found but is dated and literary. *A parting shot* is preferred by most speakers and authors.

Yesterday these two gentle giants [horses] were celebrating the end of a lifetime of hard work as they settled into pastures new. The horses – once used for pulling beer drays – trotted along to the Whitbread Hop Farm at Paddock Wood, Kent, because the firm is closing its Central London brewery, home to shires since 1897.
DAILY MAIL, August 7, 1991.

pastures new

a change of place or activity

This is part of a line from *Lycidas* (1637), a poem by John Milton:

At last he rose, and twitch'd his mantle blue;
Tomorrow to fresh Woods, and Pastures new.

The full expression should be *fresh woods and pastures new*, though *fresh fields and pastures new* is a common misquotation. Fortunately the shorter *pastures new* stands all by itself and is heard more often these days.

About 1875, Boston had reached an equilibrium. Its finality was a proof of the laws of physics. This was truly true, at least, sufficiently so for Howells, who felt an insistent need of pastures new.
V. W. BROOKS, New England: Indian Summer, 1940.

Nor did the intellectuals rise in furious defense of freedom of expression when the Catholic Legion of Decency imposed a censorship upon the movies in 1934–35. They were tired of all that, and their protests were faint. They had turned to fresh woods and pastures new.
F. L. ALLEN, Since Yesterday, 1940.

pecking order, the

the social hierarchy which dictates one's relationship to those above and below one

A strict hierarchy known as *the pecking order* operates within the hen coop. *The pecking order* is dominated by one particular hen who has the right to peck all the others indiscriminately without being pecked back. The other hens all have their places below her and know that they may peck any bird lower in the order but never one above them. Inevitably there is one lowly creature who is pecked viciously by all her sisters but may herself only peck grain. Similar patterns of dominance exist both in human society as a whole and within the groups and organisations it divides itself into and, by analogy, these structures have come to be known as *pecking orders*.

At both houses and at Philips, selling on Wednesday, there are cast-offs galore. Elvis Presley's bathrobe, Sylvester Stallone's denim anorak from First Blood, Michael Jackson's sequinned jackets, hat, belt and boots, Mama Cass's kaftan and that Madonna basque have estimates varying from hundreds to thousands, according to pecking order.
THE SUNDAY TIMES, August 11, 1991.

There is a pecking order among those weird young people who smile at you sadly when your terminal starts playing up, and then sit down and engage the machine in a conversation that is way beyond your ken. They know what the 'right stuff' is, as Tom Wolfe called it, and they acknowledge, and are suitably reverential towards, those who have it. There is the girl who writes 'elegant code', that guy who writes 'beautiful code' and the hot-shot who writes 'inspired code', but who is also terribly untidy and needs a lot of de-bugging.
DAILY TELEGRAPH, May 1992.

Humans generally produce single offspring, and the pecking order grows more complicated when your first born feels his sovereignty is being usurped by a new arrival. Both parents are tired, everyone is going around on tiptoe, and no one consulted the existing child anyway.
DAILY TELEGRAPH, May 29, 1992.

penny dropped, the

the joke, remark or point of the argument has suddenly been grasped

The phrase probably alludes to the slot machines found on piers and in penny arcades. They are motionless and unresponsive until the penny drops inside but then they come to life. Similarly a person who does not understand a joke or remark made to him does not react as one would expect until *the penny drops*. The earliest machines date back to the 1880s but their popularity increased until there were more than two hundred models on offer by the 1930s. Scenes on early cinematographic machines hinted at the macabre or the titillating; to find out what the butler saw, be part of the crowd at an execution or admire the charms of 'The

Tiger Lady', all one needed to do was drop a penny in the slot. By 1935 it was possible to ogle 'That Boy on Palm Beach' for the same price, just one penny.

He had reached Naples before the penny dropped. As she would, given time, have told him, she couldn't possibly fly out: all her cash had gone on the wasted ticket to Rome.
OBSERVER REVIEW, July 28, 1991.

Attitudes were changing in both countries. 'The penny has slowly dropped that far from it being an advantage to be associated with hostages, it is a positive millstone,' said a British diplomat.
THE SUNDAY TIMES, August 11, 1991.

pickle: in a pickle

in a difficult situation, in a mess

Pickled and salted vegetables and meat were an important part of the diet in the Middle Ages. There would be no fresh food to be had during the long hard winter months and pickled produce not only added a little variety to a plain and tedious diet but also disguised the flavour of food which was starting to go bad. *To be in a pickle* came over from Holland in the sixteenth century. The Dutch version was *in de pekel zitten*, 'to sit in the pickle', *pekel* being the liquid, brine or vinegar, in which the food was preserved. In past centuries people have sought to emphasise the phrase with a variety of adjectives, amongst them *ill*, *sad* and *sweet*. Today we might say *in a fine* or *pretty pickle* if we wanted to stress the difficulty we found ourselves in.

The two same intensifiers, *fine* and *pretty*, are also commonly found in *kettle of fish*, another phrase with a similar meaning.

Thou shalt be whipt with wire, and stew'd in brine,
Smarting in lingering pickle.
WILLIAM SHAKESPEARE, Antony and Cleopatra, 1606.

Mr Menaby was, as he put it, in pickle. He knew that he could sell the new arrival [the calf] to his cousin Ralph, in Virginia; but, on the other hand, had he a right to do it?
ROBERT NATHAN, The Enchanted Voyage, 1937.

At that opportune moment the stool report came back showing roundworms and hookworms, whereupon I grandly announced that all her problems were due to these little parasites living in her intestines and that she'd be well in a jiffy. There's nothing like a timely stool exam to get you out of a pickle.
THOMAS HALE, On the Far Side of Liglig Mountain, 1989.

usage: colloquial

see also: kettle of fish

pig in a poke, a

a purchase that was not properly examined before it was made

It was the custom in old country fairs to sell suckling pigs. The trader would have one pig on show and the rest would be neatly tied in sacks, or 'pokes', ready to take away. Not all traders were honest, however, and some would put cats into the 'pokes'. The unwary customer would pay for his pig only to discover the deception later, but the more wary fellow would untie his sack to check his purchase. *(See to let the cat out of the bag.)*

The phrase is semi-proverbial and reflects the wisdom of European peoples over many centuries. The earliest forms of the phrase throughout Europe speak only of 'buying in a sack', that is of buying without first inspecting. Later forms warn against 'buying a cat in a poke', and this is the version that has remained in other European languages. The pig is an English variation. Although the phrase is an old one, the accompanying expression *to let the cat out of the bag* is much more recent and does not appear to have equivalents in other languages.

Incidentally, the Middle English word *poke* is also the root of our present-day word *pocket*, meaning 'little poke'.

I can't buy a pig in a poke . . . Let me know what you've got to sell, and then maybe I'll make a bid for it.
MURRAY, John Vale's Guardian, 1890.

Miss Trant had seen an advertisement in The Stage, offering this theatre at a fairly moderate rent, and had taken it for a week, in spite of Jimmy's advice. 'It's buying a pig in a poke,' he said darkly, but Miss Trant refused to be warned, and was encouraged by most of the others, who were anxious to see themselves on the stage of a real theatre.
J. B. PRIESTLEY, The Good Companions, 1929.

All he can do is feel around in the dark. That's the surest way I know to buy a pig in a poke.
ERSKINE CALDWELL, Love and Money, 1954.

Well, I wasn't going to buy a pig in a poke for Auntie Gladys and there was much nasal cogitation before I eventually settled on Evening Impressions . . .
MID SUSSEX TIMES, November 1, 1991.

see also: to let the cat out of the bag

pigeon-hole someone, to

to classify; to put on one side

Our medieval ancestors kept pigeons as domestic birds, not for racing but for their meat. Pigeon holes were the openings set in a wall or a purpose-built dovecote in which the birds nested. By 1789 the arrangement of compartments in writing cabinets and offices used to sort and file documents had come to be known as pigeon holes because of their resemblance to the pigeon cote. By the mid nineteenth century *pigeon hole* was being used as a verb meaning either to put a matter to one side with the intention of coming back to it later, or to classify information.

How do you behave at fortysomething? Your lifestyle, children and job will often dictate much of what you do. But that's not like saying you should pigeon-hole yourself into adopting a 'typically middle-aged' outlook on life.
DAILY EXPRESS, October 8, 1991.

usage: When people are *pigeon-holed*, there is a nuance that the judgement of them implicit in classification might well be wrong. It suggests categorising someone on a partial or unfair basis. The hyphen may be omitted.

piggy in the middle

a third party between two opposing groups

There is an old children's game called *pig*, or *piggy*, *in the middle* in which two or more players throw a ball to each other, trying hard to keep it out of the reach of the hapless child who has been chosen to be *pig in the middle*. The frustrated 'pig' shadows the other players, trying all the while to catch the ball.

By extension the context of use can now be rival politicians, factions in an office, etc. Someone who feels between the groups, trapped and pressured from both sides, is *piggy in the middle*. In the original game, children might choose to be the *piggy*; in the adult version it is not an enviable situation.

'When Larry and the children are all here I feel like a pig in the middle,' says Wendy Miller.
GOOD HOUSEKEEPING, September 1991.

usage: informal

pikestaff: as plain as a pikestaff

totally obvious, evident; easy to understand

Some authorities believe that the phrase refers to the pike, a weapon used by the infantry. The pike was rather like a spear, but its shaft was so very long that it was easily visible to all around.

This explanation fits in very neatly with the modern meaning of 'extremely obvious'. However, another theory put forward, and supported by sixteenth-century references, suggests that the expression has changed in form and shifted in meaning over the years. Pedlars shouldered a sturdy staff, known as a packstaff, on to which they tied their bundle. Constant use wore the wood plain, and so we find the comparison *plain as a packstaff*: *'Pack-staffe plaine, uttring the thing they ment'* (Bishop Joseph Hall, *Satires*, 1597).

Plain as a pikestaff was a later sixteenth-century variant.

The comparison with a second kind of staff refers to the use in the Middle Ages by those who travelled on foot of a pikestaff, a stout stick with a metal tip, to help them along the way. The pikestaff was a simple, utilitarian affair, and the simile *plain as a pikestaff* originally meant just that, 'basic, unelaborate'. Thus, in Charles Cotton's *Scarronides* (1664) we find *'plain as a pike-staff without gilding'*. When Trollope writes, *'The evidence against him was as plain as a pike-staff'* (*The Last Chronicle of Barset*, 1867), he means not that the evidence was obvious, but that it was simple and to the point, even blunt.

He would not give way till he saw young Bosinney with an income of his own. That June would have trouble with the fellow was as plain as a pikestaff; he had no more idea of money than a cow.
JOHN GALSWORTHY. The Man of Property, 1906.

Yet it is plain as a pikestaff that our judges' problem is not their wigs but their lack of a real hard resolve to deter the criminal. On with your wigs and up with your sentences, I say.
DAILY EXPRESS. April 30, 1992.

usage: Despite its long ancestry, the phrase remains colloquial.

pipeline: in the pipeline

on the way, about to happen, about to be implemented

The phrase is from the oil trade and refers to the systems of piping which were installed from the 1880s to carry petroleum from oil-wells to the refineries. Oil which is already *in the pipeline* is on its way to the consumer.

Now there are six Kookai shops in London, with three soon to open in Bromley, Hatfield and Sheffield and yet more in the pipeline.
DAILY MAIL. August 8, 1991.

poker-faced

straight faced, expressionless

This phrase is from the gaming tables in America and has been in use since 1885. It refers to the bland expression adopted by a poker shark, determined not to betray the value of his hand.

It should be added that the film is a comedy of sorts, less poker-faced than numb.
DAILY MAIL. August 9, 1991.

The more persuasive sociological explanation is that snooker is the game made for television. Like an old-fashioned B-movie Western, it offers its poker-faced young heroes and its bruised old pros.
THE TIMES. May 6, 1992.

'Eventually he simply said, "ICI is down a pound," even though he must have seen the value of his own properties plunging by the minute,' recalls Kinloch. 'He had a complete poker face.'
DAILY TELEGRAPH. May 16, 1992.

pole: up the pole

out of one's senses, mad; in difficulty

A pole is another term for a ship's mast and, more especially, for that part of the mast which is above the rigging. It is hard to imagine a more precarious place to be; one would have to have taken leave of one's senses to shin up there at all as a single wrong move might well prove disastrous.

One can be *driven* or *sent up the pole*, that is enraged or maddened by someone or something. One can even find oneself *up the wrong pole*, meaning that one has totally the wrong idea about something.

I think we may take it for granted that our friend Weldon is a bit up the pole, financially. However, that's not what I came round about.
DOROTHY L. SAYERS, Have His Carcase, 1932.

'What poets do you like?' he asked. 'Blunden,' I said. 'Not bad. Who else?' I mentioned another name. 'Up the wrong pole.' Another. 'Written ravishing lines but has the mind of a ninny.'
STEPHEN SPENDER, World within World, 1951.

Fax Machines can drive you up the Pole. *Waiting to send an often blurred, sometimes unreadable fax can be a frustrating business – not to mention time wasting and inefficient. And yet, you can't work without them. It's enough to drive you up the pole.*
ADVERTISEMENT, MACWORLD, October 1991.

usage: Informal. A flexible expression that can be used in a variety of forms with several different senses.

post haste

immediately, with urgency

In the sixteenth century letters were delivered by a relay system of postal messengers on horseback. The horses would be ridden hard and would need to be changed every twenty miles or so. Fresh horses were kept ready at various posthouses or inns along the way, available to ordinary travellers as well as to the post-boys. To gain prompt attention and priority choice of horse, a messenger with a packet to deliver would cry, *'Post haste!'* when he entered the stable yard.

By return of post, the phrase we now use to request an immediate answer to a letter, had a much more literal meaning when the service was in its infancy. It meant that the reply should be carried back by the very messenger – that is, the 'post' – who had just delivered the message.

End to monopolies, post haste.
HEADLINE, TODAY, October 11, 1991.

The Minister for Overseas Development, Mrs Chalker, says she's now gone posthaste to Jordan to find out for herself what's happening and what more needs to be done.
COBUILD CORPUS: BBC World Service, 1989.

usage: The phrase is sometimes hyphenated.

pot: to go to pot

to fall to pieces, to go to ruin

The sixteenth-century use of the expression suggests a stewpot. The original expression seems to have been 'go to the pot' and alludes to meat being cut up into pieces ready to put into the pot. Another explanation is that it was a melting pot into which broken metal objects, or even stolen articles, were thrown to be melted down.

I shouldn't wonder if the Empire split up and went to pot. And this vision of the Empire going to pot filled a full quarter of an hour with qualms of the most serious character.
JOHN GALSWORTHY, In Chancery, 1920.

He makes the world and then he goes and rests on the seventh day and his creation can go to pot that day for all he cares.
GRAHAM GREENE, Loser Takes All, 1955.

usage: informal

rain cats and dogs, to

to rain heavily

Three theories present themselves for this picturesque expression.

The most vivid suggests that drainage in the streets in bygone centuries was so inadequate that, during storms, stray dogs and cats drowned in the flood. When the water level went down, their carcases littered the streets. Swift's *Description of a City Shower* (1710) gives us a flavour of what it was like:

Now from all parts the swelling kennels flow,
And bear their trophies with them as they go.

The 'trophies' are numerous, but amongst them are:

Drown'd puppies, stinking sprats, all drench'd in mud,
Dead cats and turnip tops, come tumbling down the flood.

The first written record of the phrase as we know it comes in Swift's *Polite Conversation* (1738) and it might be supposed that he was merely making an allusion to his earlier verse, which would confirm this theory and make Swift the author of the metaphor. Unfortunately the expression was used in a slightly different form in the previous century when Richard Brome wrote: '*It shall raine . . . dogs and polecats*' (*The City Wit*, 1653).

Alternatively, some authorities believe that the phrase may be a corruption of the Greek word *catadupe*, meaning 'cataract' or 'waterfall'. In other words the original expression had the meaning 'rain is coming down like a waterfall'.

Still others suggest a connection with Norse mythology in which witches in the guise of cats rode upon storms and the storm-god Odin was accompanied by a dog.

There was a danger, when the bumpers were raining like cats and dogs, that Viv Richards would end his final Test with English blood on his hands.
DAILY MAIL, August 9, 1991.

usage: informal

rank and file, the

the common people, those not in leadership

Rank and file describes the way a body of soldiers is drawn up for inspection. 'Rank' is a line of men standing side by side in close order and 'file' a line standing one behind the other. The expression refers to private, non-commissioned soldiers who carry out the orders of those in command. It is no longer a purely military term and is now used to describe the ordinary members of a large organisation or political party.

Flags and banners and catchwords are all very well for the rank and file, but the leaders know that a political campaign can't be carried on without money.
CHRISTOPHER ISHERWOOD, Mr Norris Changes Trains, 1935).

usage: Particularly common in journalism.

re-invent the wheel, to

to re-introduce a former practice, to do the same again (particularly unnecessarily)

There is no point in putting a lot of effort into inventing something if it is already in existence. This applies to any invention, though the one fixed in the idiom is a most fundamental discovery. This common phrase is often used in business contexts – a cynic might say because the emphasis on constant change means going back to a previous state or system but calling it something different.

To make it financially worthwhile for other people to re-invent your wheel is commercial suicide. Apple almost fell into that trap a couple of years ago, but pulled itself back at the last moment by bringing out its low-end Macs and printers.
MACUSER, October 4, 1991.

usage: informal

red herring, a

anything which diverts (often intentionally) people's attention away from the main argument

This is a nineteenth-century expression, but we must look at earlier centuries to understand its origin.
   A herring that has been dried, salted and smoked turns a reddish colour. These cured fish have a particularly strong smell so, in medieval times, they were useful as a lure for training hounds in stag-hunting. Later people who were opposed to hunting, fox-hunting in particular, would drag a red herring across the fox's trail and entice the hounds away from the scent of their quarry.

He's been dragging red herrings round this house until it smells like Fisherman's Wharf.
CLIFFORD KNIGHT, The Affair of the Fainting Butler, 1943.

In recent years, there has been much speculation about the possible role of fish oils in the prevention of Britain's number one killer, coronary heart disease. As a result, the sale of fish oil supplements has almost doubled in the last two years. But are they a miracle cure or simply a red herring? Many scientists are still undecided.
GOOD HOUSEKEEPING, March 1991.

usage: To draw a red herring across someone's path is a less common, older form.

red letter day, a

a day to celebrate

During the fifteenth century it became customary to mark all feast days and saints' days in red on the calendar whilst other days were in black. These were days for rejoicing and celebration and so people began to refer to days which had particular significance for them personally as *red letter days*.

I'm mighty proud of this privilege to meet you. This's a red-letter day for me, and I'll remember it as long as I live.
ERSKINE CALDWELL, Love and Money, 1954).

August 26th, 1871, had been some sort of red-letter day for her. She had said to herself then that never would she forget that date; and indeed, she remembered it well, but she no longer had the faintest notion

what had happened to stamp it on her memory.
K. A. PORTER, 'The Old Order', 1930.

usage: As the practice of highlighting days in red on calendars has diminished in recent years, so has the frequency of the expression. The use of the hyphen is now optional.

red tape

excessive bureaucracy, form-filling

The phrase originates in the former practice of tying together papers and official documents with red tape. This procedure goes back to the seventeenth century, as instanced by an advertisement in the *Public Intelligencer* (December 6, 1658), which offered a reward for *'a little bundle of papers tied with a red tape which were lost on Friday last . . .'* Possibly it was Sydney Smith who first used the term to satirical effect. Discussing Sir J. Makintosh he writes:

What a man that would be, had he a particle of gall, or the least knowledge of the value of red tape! As Curran said of Grattan, 'he would have governed the world.'

Modern usage has reinforced its use as a condemnatory phrase, often an insult of a frustrated man doing battle with officialdom.

Council chiefs were accused yesterday of 'robbing' schools to spend more on red tape.
DAILY MAIL, August 9, 1991.

British Red Tape Blocks Colony's Escape Route *Key workers are fleeing Hong Kong for Australia, Singapore and else-*

where because civil servants could take up to three years to deal with their applications for British citizenship.
OBSERVER, August 25, 1991.

The Government, due to unveil its proposals for extending competition next month, also plans to crack down on councils which reluctantly invite bids for a tender and then put red tape in the way of private companies, ensuring that the authority's own workforce wins the contract.
DAILY MAIL, October 11, 1991.

ride roughshod over, to

to treat someone harshly, to behave in an arrogant and domineering manner towards someone

Horses which were roughshod had shoes from which the nail-heads projected a little. Practically speaking, this helped to prevent their feet from slipping on loose ground or in wet weather, but to be trampled upon or kicked by a roughshod horse was no laughing matter.

It has been claimed that the cavalry of a number of different countries tried to use their horses as weapons by fitting them with shoes fashioned with sharp projecting edges. It was calculated that the warhorses would damage the steeds in the enemy ranks. Instead the idea proved impractical since the horses cut into not only the adversaries' mounts but those of their own company.

They thought they had only a girl to deal with and that, therefore, they could ride roughshod over her. But she would show them their mistake. They wouldn't have dared to have treated her like that if she had been a man.
JAMES JOYCE, Dubliners, 'A Mother', 1914.

The young royalist squires who now rode roughshod over the land had been ill-schooled for the parts they were to play.
G. M. TREVELYAN, History of England, 1926.

ring a bell, to

to remind someone of something, to jog someone's memory (of a shared experience)

Speculation abounds as to what kind of bell rings when the memory is jogged. Some say that the bell is that which attracts the attention of a clerk, receptionist or servant and that, in the same way, something seen or said may suddenly focus our attention on a person or event stored away in our memory.

Another offering says that the bell could be the one which rings in a shooting gallery at the fair when a bull's eye is scored. This is dismissed by Funk (1955) who feels the expression would have to be 'to ring *the* bell' in order to fit in with this theory. Instead he proposes a bell which rings a more nostalgic note and suggests a school or church bell.

What this boils down to is that no one really knows how the expression came about.

Your letter rang more than a few bells. I'm 25 and haven't had a normal relationship with my mother since I was 14.
BEST, August 15, 1991.

usage: informal

ring of truth, the

a convincing, authentic account

See *to ring true*

It may be that Simpson is inclined to exaggerate the degree of disaffection from the Saddam regime that he detected among ordinary Iraqis, but his individual vignettes have the ring of truth.
THE SUNDAY TIMES, August 11, 1991.

ring the changes, to

to do things in as many different ways as possible for the sake of variation; to reiterate the same message in different ways

The term comes from bell-ringing. The seventeenth century saw 'change ringing' practised in churches and cathedrals. 'Changes' are the different orders in which bells can be rung. A set of three bells, for instance, can be rung in a series of six different changes. The more bells there are in the belfry, the greater the number of possible changes. In a bell tower boasting twelve bells it would be possible to ring a total of 479,001,600 changes, which would take some thirty-eight years.

Dixon has a nice story about *ringing the changes*, although in a different sense: '*He buys sixpence worth of currants, tenders half a crown, and gets back two shillings as change. Then he says, "Oh, here is a sixpence; give me back the half-crown," which the shopkeeper, taken unawares, probably does, and the cheat makes off with two shillings.*'

He could apply flattery with so unsparing a hand that even Princes of the Church found it sufficient; and, on occasion, he could ring the changes of torture on a human soul with a tact which called forth universal approbation.
LYTTON STRACHEY, Eminent Victorians, 'Cardinal Manning', 1918.

On these and other charges against the Administration endless changes were rung in the conservative press, in the speeches of conservative business men and political leaders.
F. L. ALLEN, Since Yesterday, 1940.

Shops ring changes to counter slump.
HEADLINE, DAILY EXPRESS, October 8, 1991.

ring true/false, to

to give the appearance of being genuine and authentic, or not

When coins were made of pure metal, and not alloys as they are today, it was possible to test whether or not they were genuine by the sound they made when dropped. A pure silver coin had a sonorous ring, a counterfeit coin made a dull sound.

I think I can tell a good story and I can create characters that ring true.
W. SOMERSET MAUGHAM, Cakes and Ale, 1930.

As soon as he said it he knew it rang false; it sounded like some sentimental Old Boy revisiting his alma mater.
JAMES HILTON, Time and Time Again, 'Till It Was All Over', 1953.

But somehow the idea that undertakers are sensitive souls does not ring true. These undertakers have many fine qualities but they keep their trade-exhibition champagne in mortuary refrigerators. They hold impromptu cocktail parties on stands surrounded by revolving coffins, they leave dishes of Smarties on the bonnets of their hearses.
INDEPENDENT, April 30, 1992.

riot act: to read someone the riot act

to quell rowdy or objectionable behaviour by remonstrating and making the consequences clear

The *Act for Preventing Tumults and Riotous Assemblies*, or Riot Act, was decreed in 1715 in the reign of George I. The act made it unlawful for twelve or more people to disturb the public peace through riotous behaviour. Such a crowd could be ordered to disperse by a magistrate reading aloud the following proclamation:

Our Sovereign Lord the King chargeth and commandeth all persons being assembled immediately to disperse themselves, and peaceably to depart to their habitations or to their lawful business.

Those who had not obeyed the command an hour later were sentenced to imprisonment with hard labour.

'You've never gone short, Joseph.'
My mother always called me by my full name when she wanted to read the riot act.
ROBERT BROWNING, The Lost Leader, 1845.

· · · · · · · · · · · · · · · · · ·
What grammatical characteristics do the following phrases have in common: *to give somebody the boot* and *to give it somebody hot and strong*? Each phrase allows the indirect object to be the subject of a passive construction: *he was given the boot* and *he was given it hot and strong* are equally acceptable. It is relatively unusual for the fixed idiom to show this degree of flexibility (see **what is an idiom**?, page 6).
· · · · · · · · · · · · · · · · · ·

There are 25 sombre, cold sober Kennedys gathered . . . at Palm Beach. For once the Kennedy women have read them the riot act. The rule is no drinking, no dating and no high-jinks.
DAILY MAIL, November 20, 1991.

And I owe a lot to a doctor who read me the riot act about two years after David died. He said, 'There's nothing wrong with you; you should see half the human misery and suffering that I do in the course of a week. You're only 30, pull yourself together and get on with it.' And it was actually what I needed.
GOOD HOUSEKEEPING, April 1992.

---

rob Peter to pay Paul, to

to benefit one person or enterprise at the expense of another

On December 17, 1540 the Church of St Peter at Westminster became a cathedral. It enjoyed its elevated status for only ten years before the privilege was withdrawn and the diocese of Westminster fell once again within that of St Paul's cathedral. Ill feeling was further exacerbated when a good portion of revenue from St Peter's land was then used to finance repairs to St Paul's. They had *robbed Peter to pay Paul*.

This story is so convincing that there is probably an element of truth in it. An astute mind doubtless applied this apt, but already current, saying to the contemporary *cause célèbre* – for the expression, in various forms, has in fact been in use since long before 1540. In 1380 John Wyclif wrote: *'Lord, hou schulde God approve that thou robbe Petur, and gif this robbere to Poule in the name of Crist?'*; and Herbert of Bosham as early as the 1170s uses a similar phrase relating to the

two apostles: *'As one who crucified Paul that Peter might go free'* (*Life of St Thomas of Canterbury*).

Usually it is Peter who loses and Paul who gains; here it is the reverse. Perhaps the saying is hinting at some old theological debate or rivalry within the Christian church in which the relative merits of the two apostles were discussed.

Neither is the expression confined to English. French owns a similar saying – *descouvrir S Pierre pour couvrir S Pol* (strip St Peter to clothe St Paul) – and so does German.

The true origin of this centuries-old expression has been buried in time.

When taxation is utilised to secure healthy conditions of existence to the mass of the people it is clear that this is no case of robbing Peter to pay Paul.
L. T. HOBHOUSE, Liberalism, c1920.

It began to dawn upon the boosters that attracting industries bore some resemblance to robbing Peter to pay Paul, and that if all of them were converted to boosting, each of them was as likely to find itself in the role of Peter as in that of Paul.
F. L. ALLEN, Only Yesterday, 1931.

---

root for someone, to

to desire success for someone

This is a piece of American slang from the turn of the century. It originated amongst supporters on the sportsfield who were urging their team on to win. Possibly it is a corruption of the word 'rout' meaning to make an uproar.

Signing the latest in the vast number of replies to worried listeners – 'I can assure you that we will still be there every day for

Memorable events

Out of the welter of events and people we daily experience or hear of, a very few stick in the memory and are referred to in speech. A tiny proportion of these are so regularly mentioned that they become fixtures in the language, captured in a particular form of words. Their meaning, too, may well develop, such that before long the original incident that inspired them has become a hazy memory and the new sense has taken over. This is the process through which some idioms are formed. Those discussed below concern events where the location is preserved in the phrase and incidents where the protagonist lives on in the expression.

Events and place names

Places sometimes got their names from a historical incident. On December 24, 1777, Captain Cook arrived at an island in the Pacific. We now know it to be the largest atoll in the world, one of the Line Islands. Not surprisingly, he called his discovery Christmas Island. In similar fashion, idioms may include a place which refers to an incident that took place there. Many are of a military character. The famous Greek victory over Troy – thanks to *a Trojan horse* – is universally known. The battle of Waterloo is probably familiar, too – but what military incidents occurred at the river Rubicon and at Coventry? See **to meet one's Waterloo, to cross the Rubicon, to send somebody to Coventry**. The sad results of military exploits in a former colony produced this example:

like the black hole of Calcutta: Surajah Dowlah, Nawab of Bengal, is generally taken to be the villain of this story, although in all probability he had no idea of the results of his command. On June 20, 1756, following the seizure of the East India Company's Fort William, he gave orders for 146 British captives to be incarcerated in the prison there. The miserable cell measured eighteen feet by four feet ten inches. By morning only twenty-two men and the one woman prisoner had escaped a horrifying death by suffocation. This colloquial phrase has often been shortened, as in this example:

> *Do you think Miss Pinkerton will come out and order me back to the black hole?* (W. M. Thackeray, *Vanity Fair*, 1848)

Its continued use is doubtless helped by the *black holes* that astronomers have found in outer space over recent years, into which people and things metaphorically disappear, never to return. It is possible that in contemporary usage there is a coalescence of the two sources into one phrase, *a black hole*.

Sometimes the apparent reference to a famous historical event can be misleading.

To set the Thames on fire seems to refer to the Great Fire of London. One can imagine a vivid picture of flaming buildings falling into the Thames and the lurid reflection of the inferno around making it look as though the Thames itself were aflame. Alas, *Thames* is in fact *temse*, an old word for a sieve for corn. In the eighteenth century a hard-working farm labourer might have his leg pulled for going at such a pace that he *set his temse on fire*.

Events and people

Some idioms preserve the name of the person concerned in the action or incident, rather than the place where it occurred. There are examples from classical times which are today somewhat literary in use.

a Pyrrhic victory is 'a hollow victory, won at too high a price'. King Pyrrhus won the battle at Asculum in 279 BC, yet in the process he lost all his best officers and many men. '*One more such victory*,' he said afterwards, '*and we are lost.*'

to cut the Gordian knot: Gordius, the king of Phrygia, had tied such a complex knot that no one could untie it. Anyone who did would become the ruler of Asia. Alexander the Great came across this puzzle in his conquests and solved it by cutting through the knot with a blow of his sword. Quick, decisive action, perhaps by unexpected and unorthodox means, is the sense the phrase has had in English since the days of Shakespeare:

> Turn him to any cause of policy,
> The Gordian knot of it he will unloose
> *(Henry V, Act 1, scene i)*

It is by no means necessary to go back always to classical times or look for a military context. Religion offers at least two examples:

Dr Livingstone, I presume? Dr David Livingstone was a missionary and explorer in Africa. He had disappeared, so an American journalist, Henry

Memorable events continued

Morton Stanley, set out to find him. In 1871, he succeeded and uttered the immortal phrase *Dr Livingstone, I presume?* Ever since it has been used for humorous effect on meeting friends and acquaintances, usually after a long separation or in an unlikely place.

A catherine wheel: In AD 307, St Catherine of Alexandria had spoken up on behalf of some persecuted Christians. For her pains the Emperor Maximus ordered her to be placed on a spiked wheel, tortured and killed. After a miracle she was ultimately beheaded. To spoil a good story, there is sufficient doubt of her existence that the Catholic Church withdrew its official recognition of her in 1969. Her popular fame lives on, however, in the form of that humble firework, *the catherine wheel*.

Peeping Tom is another fictitious character who has become part of the language. In 1040 Leofric, Earl of Mercia, imposed swingeing taxes upon the people of Coventry. His wife, Godiva, took the citizens' part and pleaded with her husband to cut the amount levied, but he retorted that she must ride naked through the streets before he would do so. This Lady Godiva did, and the earl kept his promise.

This well-known tale was expanded in the eighteenth century. The townsfolk, in accordance with Lady Godiva's wishes, stayed at home with their doors and shutters closed tight. But one man, Tom the Tailor, was so overcome by curiosity that he spied at his lady through a window, whereupon he was struck blind.

Even though Peeping Tom is a figment of the eighteenth-century imagination, his fame is such that he appears hourly with Lady Godiva on a clock set over an archway in Coventry, and he plays a part in an annual procession that has taken place since 1768 in commemoration of the event.

All the time new phrases are being coined after an incident captures the public's imagination. However, very many of them fall out of use in a decade or two.

to do a Bannister: For a few years after 1954, anyone running fairly fast might humorously be described as *doing a Bannister*. This refers to Dr Roger Bannister's record of being the first man ever to run a mile in under four minutes. Today it is more a sporting allusion than an idiom.

to give somebody a Harvey Smith: This phrase of the 1970s will surely follow the same path and end up being forgotten. But it may perhaps stay with us in the language for a few years more. After all, Harvey Smith and his son are still prominent in show-jumping. There is also a linguistic reason why the phrase might linger on: the natural tendency to use euphemisms and avoid offensive language. We sometimes say *Gosh* instead of *God, Heck* instead of *Hell* and **the dickens** instead of *the devil*. So when in August 1971 Harvey Smith raised two fingers in a strong gesture of contempt at Mr Douglas Bunn, one of the judges of the show-jumping competition, the English public saw the incident on TV and were delighted to use the new phrase *to give somebody the old Harvey Smith* in a humorous, euphemistic way.

Some phrases do indeed have a short life, often till the generation that witnessed the event has itself passed away. Yet others persist. Some thrive in the spoken language, without the help of the literary form or classical status that **Achilles' heel**, for example, has enjoyed. *Bob's your uncle* is one. A political scandal is suggested for this British quip. In 1886 Prime Minister Robert Cecil, Lord Salisbury, appointed his nephew, Arthur Balfour, Chief Secretary for Ireland. Mr Balfour's abilities were considered inappropriate for the post and nepotism was suspected. Popular opinion suggested that he had been selected purely because Bob was his uncle. In the event, Lord Salisbury's judgement was vindicated, as Balfour turned out to be an outstanding politician and ultimately became Prime Minister himself.

Memorable events are an excellent trigger for the formation of new idioms, but there is a high drop-out rate. There is no known explanation why one or two survive whilst the majority fail. In this, idioms reflect the rest of language. Historical dictionaries are littered with neologisms that briefly darted across the linguistic firmament like shooting stars, only to fizzle and fade. Idioms and words alike leave their burnt-out shells as entries labelled 'obsolete' in the great dictionaries of the language.

an hour' – women everywhere should be rooting for her.
GUARDIAN, September 2, 1991.

usage: An obvious Americanism that is taking hold in Britain.

ropes: to know/learn the ropes

to be conversant with the practices and idiosyncrasies of an organisation, an activity, etc.

This is a nautical term of nineteenth-century origin. The rigging on a vast sailing vessel was a complicated system of ropes with which every sailor had to become familiar because 'to handle a ship, you must know all the ropes' (T. C. Haliburton, *Wise Saws*, 1843). From its nautical context the phrase was then applied to other areas of expertise.

To show someone the ropes has the same origin.

Every week a new influx of young, naive girls whose hopes of careers in modelling have turned to dust – or whose rent needs paying – go on the game. Each of them will be severely beaten several times before they learn the ropes.
OBSERVER, August 25, 1991.

usage: informal

Rubicon: to cross the Rubicon

to take a step or decision from which there is no turning back

In ancient times, the little river Rubicon made up part of the boundary separating Italy and Cisalpine Gaul, the province

governed by Julius Caesar. In 49 BC, Caesar, after taking time to reflect on the consequences of his action, crossed the Rubicon into the republic with his army, fully aware that this constituted a declaration of war. *'Jacta alea est'* – 'the die is cast' – were the words he is said to have spoken as he crossed over and began his successful campaign against Pompey and the Senate.

It is thought that the Rubicon is the trickle of water now known as the Fluminico. In 1934 Mussolini ordered a monument to be put up on its bank, supposedly at the exact place where Caesar had crossed.

Compelled to choose between two alternatives, he laid the matter before his wife, and awaited the verdict from her lips. It came without hesitation. 'It is your duty; the consequences we must leave. Go forward, and to victory.' The die was thus cast, the Rubicon crossed.
QUARTERLY REVIEW, 1887.

The young man now appeared to have crossed, as it were, some Rubicon in his mind and was speaking more fluently.
REX WARNER, The Professor, 1938.

usage: literary

see also: to burn one's boats/bridges

rule of thumb, a

guesswork, rough calculation, estimate based on experience rather than careful calculation

The phrase has been in figurative use since the late seventeenth century. There are two theories for its origin, both concerned with types of measurement.

In Roman times it was estimated that the measure of the last part of the thumb above the top joint would fit roughly twelve times into the larger measure of a foot. Thus the foot was split into twelve 'inches' (the French called them 'pouces', meaning 'thumbs') and remained a standard measure for centuries. Careful measurement required a standard rule but where an estimated length would do the thumb sufficed. Now that the metric system has been adopted, the need to measure in inches is diminishing and the practice, if not the phrase, has died out.

An alternative, though not so well-known, theory is that the temperature of fermenting ale was checked by dipping the thumb into the brew. It is said that, in Yorkshire, such ale was referred to as 'Thumb Brewed'.

What he doth, he doth by rule of Thumb, and not by art.
SIR WILLIAM HOPE, The Compleat Fencing-Master, 1692.

No rule so good as rule of thumb, if it hit.
JAMES KELLY, Scottish Proverbs, 1721.

rule the roost, to

to be dominant, to display one's authority

In the hencoop the cock makes an obvious display of his dominance over the hens to show that he *rules the roost*. There is, however, an older expression than this. As early as the fifteenth century *rule the roast* was current. Shakespeare writes of '*Suffolk, the new-made man that rules the roast*' (*Henry VI Part II*, 1590). Some authorities say that it was the master of the house who saw to the carving of the roast meat at table. He who *ruled the roast* ruled the household. There is evi-

dence to support this theory in Thomas Nabbes' *Microcosmus* (1637): '*I am my ladies cooke, and king of the kitchen, where I rule the roast.*'

Other authorities suggest, however, that *roast* was an alternative spelling for *roost* which was originally pronounced with a long *o*. Evidence for this comes from *Jewell's Defence of the Apologie* which has a spelling confirming the long medial *o* in the medieval pronunciation of *roost*: '*Geate you nowe vp into your pulpites like bragginge cockes on the rowst, flappe your whinges, and crow out aloude.*' So the likelihood is that the origin lies in the comparison with the cockerel.

Home from school, Junior continues to rule the roost. He is supposed to be allowed one hour of television between school and supper. After a long wrangle, Junior begins his television session immediately, and since Mother is busy with visitors, he stays glued to the television set until suppertime.
H. & S. NEARING, USA Today.

The production also stars Paul Eddington as Orgon and Felicity Kendal as razor-tongued Dorine, the maidservant who rules the roost.
GOOD HOUSEKEEPING, November 1991.

sack: to get the sack

to be dismissed from one's job

At one time a workman kept all his tools in a sack and took them with him to his job where he would leave them with his employer. If he were dismissed, whether through his own fault or lack of work, the employer would *give him the sack*, that is, he would return the workman's sack of tools.

The expression did not appear in written English until 1825, but was current in Dutch from the early seventeenth century and was also known in French.

If I just give him the sack he won't get another job and will get into a brawl and be sent to prison again. And I shall be morally responsible. A very little help now might save him from becoming an habitual criminal.
DAVID GARNETT, Beany-Eye, 1935.

If they failed to secure a minimum of twenty orders a day, they got the sack. So long as they kept up their twenty orders a day they received a small salary – two pounds a week, I think.
GEORGE ORWELL, The Road to Wigan Pier, 1937.

usage: To give someone the sack, the converse of to get the sack, is commonly replaced by the simple verb, to sack.

sackcloth: to wear sackcloth and ashes

to be penitent

The phrase alludes to the ancient Hebrew custom of wearing sackcloth and ashes as a sign of mourning or penitence. The sackcloth was black, coarse goathair cloth which was used to make grain bags. To wear it was a sign of humility.

The Hebrew word for sackcloth was saq and the Greek sakkos. The English word sack is derived from these.

'*I am not advocating a general wailing and gnashing of teeth or sackcloth and ashes. But emotional outbursts might be less dra-*

matic or violent if a little steam were occasionally vented harmlessly.'
HRH PRINCESS OF WALES, Daily Mail, September 12, 1991.

salt of the earth

a dependable, kind-hearted person

The expression is a biblical one and can be found in the Sermon on the Mount (Matthew 5:13) where Jesus says:

Ye are the salt of the earth: but if the salt have lost his savour, wherewith shall it be salted? It is thenceforth good for nothing, but to be cast out, and to be trodden under foot of men.

The Hebrews found their salt supply in the Dead Sea and in the Hill of Salt (*Jebel Usdum*) nearby. It was rock salt and subject to chemical changes which meant that the outer layer, besides being full of impurities, had very little flavour and was usually thrown away. This was the salt that Jesus was referring to in the Sermon.

We no longer accept these country gentlemen, these opulent ladies who drive about in barouches, as the salt of the earth, and their behaviour too often strikes us as vulgar and trivial.
W. SOMERSET MAUGHAM, Books and You, 'Preface', 1940.

Eve was a mighty fine girl, and her mother is the salt of the earth.
ERLE STANLEY GARDNER, The DA Takes a Chance, 1948.

I wouldn't trust myself to a movie company. You dine with the President on Monday, and he slaps you on the back and tells you you are the salt of the earth, and on Tuesday morning you get a letter from him saying you are fired.
P. G. WODEHOUSE, Performing Flea, 1953.

salt: worth one's salt

deserving of one's position or salary

Salt has not always been in cheap and plentiful supply. *Salarium* (Latin *sal*, salt), from which our word 'salary' derives, was 'salt money', a sum paid to a Roman soldier so that he could buy salt and remain healthy. Someone who is *worth his salt* is therefore hardworking and diligent and thoroughly deserves his salary, privilege or position. The expression has only been in use since the nineteenth century, however, when the phrase was coined from the origins of the word 'salary'.

It seems that, after all, the police are good for something. But this is the first time I ever knew them to be worth their salt. There is to be a thorough and systematic search of the hotel tomorrow.
ARNOLD BENNETT, The Grand Babylon Hotel, 1902.

The propagandist, if he is worth his salt, must create new faith, must know how to bring the indifferent and the undecided over to his side, must be able to mollify and perhaps even convert the hostile.
ALDOUS HUXLEY, Brave New World Revisited, 1958.

It is plain that being beaten by Koch hurts the established figures in the Cup. Koch plays the game harder than anyone. When he claimed his Guzzini spyship carried nothing other than wind and current measuring instruments, Cayard's eyes rolled heavenwards in disbelief. Koch even admitted that 'any syndicate worth its salt' should hire divers to 'snoop at their rivals' keels'. Cayard replied wryly: 'I guess we're not worth our salt. We have never hired divers.'
DAILY TELEGRAPH, May 18, 1992.

salt: to rub salt in the wound

intentionally to increase someone's pain, discomfort

It is a long-standing belief, dating back to Cicero, Horace and Livy, that wounds will not heal unless re-opened and cleaned. The application of salt was one way of doing this – at a cost of some pain. Today there is no implication of healing, just the imposition of discomfort.

It is possible that the phrasal verb *to rub it in* is connected.

She sprinkles salt upon my wound and opens the sore afresh.
SADI, Gulistan, c1258.

David Mellor: 'I'm not one of those people who want to rub salt in the wounds but I did say last night that the bandwagon had become the tumbril. I'm not into personal vendettas – but I can't see how he [Kinnock] can stay on.'
EVENING STANDARD, April 10, 1992.

salt: to take something with a pinch/grain of salt

to take it with a degree of reservation, with some scepticism

This phrase is held by many to be from the Latin *addito salis grano* penned by Pliny the Elder (cAD 77). He had come across a story that King Mithridates VI, King of Pontus, had built up immunity to poisoning by fasting and swallowing small, regular doses of poison with a grain of salt (*cum grano salis*) to make them more palatable. Other authorities, however, take this suggestion with a pinch of salt, pointing out that Pliny intended the phrase to be taken literally and that nowhere in classical Latin does the word 'salt' appear as a figurative expression of scepticism. Indeed, the English expression would seem to date back no further than the Middle Ages, giving rise to speculation that *cum grano salis* is, in fact, a piece of medieval Latin. Nevertheless, the idiom is easily understood; just as a sprinkling of salt makes one's meal more enjoyable, so a doubtful story or excuse goes down easier with a pinch of salt.

John Foxe, the martyrologist, reports that Cromwell learned the whole of Erasmus's New Testament by heart while travelling to Rome and back, and although this story ought to be taken with a pinch of salt there is evidence that Cromwell was in touch with Miles Coverdale when Coverdale was still a friar at Cambridge.
ROGER LOCKYER, Tudor and Stuart Britain, 1964.

They will tell you over and over again that there is no better conservationist than a fisherman, because his livelihood depends on it. That needs to be taken with a pinch of salt; this is the world of overstatement.
THE TIMES SATURDAY REVIEW, August 31, 1991.

There are even claims that [borage] rivals the restoratives that Jeeves would shimmy in with at a well-chosen moment on the morning after – but, as with all such tonics, these claims are best taken with a pinch of salt.
COUNTRY LIVING, September 1991.

scot-free: to go/get off scot-free

to escape punishment or having to pay for the consequences of one's misdeeds

Scot means 'payment' and was the name given to municipal taxes as early as the thirteenth century. People paid according to their means. The very poor were exempt from payment and *went scot-free*. Tavern scores were known as *scots* and *to go scot-free* meant to be given one's ale on the house or to have one's bill paid by a drinking companion. There is some doubt as to which use came first: relief from taxes or from drinking bills. In either case it would be welcome!

Tindale used the phrase figuratively in his *Exposition* of 1 John 2:2 (1531): '*The poore synner shulde go Skot fre*', and it is in this sense of being allowed to go free and unpunished that it is still used today.

Monsieur would not stand by and see her falsely accused, while that infamous chambermaid was allowed to go scot-free.
AGATHA CHRISTIE, Poirot Investigates, 'The Jewel Robbery at the Grand Metropolitan', 1925.

What made the Marian persecution so unpopular was the way in which it struck down the small offender while letting most of the big ones go scot-free.
ROGER LOCKYER, Tudor and Stuart Britain, 1964

scrape: to get into a scrape

to get into an embarrassing situation, usually as a result of one's own carelessness

A story sent in to *Notes and Queries* relates how, in 1803, a woman, Frances Tucker, was killed by a stag in Powderham Park, Devon where she inadvertently crossed the stag's scrape and met with the animal's fury. Scrapes are holes which deer habitually dig out with their forefeet. They can be up to a foot or eighteen inches in depth so that an unwary passer-by might easily fall into one and even injure himself. Anyone unlucky enough to do so has *got himself into a scrape*.

Justice for the Scots!

To go or **get off scot-free** means that you get off without payment or without punishment. Why should the Scots be singled out for such a negative reputation? The answer is simply that the *scot* in the expression has nothing to do with Scotland, or with Scotsmen, but is an example of what is technically known as homonymy. That is, a word that is spelled and sounds the same as another one but has a different meaning. There are plenty of them in the English language, like 'bank of the river' and 'bank you put your money in', for instance. Similarly, *Scot* and *scot* are quite different words. The full story for *scot* is in the entry.

There is another old phrase which is not so frequent today, *scot and lot*. It occurs quite commonly in Dickens and other nineteenth-century literature. *Scot* means tax, and *lot* means something similar. It is connected with allotment, the allotted portion, the share you had to pay. So *scot and lot*, in fact, were medieval rates. In recent years householders have paid rates, poll tax or a community charge, and council tax for all the services they receive, such as education, water and so forth. Centuries ago, they paid *scot and lot*, which also qualified them to vote in elections. But this expression has fallen into disuse; today we are left only with the phrase **to get off scot-free**. It is indeed about medieval tax-dodging, but (through homonymy) the Scots are exonerated from blame!

The deer which . . . were addicted, at certain seasons, to dig up the land with their fore feet, in holes to the depth of . . . half a yard, contributed a new word to our language. These were called 'scrapes'.
THE ATHENAEUM, September 27, 1862.

usage: A *scrape* implies a relatively minor problem.

scratch: to come up to scratch

to meet the required standard

The expression *to come up to scratch* was originally *to come up to the scratch*.

Early boxing knew none of the sophistication of the sport today. Bouts took place in the open air and contestants fought with their bare fists. Both fighters began the bout with their left foot on a line, known as 'the scratch', scored in the earth between them. The fight was not divided up into rounds but simply went on until one contestant was knocked down. The fighters were then permitted to break for thirty seconds before being given a count of eight during which they both had to *come up to the scratch* once more. A fighter who was unable to do so was no longer fit to continue and his opponent was declared the winner.

Today, if a boxer is not dedicated enough to submit to a rigorous training programme, then it is unlikely that he will ever *come up to scratch* and reach a high enough standard to be selected to fight. By extension, candidates for a job, concert pianists, theses and reports all need to *come up to scratch*, to meet the basic requirements for success.

I agree with them that they are not legally responsible, and this makes it all the better to see them compensating you purely because their service was not up to scratch.
THE SUNDAY TIMES, August 11, 1991.

Decorators are bringing the property in the Thames-side village of Bray, Berkshire, up to scratch before Mr Ratner, his second wife Moira and their son and daughter move in.
DAILY EXPRESS, May 26, 1992.

usage: Informal. *Not up to scratch*, used of a person, is a common, derogatory, colloquial variant.

see also: to start from scratch

scratch: to start from scratch

to start from the very beginning and with no help or advantage.

The *scratch* is the starting point of a race, originally just a line scored out in the earth. A sportsman *starting from scratch* begins his event from the very beginning without any benefit from a handicap system, as in this news item:

> *Hector Padgham's father was a scratch golfer with the Cantelupe Club, the artisan section of Royal Ashdown Forest Golf Club . . . He himself joined the Cantelupe Club at the age of 16 and was soon playing off scratch.*
> (Daily Mail, October 2, 1991)

Horses in a race were also said to start equally from a scratch line on the ground. *The scratch* in boxing is explained in *to come up to scratch*.

The phrase is now widely used outside sport to refer to any project which started from nothing.

I do not mean to suggest that in putting his materials together the composer necessarily begins from scratch.
AARON COPLAND, What to Listen for in Music, 1939.

We'd no fishing tackle of any kind, not even a pin or a bit of string. We had to start from scratch. And the pool was swarming with fish!
GEORGE ORWELL, Coming Up for Air, 1939.

see also: to come up to scratch

seal of approval

a sign of official recognition and approval

Seals have been used for millennia to authenticate documents. They have at different periods been carved precious stones impressed on clay, lead and wax seals, and signet rings. A document with a seal, then, was approved. The seal gave it legal status, as in the contracts of medieval times, or simply ensured confidentiality, as with personal correspondence.

Other phrases refer back to some of these procedures: *signed, sealed and delivered* comes from legal practice; *sealed orders*; *a sealed book*.

Mr Maude also announced a scheme which will stamp an official seal of approval on organisations providing high quality public services. Applicants will have a year to show they can meet targets set out in the charter and if successful will be able to display the Chartermark.
DAILY MAIL, October 11, 1991.

usage: Not surprisingly, as seals are superseded by other devices for the same purpose, a modern variant is *stamp of approval*.

seventh heaven, in the

in ecstasy, in sheer delight

Muslims maintain that there are seven heavens which correspond to the seven planets ruling the universe. Seven is widely considered to be symbolically the perfect number. They believe that each level of heaven is made of a precious metal or stone and that each is the domain of a servant of the Most High. The seventh heaven is the most glorious and is governed by Abraham, who presides over creatures eternally singing the praises of God.

Towards the end of the Middle Ages the cabbalists, steeped in the occult, reinforced this ancient tradition by making mystical interpretations of the Jewish *cabbala* (the oral tradition passed down through Moses). They concurred that there were seven heavens, the seventh being the dwelling place of God and his most holy angels. Someone *in the seventh heaven*, therefore, is in a realm of complete bliss.

Presently the bells were ringing out in Meg Speedwell's honour, and the children were strewing daisies on which Meg Speedwell trod, a proud young hoyden of a bride with her head in the air and her heart in the seventh heaven.
MAX BEERBOHM, Zuleika Dobson, 1912.

They motored up, taking Michael Mont who, being in his seventh heaven, was found by Winifred 'very amusing'.
JOHN GALSWORTHY, To Let, 1921.

see also: on cloud nine

shambles, in a

in complete chaos, disarray

This is a favourite expression of politicians when criticising the policies and performance of another party. *Shambles* comes from the Anglo-Saxon *scamel*, meaning 'stool' and in the singular form *a shamble* was a little counter or bench where a butcher displayed his goods. In medieval towns each street would be occupied by a particular trade or guild. Several British towns, Nottingham and York among them, still have streets named *The Shambles* which would once have had a whole row of butchers' stalls. From here *shambles* was used to describe a slaughterhouse and, figuratively, a place of carnage and bloodshed. Modern usage has weakened the sense to 'a state of disorder, a mess'.

As summer-flies are in the shambles.
WILLIAM SHAKESPEARE, Othello, Act IV, Scene ii.

Beazer's house in a shambles Beazer shares slipped another 2p to 86p – capitalising Beazer at half the subsidiary it is about to float. What a shambles.
DAILY TELEGRAPH, September 12, 1991.

usage: Although plural in form, it is construed as singular.

sheep: to separate the sheep from the goats

to separate the good from the bad

This phrase comes from the Bible. Matthew 25:32 reads: *'And before him shall be gathered all nations: and he shall separate them one from another as a shepherd divideth his sheep from the goats.'*

Sheep and goats were equally valued in Palestine for their provision of cheese, milk and meat. In addition, sheep were kept for their wool, and goats' hair could be twisted into ropes or woven into cloth. Goatskins were made into bottles to hold water or wine.

There is a figurative distinction made between the animals, however. In biblical parables sheep are helpless creatures in need of care, guidance and protection. Goats, on the other hand, often represent sin or condemnation (e.g. scapegoat). And so it is with this parable; the sheep are those who belong to God and the goats are those who are judged unworthy.

The examples of uses of this phrase show that sheep and goats need not necessarily refer to people. The expression can be used to categorise anything into sets of 'good, worthwhile' and 'bad, not worth bothering with'.

No two persons can agree on what is good art, so it is not possible to make a sheep-and-goat division between religious and individualistic art.
H. READ, The Meaning of Art, 1931.

What an amazing thing. I suppose you could walk down a line of people, giving each of them a quick glance, and separate the sheep from the goats like shelling peas.
P. G. WODEHOUSE, Uncle Fred in the Springtime, 1939.

I tried repeatedly to analyse my emotions coldly and clearly; to still my anxieties by segregating them, by separating the sheep from the goats.
NOËL COWARD, Future Indefinite, 1954.

usage: literary

see also: to separate the wheat from the chaff

shell-shocked

Shell shock is a medical condition suffered by those traumatised by being under fire in war. By metaphorical extension, it can now be applied to any situation of shock: divorce, redundancy, death.

'People are so shell-shocked they don't think to look beyond similar work,' says Sue Morris, who leads workshops for people who have been made redundant.
GOOD HOUSEKEEPING, September 1991.

usage: informal

shilly-shally, to

to be undecided, to vacillate

The original form of the eighteenth-century term was *shill I, shall I*. It was used as a noun, an adjective and an adverb but it was not until the end of the eighteenth century that it was used as a verb in the way we use it today. The expression is very evocative of the person who cannot make his mind up.

A similar phrase is *willy-nilly*.

The others, his immediate councillors, were timid, mediocre and irresolute. Their policy was to hesitate, to shilly-shally, to temporise.
COBUILD CORPUS.

usage: Informal. Regularly hyphenated.

shipshape: (all) shipshape and Bristol fashion

neatly in its place and ready, organised

The phrase was used as a boast among seamen proud of their vessels. It meant that the ship was well organised and maintained and ready for sea. For many centuries Bristol was a centre for explorers, for maritime trade and for the navy. It was recognised as having exemplary standards and gained a particularly keen reputation for efficiency.

The adjective ship-shape (originally *ship-shapen*) was already in use in the first half of the seventeenth century. *Bristol fashion* was a nineteenth-century addition.

Her decks were wide and roomy . . . There was no foolish gilding and ginger-bread work . . . but everything was 'ship-shape and Bristol fashion'.
R. H. DANA, Two Years Before the Mast, 1840.

I laid it out shipshape and Bristol fashion.
FRANCIS BRETT YOUNG, A Man About the House, 1942.

Compton End reflects the preference shown by the garden makers of the Arts and Crafts movement for old-fashioned flowers, topiary, fruit trees and traditional cottage-garden plants. Topiary is Captain Kitchin's great passion. 'I like things ship-shape,' he says.
OBSERVER MAGAZINE, April 19, 1992.

usage: Often reduced to *shipshape*, or *all shipshape*. It is still found hyphenated: *ship-shape*.

The full form has a distinctly dated air about it, harking back to the past glories of sail. The short form shares these over-tones to a lesser extent.

see also: in apple-pie order, spick and span

shoestring: to live on a shoestring

to manage on very little money

On a shoestring was first used in America in the late 1800s when it referred to a business operated on a very restricted budget.

This is one of those phrases whose origin is left to anybody's interpretation. One suggestion is that a person is managing on so little money that he cannot afford to buy anything more expensive than a shoelace. Webster's Dictionary mentions that shoestrings were amongst the articles commonly carried by street vendors. Perhaps living or running a business on a shoestring refers to the lowliest business of all – that of the street sales-man who eats or buys new stock only if his sales of these humble items are sufficient.

Look at what you spend each month. Unless you've been living on a shoestring, analyse where you can make savings.
GOOD HOUSEKEEPING, September 1991.

usage: informal

short shrift, to give/get

to dismiss someone brusquely without hearing them out/to be dismissed in this way

A *shrift* is a confession made to a priest after which absolution is given. In the seventeenth century criminals were taken out and executed upon receiving sentence. They were entitled to make their confession but were often given only a few moments to do so and so a *short shrift* was made.

The word *shrift* comes from the verb *shrive* meaning 'to hear confession'. The past tense of the verb is *shrove*, hence *Shrove Tuesday*, the day immediately before Lent and a holiday when people went to confession, then made merry with sport and feasting.

The general sense has changed little since its early use, though the context is much wider. The English footballer in the *Daily Mail* quotation below, however much disapproved of by the selectors, would hardly expect to be marched out to be executed! .

My feeling for my friends was intense but unsentimental – Charles's astringent approach and Rex's homeric boisterousness would have given short shrift to sentimentality.
C. DAY-LEWIS, The Buried Day, 1960.

He was, by his own admission, a Jack the Lad. The species tends to be given very short shrift by an England set-up which refuses to let anything distract itself from the pursuit of excellence.
DAILY MAIL, October 22, 1991.

show a leg

get up, get moving

The expression goes back to the days when women were allowed to stay on board ship whilst it was in port and even, with permission, to remain for the voyage. In the mornings when the call came to '*show a leg*' the crew were expected to get up and look lively but a woman who wished to sleep in had to dangle a leg over the edge of the hammock to prove that she, and not a rating, was the occupant.

A similar phrase, *shake a leg*, means 'to hurry up, to get a job done faster'. In an obsolete sense, it once meant 'to dance'.

usage: Both *shake* and *show a leg* are somewhat dated colloquialisms, used as an imperative to encourage someone to get up or get moving.

sign the pledge, to

to give up alcoholic drink

At the height of the temperance movement in the nineteenth century, someone wishing to give up strong drink made a public declaration of resolve by signing a pledge not to touch it again.

Though the Temperance Movement long since gave way to Alcoholics Anonymous, it is still possible to hear of people *signing the pledge*. More widely, it may refer to any public declaration of renouncing something.

There is also an enormous number of people, now over one million people, who've signed what we call our 'Ivory Out' pledge form, which pledges that they won't buy or wear ivory ever again.
COBUILD CORPUS: BBC World Service, 1989.

usage: One can also *take* and *keep the pledge*

see also: on the wagon, to go cold turkey

silly season, the

the months of August and September when Parliament is not in session

At one time newspapers did just what their name suggests – they reported the news, informing the population about political debate and decision. When Parliament rose for the months of August and September, the *silly season*, also known in earlier years as *the Big Gooseberry Season*, began. Deprived of Parliament for its steady provision of newsworthy items such as political rows, leaks to the press, errors of judgement and interference in the affairs of other countries, desperate journalists were forced to make much of giant gooseberries, the Loch Ness monster and the like, to keep the paper in print. The *silly season* still comes round each year but the British public is now fed a year-round diet of trivia and so hardly notices.

Meanwhile, out and about, the silly season was bursting into action.
DAILY EXPRESS, August 30, 1991.

sitting duck, a

an easy target

Someone described as a *sitting duck* is vulnerable to verbal or physical attack. A literal *sitting duck* makes an easy target for the huntsman, since it is neither swimming nor dabbling but is simply reposing on the water.

She didn't care to be out of touch with the human race for more than a few minutes at a time, which made me, working at home, a sitting duck.
GOOD HOUSEKEEPING, September 1991.

usage: colloquial

skeleton in the cupboard, a

a painful or shameful secret

This expression allows for all sorts of hideous imaginings since its origin is a mystery. Funk (1955) says it may refer to an actual discovery of a skeleton boarded up in a dark corner of some fusty cupboard. Certainly it is not unknown for gruesome remains to come to light in later years and

stir up much investigation and speculation.

Then again, its roots may lie in the study of anatomy. It was not until 1832 that the dissection of a body for study and research was permitted by law. The demand for bodies soared, but there were few to be had. Some doctors resorted to unscrupulous dealings with grave robbers who dug up corpses and sold them at exorbitant prices. This macabre exchange was a matter of utmost secrecy and many an ambitious physician had *a skeleton in his cupboard*.

The expression appeared in print in 1845 in an article by Thackeray for *Punch* magazine. Thackeray used it again ten years later in a piece attacking the Newcome family. But they must have our sympathy, for there can be few families then or since who do not nurse little secrets they would rather not publish abroad.

They are dull. Everybody knows them. They are not the skeleton in everybody's cupboard, for the skeleton is usually some relative who is a cheerful wastrel and turns up at inconvenient moments to borrow five shillings; the skeleton is exciting.
J. B. PRIESTLEY, Self-Selected Essays, 'A Defence of Dull Company', 1932.

[The novel] features a biographer agonising over whether or not to write about three well-known men in the publishing world, purportedly friends. Every step into his research has him stumbling upon more skeletons in their cupboards, not to mention more gossip and backbiting than he would have thought possible.
GOOD HOUSEKEEPING, May 1991.

His probing throws up the usual dark conspiracies and skeletons in family cupboards.
THE SUNDAY TIMES, August 11, 1991.

The meeting between Emily and her two half-brothers was initially tentative. 'They were diffident at first, which upset Emily. What have she and my boys got in common, after all? She's had a totally different upbringing. She's a skeleton from their mother's cupboard if you like. But in fact, they liked her and she liked them, which is a source of great joy to me.'
GOOD HOUSEKEEPING, May 1992.

usage: American usage has *a skeleton in the closet*.

skin: by the skin of one's teeth

just about, by the narrowest of margins

This evocative phrase is biblical but it is also a misquotation. Job 19:20 reads: *'My bone cleaveth to my skin and to my flesh, and I am escaped with the skin of my teeth.'* Job meant that *all* he had escaped with was the skin of his teeth. Everything else had been taken away from him: his family, his possessions, his friends and his health. The misquotation *by the skin of my teeth* leads us into a different interpretation of the phrase from the original: that the speaker has just about escaped, that it was a close run thing.

Nevertheless, the misquotation is here to stay.

I got away with it that time, but only by the skin of my teeth.
O'FARRELL, Repeat Performance, 1942.

usage: It is a shame that a phrase so evocative should become so hackneyed. *With the skin of one's teeth* is not common. Informal.

smithereens: to blow to smithereens

to shatter into tiny pieces

Smithereens is a borrowing from Irish Gaelic, the word having an Irish diminutive ending, and simply means 'tiny pieces'.

In Lethal Weapon 3, *which is said to have much more comedy and twice as many thrills, Riggs and Murtaugh, Glover's character, have been demoted to walking the beat but that's still not enough to prevent the city from being blown to smithereens again.*
DAILY MAIL, October 11, 1991.

usage: Smithereens may be preceded by a number of other verbs, such as *to knock into, to smash to*.

sour grapes

comfort sought in despising what one longs for and cannot have

In one of Aesop's fables entitled *The Fox and the Grapes,* the fox finds herself unable to reach the succulent grapes growing high on a vine above her and, in a fit of pique, declares that they are sour. The implication is clear. He who longs for the unattainable may be goaded by his lack of success into making ungenerous and scornful remarks to soothe his anger.

What can be more reasonable than that the successful should shape the future? Would you have the failures decide it? That would be merely sour grapes.
ANEURIN BEVAN, In Place of Fear, 1952.

Advertisements

Perhaps the most creative use of language in newspapers isn't in the articles or news items, it's in the advertisements. Advertising copywriters know they have to catch and hold the reader's attention. They often do this, for instance, with a clever play on words. You read the words and understand them one way and then, suddenly, you realise that another interpretation is possible. Through that ambiguity the advertiser has caught your attention and in the end, he hopes, you'll buy his product.

Under the picture of a new car recently available on the market are the words: 'Not another family saloon.' The dual interpretation of that phrase depends on the stress, rhythm and intonation of how it is pronounced. Misread it by putting the stress on the second word, thereby projecting a message the advertiser clearly would not want, and that incongruity makes you look again and pay conscious attention to the alternative pronunciation and message that he does want to get across.

Idioms are part of the stock-in-trade of the advertiser's art. One poster on the London Underground showed some girls wearing different coloured jeans, but none the traditional blue ones. Underneath were the words: 'Jeanius is having ideas out of the blue.'

On one level, that means the jeans are not the ordinary blue jeans but ones in a range of other colours. But there is also the suggestion that these new jeans are a sudden piece of inspiration, a stroke of genius. For **out of the blue** is an idiom which means 'quite unexpectedly' and genius often involves getting a brilliant idea suddenly, in a flash of illumination. That's very clever, but that's not quite the end of it, because it's not *genius* that they are talking about, but *jeanius*. That is another play on words, for the product they are selling, after all, is a pair of *jean*s.

Many people think that **dickens** is linked in some way with the Victorian novelist. It isn't, as the entry in this book makes clear. However, a minor inaccuracy of that kind should not take away from this very clever play on words:

> *When it came to selecting books for a journey, Victorian travellers had to contend with novels that came in three-volume editions and cost thirty shillings. A dickens of a price. (W. H. Smith advertisement,* Daily Mail, *October 2, 1991)*

Next time you are reading a magazine, do look at the advertisements. You may not buy the product, but you will enjoy the advertiser's skill in playing with words and idioms.

I have never been able to understand the fascination which makes my brother Philip and others wish to spend their entire lives in this neighbourhood. I once said as much to Hannah, and she replied that it was sour grapes on my part.
C. P. SNOW, The Conscience of the Rich, 1958.

'You tend to make a bit of an ass of yourself if you start complaining about how you've been treated. It appears sour grapes-ish. I mean just look at the fool Mrs Thatcher is making of herself.'
GUARDIAN, April 29, 1992.

Dennis Canavan urged . . . the appointment of Baroness Thatcher as Governor of the Falklands.

Mr Major drily replied that we already had a governor.

No matter: she'd soon get him out.

Robert Adley portentously warned the baroness that the best wine is not made from sour grapes. What, then, about the grapes of wrath?
DAILY MAIL, June 30, 1992.

sow one's wild oats, to

to pursue illegal or immoral practices when young

The vices of youth are varnished over by the saying, that there must be a time for 'sowing of wild oats'.

So wrote William Cobbett in 1829. The excuse was not a new one. For at least three centuries before that, young men made light of their youthful dissipation and sexual indiscretions with the same phrase. The allusion is to the young and impulsive lad who sows wild seed on good ground where a mature and experienced man would have sown fine seed. Like the weeds they are, wild oats take hold

rapidly but are extremely difficult to get rid of, rather like the consequences of youthful folly.

A contemporary British variant emphasises sexual activity: men (usually not women) who *get their oats* have regular sexual encounters. Neither is the suggestion any more that they are necessarily young.

Perhaps it was essential to him, as to some men, to sow wild oats; and afterwards, when he was satisfied, he would not rage with restlessness any more, but could settle down and give her his life in her hands.
D. H. LAWRENCE, Sons and Lovers, 1913.

Charles believed that a trial crop of wild oats should be sown under experienced sponsorship – nothing extreme, of course – just a visit to one of those rather absurd places where it could do a young man no harm to get his first sight of a row of nude women cavorting.
JAMES HILTON, Time and Time Again, 'Paris I', 1953.

Mr Portillo cruelly reminded Mrs Beckett of her wild oats, now shyly putting out a second crop, presumably designed to woo the Left. She speaks now well again of Clause Four, trade union power, CND, Benn and Scargill – the lot.
DAILY MAIL, May 8, 1992.

usage: *To get one's oats* is very colloquial, the older phrase is standard.

spade: to call a spade a spade

to speak one's mind, to put things bluntly

The ancient Greeks had a popular proverb for plain speaking, 'to call figs figs, and a tub a tub'. Plutarch quoted the expression in an episode of *Sayings* of *Kings and Commanders* but, when the scholar Erasmus drew upon the work in 1500 for his *Adagia* (a collection of Greek and Latin proverbs traced back to their origins), he substituted 'spade' for 'tub'. Erasmus' version stuck and *to call a spade a spade* has been in popular use ever since.

Sometimes I get so fed up with all the mumbojumbo and abracadabra and making of holy mysteries about simple things that I like to call a spade a shovel.
NIGEL BALCHIN, Mine Own Executioner, 1945.

There are others, and they are numberless as the sands, who are mortally afraid to call a spade a spade, because that would be the natural word, and to be natural, in their eyes, would be common, and by this declension they would fall into the pot of vulgarity.
VALERIE GROVE, The Language Bar, 1980s.

spick and span

clean and neat, in perfect order

It was only in the mid nineteenth century that *spick and span* came to mean 'tidy, clean and orderly'. Formerly the phrase was *spick and span-new*, equivalent to *brand new*.

The phrase has its origins in an Icelandic word *spannyr*, itself compounded from *span* (a chip of wood) and *nyr* (new). The sense was 'as new as a shaving freshly cut from the block'. Middle English had the expression *span-new*. Chaucer uses the phrase in *Troylus and Cryseyde*: '*This take was aie span-newe to begin.*'

Spick (spike or nail) was added to form the extended expression in the sixteenth century. Samuel Pepys remarked

happily on '*My Lady Batten walking through the dirty lane with new spicke and span white shoes*' (*Diary*, November 15, 1665), but Dr Johnson included *spick-and-span* in his dictionary of 1755 only after much hesitation. It was his opinion that the word was too 'low' to be used by a polite writer.

He sought his room slowly. They never gave him the same, and he could not get used to these 'spick-and-spandy' bedrooms with new furniture and grey-green carpets sprinkled all over with pink roses.
JOHN GALSWORTHY, Indian Summer of a Forsyte, 1918.

His uniform was spick and span, but he wore it shabbily.
W. SOMERSET MAUGHAM, Ashenden, 1928.

usage: Less commonly hyphenated today.

see also: in apple-pie order, brand new

spill the beans, to

to tell a secret, whether inadvertently or not

The story goes that ancient Greeks were very particular about the sort of person they allowed into membership of their numerous secret societies. If a candidate presented himself to a group, his application was put to the vote. A discreet voting system was devised whereby members walked past a jar and dropped a single bean into it. White showed approval and black registered disapproval. Just a few negative votes would be enough to reject the candidate. Only officials in the society had the right to know how many black beans the jar contained but, occasionally,

176 · spoke · ·

someone's arm would catch the pot and
the contents would spill out for all to see.
The beans were spilt, the secret was
known.

The story is both appealing
and credible. An ancient Greek maxim
'Abstain from beans' was interpreted by
Plutarch as a warning to keep out of politics *'for beans were used in earlier times
for voting upon the removal of magistrates
from office'* (*Moralia: Education of Children*, cAD 95), and the proverb was
known in sixteenth-century England. In
the eighteenth century certain British
clubs used a similar method of selecting
members (see *to blackball someone*).

Unfortunately, the expression itself has
only been in circulation since the 1920s
when it gained popularity in America
before coming to Britain. Perhaps it has
more to do with a farmer or storekeeper
being invited to reveal the quality of his
crop or merchandise than with the world
of the ancients.

*Michael has spilled the beans to Gadsby,
who is even now distributing them (in the
strictest confidence) to his colleagues.*
NICHOLAS BLAKE, A Question of Proof, 1935.

*Her resistance proved futile. Other less
sensitive hacks spilled the beans and Paxos
is now about as obscure as Disneyland.*
OBSERVER, July 28, 1991.

Little more than 24 hours after the Mail
*finally spilled the beans, the Queen issued
her short statement confirming the break-
up of the 5½-year marriage, stressing that
she did not wish newspaper speculation to
detract from the general election
campaign.*
THE SUNDAY TIMES, March 22, 1992.

Entitled The Naked Spy, *the book (to be
serialised in this newspaper) promised to
spill several beans – so much so that*

*Ivanov, fearing a visit from MI5, resisted
the temptation to come over here to promote the book.*
THE SUNDAY TIMES, March 22, 1992.

usage: informal

spoke: to put a spoke in some-one's wheel

purposely to hinder someone's plans or
success

Formerly cartwheels were solid circles of
wood. The front wheels on a cart would
have holes in them through which a stout
bar of wood, known as a *spoke*, could be
thrust in order to check the cart's speed
when rolling downhill, or brake it
altogether.

In the original expression, the carter
checked his own speed. In modern usage,
someone else's projects are deliberately
sabotaged.

*He ought perhaps to have put a spoke in
the wheel of their marriage; they were too
young; but after that experience of Jo's
susceptibility he had been only too anxious
to see him married.*
JOHN GALSWORTHY, The Man of Property, 1906.

*It is well known that to praise someone
whose rivalry you do not dread is often a
very good way of putting a spoke in the
wheel of someone whose rivalry you do.*
W. SOMERSET MAUGHAM, Cakes and Ale, 1930.

usage: Colloquial, despite its long
pedigree.

spots: to knock (the) spots off

to defeat with ease

That the idiom is an American one from the middle of the nineteenth century is certain. Less certain is its origin. It probably goes back to the days when men would engage in shooting contests to find the best marksman. The target would be a playing card, the idea being to hit as many of the 'spots' (the visual symbols for spades, clubs, diamonds or hearts) on the card as possible. The marksman skilful enough to *knock the spots off* the card would emerge as victor.

Addison County leads the van (or 'knocks the spots off', as we say here) in Vermont and is celebrated over the world for its fine horses.
PORTER'S Spirit of the Times, November 22, 1856.

Sue Lawley's chat show may have been axed but I hope she doesn't change her aggressive style. She knocks the spots off sycophantic Wogan.
TODAY, May 12, 1992.

usage: Informal. *To knock spots off* is very common.

spout: up the spout

wasted, spoilt, ruined, in great difficulty

The spout was a type of lift found in a pawnbroker's shop. Articles to be pawned were put into it and hauled up to the rooms above where they were stored. Belongings that had gone *up the spout* were out of service, totally useless to the owner until they were redeemed.

More recently the phrase has become a euphemism for 'pregnant', though whether it is intended to describe intercourse or simply refer to the fact that the woman is temporarily out of action is unclear.

Fifty dollars' tuition, all of our plans – my hopes and ambitions for you – just gone up the spout, just gone up the spout like that.
TENNESSEE WILLIAMS, The Glass Menagerie, 1944.

She asked herself the question that so many people, even her mother's critics, asked: Where would the Knightons be if it wasn't for Mrs Knighton? Up the spout, down the drain – anywhere but in the position of influence and honour.
L.P. HARTLEY, A Perfect Woman, 1955.

usage: Colloquial generally, and very colloquial in the narrow, euphemistic sense of 'pregnant'.

square one: back to square one

to be back where one started with a project or plan

The explanation normally given for this phrase is that before the days of televised sport, soccer enthusiasts would spend Saturday afternoons huddled round the wireless listening to live commentary. The *Radio Times* printed a plan of the pitch which was divided into squares, each with a number. In the 1930s, for example, Captain H B Wakelam gave rugby commentaries in which an assistant would murmur 'Square six' . . . 'Square two' as the ball moved about the field. Playing the ball back to square one meant losing maximum territorial advantage and, by extension, it meant 'back to the beginning'. Opponents of this explanation suggest that the phrase was in use before the days of radio commentaries and its origin is best found in hopscotch or in board games such as Snakes and Ladders, where a penalty might involve returning to the start – square one.

'He's been looking a bit better since he had a holiday in Pembroke, but if he isn't careful all the worry and bother will put him back to square one.
Doris Archer's Diary, Selections from Twenty-One Years of The Archers, 1971.

stalking horse, a

a less acceptable purpose hidden behind a more attractive façade.

The problem of any huntsman is how to get close enough to the game to take a good shot. In the Middle Ages, the stalking horse answered this need. Horses were trained to provide cover for fowlers who hid behind them whilst stealthily creeping up on their quarry. Later real horses were no longer used but were replaced by movable screens made in the shape of a horse.

In modern times there has been an extension of the meaning, particularly in politics. Sir Anthony Meyer stood in opposition to Mrs Thatcher in 1989 for the leadership of the Conservative Party. No one expected him to win; the purpose of the challenge was to demonstrate that there was opposition to the incumbent and perhaps also prepare the way for a weightier challenger on a future occasion. Sir Anthony was widely described in the press as a stalking horse. And, in the event, Mrs Thatcher was deposed the following year.

He uses his folly like a stalking-horse and under the presentation of that he shoots his wit.
WILLIAM SHAKESPEARE, As You Like It, 1599.

The cost of building a golf course is staggering. Developers claim they need leisure facilities or housing developments . . . to make it financially viable. (Hence the accu-sation that golf is being used as a stalking horse for yet more housing.)
COUNTRY LIVING, September 1991.

sterner stuff: made of sterner stuff

having a firm resolve; inflexible, unyielding

This expression is part of a line from Shakespeare's Julius Caesar. In Act III Scene ii Mark Antony, speaking at Caesar's funeral, answers the charge that he was an ambitious man:

Did this in Caesar seem ambitious?
When that the poor have cried, Caesar hath wept;
Ambition should be made of sterner stuff.

We shook hands and I watched him cross the road with his loose long-legged stride. I, being made of stuff less stern, stepped into the taxi and returned to my hotel.
W. SOMERSET MAUGHAM, The Razor's Edge, 1944.

usage: The expression can be used approvingly but it may have critical overtones through a perceived hardness and inflexibility.

stiff upper lip, a

to remain calm and composed in the face of problems or danger

Keeping a stiff upper lip is supposedly an admirable characteristic of the British. It refers to the ability to keep one's features, especially one's mouth, under control so that they do not betray the turmoil of emotion within. It is allied to resoluteness and courage of spirit, though some – the Princess of Wales included – think it no virtue at all.

'When people suffer a loss they are taught to keep a stiff upper lip and not to show their emotions. This is unhealthy because their emotions can overwhelm them at a later time.'
H.R.H. PRINCESS OF WALES, Daily Mail, September 12, 1991.

She is tactile, emotional, gently irreverent and spontaneous.' For a white-gloved, stiff-upper-lip institution with a large 'Do not touch' sign hanging from its crown, the Princess of Wales is a threat.
ANDREW MORTON, Diana: Her True Story, 1992.

stone: to leave no stone unturned

to make every effort possible to accomplish an aim

After the defeat of the Persians by the Greeks at Plataea (477 BC), Polycrates decided to look for treasure rumoured to have been left in the tent of the Persian general Mardonius. Unable to find it, he resorted to the oracle at Delphi which instructed him to 'move every stone'. Polycrates resumed his search and found the treasure.

The phrase rapidly became semi-proverbial. Aristophanes in 410 BC called it 'the old proverb' *(The Thesmophoriazusae)* and Becon in 1560 'the common proverb' *(A New Catechisme)*.

The original meaning of the expression, 'an exhaustive search', is still current, but it may be used more widely to embrace sparing no expense or effort to achieve a goal.

It humiliates me to speak to you as I am speaking. But I am heart-set on you, and to win you there is not a precious stone I would leave unturned.
MAX BEERBOHM, Zuleika Dobson, 1912.

Your idyll with that fellow Jolyon Forsyte is known to me at all events. If you pursue it, understand that I will leave no stone unturned to make things unbearable for him.
JOHN GALSWORTHY, In Chancery, 1920.

usage: The expression was heavily overused in the vogue for detective fiction during this century, turning it into a contemporary cliché.

storm in a teacup, a

a petty disagreement, much fuss made about something of little importance.

'Excitabat fluctus in simpulo' is a neat little metaphor used by Cicero. Translated it reads, 'He whipped up waves in a ladle.' Some commentators suggest that the storm in a teacup is a variation of this saying. According to Partridge, other distinguished people have played with the expression, notably the Duke of Ormond's 'storm in a cream-bowl' (1678), Grand Duke Paul of Russia's 'tempest in a glass of water' (c1790) and Lord Thurlow's 'storm in a wash-hand basin' (1830). Storms in teacups do not appear to have arisen until the nineteenth century.

For all that, his sympathies had been entirely with her in the recent squabble. 'What a ridiculous little storm in a tea-cup it was!' he thought with a laugh.
MURRAY'S MAGAZINE, 1887.

Intended as a peck it develops into a passionate embrace. A storm in a teacup results but in the context of the Edwardian period there is the theme here for a good serious comedy . . .
MID SUSSEX TIMES, August 16, 1991.

The Bible and Shakespeare

Some works have had a quite stunning impact on the cultures of the globe on which we live. For example, parts of the Old Testament of the Bible have been in existence for several thousand years and the whole Bible has been translated (in part, if not yet in its entirety) into many hundreds of languages. Similarly, great works of literature have been read in translation far beyond the confines of their original language. Molière, Cervantes and Dostoevski have had a ready audience that transcends their time and culture.

And so it is within Britain. Some works have exerted an immense influence on language and culture over centuries. As any listener to the radio programme *Desert Island Discs* would know, the two most important works are the Bible and Shakespeare.

The most prolific author

It is not very surprising that one authority lists ninety phrases coming from Shakespeare's work. That is, ninety *phrases*, not ninety quotations, of which we could all probably recognise hundreds.

Many expressions we use every day, and never for a moment think they go all the way back to Shakespeare. *In the mind's eye*, for example, *with bated breath* and *out of joint*.

There are quite a few more which sound informal to modern-day ears. Shakespeare himself wasn't afraid of contemporary colloquialisms in his plays. For instance, *to lay it on with a trowel*, which means 'to flatter somebody excessively', or 'to overdo something'. And *there's the rub*, which means 'that is where the problem lies'.

These expressions are familiar to us today through their telling appearance in Shakespeare's writings. But it does not necessarily follow that they are his invention. His plays are full of the sayings of contemporary popular speech. *There's the rub*, for instance, actually comes from the game of bowls. *Out of joint* has been found three hundred years before the date of *Hamlet*, in which it appears.

In such cases as these, he appears to have fixed these phrases in the popular mind. But on the whole, when nothing else is known, other phrases seem to bear the stamp of his invention. Clearly we owe a great idiomatic debt to Shakespeare.

The most prolific book

The works of Shakespeare have been such a rich source of idioms that it is difficult to believe that one book has been even more influential. For centuries the Bible was the book that was most read and quoted in Britain. It's no wonder, then, that many idiomatic phrases have been added to the language from its pages. Moreover, it's one particular translation – that authorised by King James in 1611 – from which they nearly all come.

in the twinkling of an eye: Generally, we are unaware of the biblical source of an expression. Only a student of early modern English, or a careful reader of the Bible, would connect this phrase with a passage in the New Testament where Paul is talking about what will happen when Christ returns to earth: *We shall all be changed in a moment, in the twinkling of an eye, at the last trumpet* (1 Corinthians 15:52).

In the twinkling of an eye is a translation of a traditional Greek phrase, suggesting 'in the time it takes to cast a glance, or to flutter an eyelid'.

to play the fool: In some cases the sense of an expression has changed since 1611. When Saul, the king, admits his guilt for following David and trying to kill him, he is obviously referring to an act of great seriousness: *I have sinned: return, my son, David: for I will no more do thee harm, because my soul was precious in thine eyes this day. Behold, I have played the fool, and have erred exceedingly* (1 Samuel 26:21).

Today we use the expression in relation to something unimportant and trivial, as Kingsley Amis does here: *Come down and stop playing the fool. I've got a few things to say to you and you'd better listen.*

These phrases are still in popular use. See page 55 for an account of **to wash one's hands of something**. All the following are dealt with in detail in this dictionary:

Adam's ale	the writing is on the wall
Adam's apple	filthy lucre
feet of clay	a fly in the ointment
at the eleventh hour	to separate the sheep from the goats
a whited sepulchre	sackcloth and ashes
to strain at a gnat and swallow a camel	till/to kingdom come
a little bird told me	a wolf in sheep's clothing
	to turn the other cheek

strain at a gnat and swallow a camel, to

to be preoccupied with the trivial rather than the important, with details rather than major matters

This biblical expression meaning 'to fuss over insignificant matters while accepting glaring faults' can be found in Matthew 23:24. Jesus criticises the scribes and Pharisees for their bad example to the people in meticulously observing less important areas of the law whilst failing to observe the weighty issues of justice, mercy and faithfulness. The law, says Jesus, should be kept in its entirety: *'These ought ye to have done, and not to leave the other undone. Ye blind guides, who strain at a gnat, and swallow a camel.'* (Authorised Version, 1611)

The expression is commonly thought to describe someone who has difficulty in swallowing a gnat but none at all in swallowing a camel. In fact the original Greek text does not read 'strain at', as the Authorised Version translates it, but 'strain out' and refers to the practice of straining wine before it was drunk to remove the tiny insects which bred in it while it was fermenting. The New International Version of the Bible (1973) correctly translates the words as 'strain out' but, of course, 'strain at' is now part of our idiomatic language and the expression's misleading wording will remain.

Mr Gosse's view seems to be, in fact, the precise antithesis of Dr Johnson's; he swallows the spirit of Browne's writing, and strains at the form.
LYTTON STRACHEY, Literary Essays, 1948.

She dismounted at the door of the humble cottage, carrying a bowl of steaming soup – I was going to say, but just as I was *wondering how she could carry it on horseback, for my imaginings, which would swallow a camel, sometimes also strained at a gnat – I heard a voice behind me that made me jump.*
L. P. HARTLEY, The Go-Between, 1953.

'That the FA should strain at a gnat and swallow a camel, that they should continue to agonise about selling their historic Cup to a sponsor – when they have already sold it out so comprehensively to TV – is surprising.'
INDEPENDENT, May 5, 1992.

usage: literary

straw poll, a

a superficial test of opinion

It is difficult to imagine a time when public opinion polls were not an ingredient in general elections. *Straw polls* were forerunners of these and originated in America. In 1824 reporters from the *Harrisburg Pennsylvanian* decided to question the people of Wilmington to try to establish their preferred presidential candidate. The idea caught on.

The name *straw poll* alludes to the custom of throwing a straw up in the air in order to determine the direction and strength of the wind. Figurative reference to this rural practice is much older than the *straw poll*, however. John Selden uses it in *Table-Talk: Libels* as early as the mid seventeenth century.

Undoubtedly, spending habits are profoundly influenced by our backgrounds; we either copy our parents or reject them. A straw poll among my friends, all postwar babies brought up in the shadow of rationing and austerity, revealed that as

children we were expected to bath in ½in of water. Now we fill our tubs deeply, and it still feels like a delicious forbidden luxury.
GOOD HOUSEKEEPING, May 1992.

Lower lip reinforced, eyes mopped, morale-boosting outfit on, I struggled into the office for Day Two. It started with a quick straw poll of the other mothers. They had all felt like resigning for the first 48 hours. Sit it out, they said, get on with it, it'll be fine. Cold, hard beasts, I thought.
WEEKEND TELEGRAPH, May 16, 1992.

straw: the last/final straw

an insignificant event which brings about a final catastrophe

The last straw is an abbreviation of the proverb *It's the last straw that breaks the laden camel's back*, and both are current. It is not the original proverb, however. In the seventeenth and eighteenth centuries people spoke of *the last feather that breaks the horse's back*. Dickens introduced the present-day variant in *Dombey and Son* (1848).

À number of languages, among them French, Spanish and Arabic, have proverbs which express the same idea in a similar way: that eventually a minute, and seemingly insignificant, increase in weight, effort or volume will bring about disaster. It seems a highly relevant expression for today's high-pressure, high-stress lifestyles.

The car ploughed into the side of Christine and Kingsley Hunt's house . . . Janice Thompson said, 'This was the last straw – the mess that was left was incredible'.
MID SUSSEX TIMES, August 16, 1991.

Holiday was too tough a test for my marriage. Sometimes that romantic idyll turns out to be the last straw in a relationship.
HEADLINE, DAILY MAIL, June 30, 1992.

'Moving in with that woman right under my nose was the straw that broke the camel's back. I wouldn't have minded in the slightest if she had been in the next county. But this is a horrible gossipy little village, and I have to pass that cottage every day.'
DAILY MIRROR, May 27, 1992.

usage: *Laden* is often omitted from the full form of the proverb.

sword of Damocles, the

impending doom, an imminent threat

Damocles' story is an ancient one recorded in the works of Horace and Persius, amongst others. It was alluded to in English literature in the sixteenth century but received scant attention until the nineteenth century.

The story tells of Dionysius, ruler of Syracuse around 400 BC, who, night and day, was compelled to listen to the sycophantic murmurings of Damocles lauding his power and riches. The exasperated Dionysius finally invited him to taste this good fortune for himself, urging him to take his own seat at the banqueting table. Damocles accepted eagerly and was enjoying the feast when, glancing upwards, he was horrified to see a large sword suspended above his head by a single hair. This, explained Dionysius, was a symbol of the insecurity which everyone holding power and position is forced to live with.

Graham Townsend is very angry: 'It's like having the Sword of Damocles hanging over my head.' The EC dairy directives have not yet been published, so Graham doesn't know where he stands. They barely make a profit as it is, and having never borrowed, he is not prepared to start now.
GOOD HOUSEKEEPING, July 1992.

tack: on the right/wrong tack

following the right/wrong course of action

When a sailing ship needs to head into the wind it has to steer a zig-zag course to make progress. This is known as tacking. A ship on the wrong tack will make no headway.

To go (off) on another tack is from the same source and means 'to take another course of action than that previously followed'.

People are quite on the wrong tack in offering less than they can afford to give; they ought to offer more, and work backward.
JOHN GALSWORTHY, To Let, 1921.

It was at this point in the conversation that Miss Thriplow became aware that she had made a huge mistake, that she was sailing altogether on the wrong tack.
ALDOUS HUXLEY, Those Barren Leaves, 1925.

usage: Through similarity of form and meaning, one sometimes finds *on the right/wrong track*.

see also: to bark up the wrong tree

tarred with the same brush

considered to show the same faults or peculiarities

This expression seems to originate with the shepherd and his flock. Formerly, sheep sores were treated by dabbing them with tar, the same brush sufficing to dress the sores of every sheep in the flock. A tar brush might also be used to daub a special mark of ownership upon every fleece, so that each sheep was identified as being a member of the same flock.

They are a' tarr'd wi' the same stick.
WALTER SCOTT, Rob Roy, 1818.

I cannot see, from my reading of history that there is a pin to choose between the morality of empires and that of republics. They are both tarred with the same brush.
W. R. INGE, More Lay Thoughts, 'Three Lectures', 1931.

Finally Dixon said: 'She does seem rather as if she's tarred with the same brush as Bertrand.'
*   She gave him a curious sardonic smile. 'I should say they've got a lot in common.'*
KINGSLEY AMIS, Lucky Jim, 1954.

usage: An uncomplimentary remark.

tell it to the marines

A remark expressing incredulity at a story

Samuel Pepys' *Diary* for 1664 supposedly reports how Charles II was once at a banquet with the diarist, who was entertaining him with anecdotes about the navy. The subject of flying fish came up in conversation and had the company laughing in disbelief, all except for an officer in the marines who claimed that he too had glimpsed these creatures. The king was convinced, saying that the marines had vast experience of the seas and customs in different lands and that should he ever again come across a strange tale he would check the truth of it by telling it to the marines.

Unfortunately, diligent searches of Pepys' *Diary* came up with no such entry and the story proved to be an ingenious hoax dreamed up by one W. P. Drury who spread it abroad in a book of naval stories he had written.

Many authorities have enthusiastically reported Drury's leg-pull, doubtless because it makes such a charming story. Less fanciful but more accurate is the explanation that the expression has its origins in the deep contempt which the sailors of the navy had for the men of the marines. The navy were jealous for their seafaring traditions and made the marines the target of ridicule, representing them as gullible idiots with no understanding of life at sea. So successful was their slander campaign that an expression *Tell it to the marines, the sailors won't believe it* became current. John Moore uses the full expression in *The Post-Captain* (1810) and Byron, writing thirteen years later, refers to it as an old saying in a note on the verse quoted below. Exactly how old, it is not possible to say.

But, Whatsoe'er betide, ah, Neuha! now
Unman me not; the hour will not allow
A tear: 'I'm thine, whatever intervenes!'
'Right,' quoth Ben; 'that will do for the
marines.'
LORD BYRON, The Island, 1823.

Talk thus to the marines, but not to me
who have seen these things.
GENERAL WILLIAM SHERMAN, Letter to General J. B. Hood, September 10, 1864.

Is that a story to tell to such a man as me!
You may tell it to the marines!
ANTHONY TROLLOPE, The Small House at Allington, 1864.

usage: Tell that to the marines is equally common.

tenterhooks, on

under strain, in a state of agitation or suspense

Formerly, cloth which had just been woven and washed was stretched out taut to dry without wrinkling or shrinkage on a wooden frame or *tenter* (from the Latin *tendere*, 'to stretch'), where it was secured by hooks. Someone who feels tense while awaiting the outcome of a situation is said to be *on tenterhooks*.

Another early use of *tenter* undoubtedly strengthened the figurative meaning. Because of its construction and stretching function, a *tenter* was also a word for that instrument of torture, the rack. *On the rack* and *on tenterhooks* are close cousins in origin and meaning.

Having ordered a light repast, they
awaited its arrival together with that of Mr
Bellby, in silent reaction after the hour and
a half's suspense on the tenterhooks of
publicity.
JOHN GALSWORTHY, In Chancery, 1920.

The post was delivered at noon and at five
minutes to she looked at her watch and
him. Though Ashenden knew very well
that no letter would ever come for her he
had not the heart to keep her on
tenter-hooks.
W. SOMERSET MAUGHAM, Ashenden, 1928.

usage: Written today as one word, without a hyphen.

tether: at the end of one's tether

at the point of frustration, at the end of one's inner resources, powers of endurance

A tether is a rope by which the freedom of grazing animals to wander is restricted, one end being fastened around the animal's neck and the other to a stake. The expression describes the frustration of the animal which strains to browse further afield and run where it will.

He proposed to call a witness to show how the prisoner, a profligate and spendthrift, had been at the end of his financial tether, and had also been carrying on an intrigue with a certain Mrs Raikes, a neighbouring farmer's wife.
AGATHA CHRISTIE, The Mysterious Affair at Styles, 1920.

I didn't need the set, withdrawn look of his face, the occasional mumbling of the lips, to tell me that he was mentally very near the end of his tether.
HAMMOND INNES, The Doomed Oasis, 1960.

My new routine has nearly established itself. I now have the blissful freedom of no longer having to make decisions about how I spend each section of the day. If it's 10 o'clock I'll be moaning about London Transport, if it's 11 I'll be at the end of my tether with the coffee machine, and if my discontent remains at this level then we shouldn't have to sell the house, disturb the children and do all the other things that would mean destroying others' routines.
WEEKEND TELEGRAPH, May 16, 1992.

three Rs, the

the basic subjects taught at school: reading, writing and arithmetic

This is attributed to Alderman Sir William Curtis (1752–1829) who rose to become Lord Mayor of London. A firm believer in education, he once proposed the toast at a public dinner given by the Board of Education with: 'The three Rs – Riting, Reading and Rithmetic.' The spelling is ascribed to Sir William's generally agreed illiteracy. However, a writer in *Notes and Queries* knew someone present at the dinner. Sir William, it appears, had a limited education but was very shrewd (as one might expect from a Lord Mayor of London and a warden of the Tower for many years). He chose the particular wording as a joke, and it was received with great applause and merriment. His political opponents seized on the phrase and used it to portray Sir William as an ignoramus. If this account, given in Walsh, is correct, then the mud has indeed stuck.

Having read the article about Education Secretary John Patten's five-year-old daughter Mary Claire and her state school, I find it worrying that there was no mention of the three Rs. Instead, religion, sex and green issues were quoted.
DAILY EXPRESS, April 30, 1992.

Spiritual and moral development is as important as mastering the three Rs and must not be left solely to a school's religious education department, said David Pascall, chairman of the National Curriculum Council.
DAILY MAIL, May 8, 1992.

usage: An alternative form is *the three R's.*

throw in the towel, to

to give in

See *to throw up/in the sponge*

But despite the unending demands, he has no regrets: 'I was only ready once to throw in the towel, and that was around three years after I started. It wasn't the demands of the job, but the clinical isolation that was wearing me down. But things began to change, and I carried on.'
WHAT'S ON TV, July 20, 1991.

usage: informal

throw up/in the sponge, to

to give up, to admit defeat

This was originally *to throw up the sponge* for, in the days of prize-fighting, when a fighter had taken enough punishment and was ready to admit defeat, his corner would toss up into the air the sponge used to refresh him between rounds. Today *to throw in the towel*, a later gesture of defeat, is perhaps more commonly heard.

As the quotation given under *to kick the bucket* indicates, the metaphor in America was extended to giving up the battle for life, hence the sense of 'to die'. It is not current on this side of the Atlantic.

If ever you are tempted to say . . . 'I am beaten and I throw up the sponge', remember Paul's wise exhortation.
ALEX MACLAREN, Philippians, 1909.

So Mummy and Daddy and Johnny and Jane book a self-catering holiday and struggle there with a carful of food and drink and nappies and clip-on highchairs . . . and wear themselves to the bone with a strenuous week of self-catering. Unless they chuck in the sponge completely and head for the Med, where hosts and

hoteliers will smile upon their children, chuck them under the chin, let them run around the kitchen and generally appreciate them as much as the parents do themselves.
AA MAGAZINE, Issue 1, 1992.

usage: Only *to throw in the sponge* is commonly used today. Informal.

see also: to throw in the towel

thumbs up/down: to give something the thumbs up/down

to show approval/disapproval for something, to give a project the go-ahead/to reject a project

Whilst it may be stated with confidence that this expression has in some way emerged from the use of the thumb to judge combats in Roman arenas, there is considerable confusion over what the signals actually were. Those signals we can be reasonably sure of are contrary to what we would expect from our modern use of *thumbs up* and *thumbs down*.

Although the thumbs-up sign signifies approval to us, it was not the gesture that a gladiator on the point of defeat wanted to see. He would have preferred the audience to turn down their thumbs or, better still, to close them up within their fists (*pollicem comprimere*), a signal that he had fought well and deserved to be spared. Other thumb positions – turned up, whirled round, turned inwards or outwards – meant disapproval: the wounded man should be shown no mercy but dispatched forthwith.

Funk (1950) attributes the reversal of meaning to a painting by the French artist Jean Léon Gérome in 1873. He misinterpreted the signal for death, *Pollice Verso* (the title he gave to his painting), as 'thumbs down' rather than 'thumbs turned'.

Which? *readers who've extended their homes give it the thumbs-up, despite potential pitfalls of costs, delays, local authority red tape and problems in getting building work done satisfactorily.*
WHICH?, February 1988.

Thumbs up, even after the hitches.
HEADLINE, OBSERVER REVIEW, July 28, 1991.

The Queen having firmly given the royal thumbs-down to any thought of abdication in either the near or the far-distant future, the murmuring classes have once again been turning their restless minds to the question of how Prince Charles will occupy himself in the coming years.
DAILY MAIL, March 5, 1992.

usage: *Thumbs up* is used more frequently than *thumbs down*. Perhaps we are all natural optimists! *Thumbs up* can be used as an encouragement to someone facing a test, like 'Good luck'.

thunder: to steal someone's thunder

to upstage someone, to take the credit properly belonging to someone else

The expression was coined by playwright and critic John Dennis (1657–1734), who discovered that, by rattling a sheet of tin, he could make the sound of thunder for dramatic effect in his play *Appius and Virginia* (1709). The play was not well received, Pope being one of its most cutting critics, and closed down after only a short run. The sound effects were more successful, however, and Dennis was infuriated to hear his thunder reproduced

not long afterwards in a production of *Macbeth*, when it is reported that he leaped to his feet in anger crying, *'See how the rascals use me! They will not let my play run, and yet they steal my thunder!'*

The chief change in English opinion during recent years has been the eclipse of Liberalism, so powerful during the nineteenth century. Labour has stolen the Radical thunder and an electoral system which allows neither Alternative Vote or Proportional Representation inevitably and unfairly destroys the weaker party of the three.
IVOR BROWN, The Heart of England, 1935.

The Government's predatory behaviour in stealing Jack Straw's thunder shows that they feel electorally vulnerable on the subject of reading – as well they might.
TIMES EDUCATIONAL SUPPLEMENT, January 10, 1992.

ticket: that's the ticket

that's just what's needed

The phrase may be a corruption of the French word *étiquette*. This means 'ticket' in translation, and a mispronounced anglicised version of *étiquette* could easily be construed as 'That's the ticket'.

Edwards suggests that the sense 'that's the right way to proceed' comes from *étiquettes*, which were programmes of events or ceremonies distributed to make sure that things ran smoothly. Another possible explanation concerns tickets which were given to the needy to exchange for food, fuel and clothing. The full phrase would be *'That's the ticket for soup'*, to distinguish between that ticket and any other.

Princess Diana yesterday showed just how determined she is to keep up her fitness regime when she took to the pool for a quick 12 laps of her favourite exercise. Her quick-fit regime is just the ticket for a busy royal tour schedule, exercising almost every muscle in her body.
TODAY, May 12, 1992.

usage: Informal. *Just the ticket* is an alternative.

tie the knot, to

to take one's marriage vows

Knots are a feature of many ancient marriage rituals throughout the world. The climax of a Hindu ceremony comes when the garments of the bride and groom are tied together and, thus bound, the couple walks round holy fire. In Sikh weddings the bride and groom both wear a scarf. During the ceremony the bride's father knots the two scarves together and the couple honour the Sikh scriptures. Chinese Buddhists revere a certain deity, *Yue-laou*, who unites with a silken cord all predestined couples; after which, nothing can prevent their union.

Knots are also part of our own ceremonies. The ribbons in a bridal bouquet traditionally should be knotted. The knots are there to symbolise love and unity and the solemn bond of marriage which cannot be broken. As the old proverb goes, *'He has tied a knot with his tongue he can't untie with all his teeth'* (John Ray, *English Proverbs*, 1670); the vows so easily tied are not so easily loosened.

A couple from Mid Sussex tied the knot in Las Vegas at the Little Church of the West.
MID SUSSEX TIMES, August 30, 1991.

Married couples are normally banned from journeying on space missions because they interfere with team spirit. But officials decided to make an exception for Jan and Mark because they tied the knot after being selected for the voyage on the Endeavour in August.
DAILY EXPRESS, February 25, 1992.

Time to be the darling bride of May. It's the first day of the rest of your lives, so tie the knot with style for magical memories.
HEADLINE, DAILY EXPRESS, May 25, 1992.

usage: In earlier years it was possible *to tie a knot*, but no longer. The definite article is now essential.

tilt at windmills, to

to face an imagined foe, to take on a fanciful enemy

The phrase is from the classical Spanish novel *Don Quixote de la Mancha* by Cervantes in which the knight attacks some windmills in the belief that they are monstrous giants. When his lance becomes entangled in one of the whirling sails, Don Quixote is snatched up from his horse before falling heavily to the ground, his act of chivalry leading only to injury. The book was published in 1605 and such was its popularity that by 1622 references to Don Quixote's battle with the windmills had started to appear in English literature with the expression 'to have windmills in one's head', meaning 'to have one's head full of fanciful notions'. This idiom, once very popular, has now slipped from use. *Tilting at windmills*, meaning battling with imagined enemies, appeared later, around 1644.

*'Rather eccentric, I'm afraid,' said Poirot.
'Most of that family are. Spoilt, of course.
Always inclined to tilt at windmills.'*
AGATHA CHRISTIE, Death on the Nile, 1937.

*He is the legatee of a tradition of opprobri-
ous persecution by spiteful laws and mean
prejudice, and thus can hardly be blamed
for tilting at demolished windmills or
ascribing his failure to secure mainstream
commissions to his homosexuality.*
THE SUNDAY TIMES, August 11, 1991.

usage: Partridge demoted the phrase to a
cliché from the mid nineteenth century.
It is now rather dated and literary.

tinker's dam/damn: not to care/ give a tinker's dam/damn

not to care at all about something, to be
totally indifferent to something

At one time itinerant tinkers were
familiar figures. They roamed the
countryside earning their living by mending pots and pans. A hole in a pan would
be surrounded by a wall, or *dam*, of clay,
or even bread, and solder poured inside.
Once the solder had set, the *dam* would
be thrown aside. So the *tinker's dam* is
worthless and trivial, something to
discard.

An alternative theory is that tinkers
had a reputation for swearing and cursing
at every other word, so much so that their
expletives, their *damns* or *cusses*, became
meaningless.

*I feel fairly confident that there cannot be
many among you who give a tinker's curse
whether you copped .003" last night or
.004". I doubt that you would know what
to do with the information even if you had*

*it. Meteorology for you is about whether
or not to take your hat.*
THE TIMES, September 4, 1991.

to a T

perfect for the purpose, exact; typical,
characteristic of

The shape of the T-square, a device used
in technical drawing, has led some authorities to associate this instrument with
the phrase. The origin does not lie here,
however, since the expression has been
in common use since the late seventeenth
century, some time before the T-square
was invented. Instead, T is thought to
stand for a 'tittle', a minute and precisely
positioned penstroke or printer's mark.
A tiny brush stroke, for instance, was all
that distinguished the two otherwise
identical Hebrew letters 'dalet' and
'resh', and 'tittle' was the word chosen
by Wycliffe to translate references to this
minuscule difference in his version of the
New Testament. Thus something which
suits *to a T* is as perfect and exact to its
purpose as the scribe's tittle.

*That's him to a 'T' – like a navvy! He's
not fit for mixing with decent folk.*
D. H. LAWRENCE, Sons and Lovers, 1913.

*Doug and Grace – they would suit each
other to a T.*
FRANK YERBY, The Serpent and the Staff, 1959.

usage: Informal. Often found as *done to
a T* and *to suit to a T*.

toe the line, to

to submit to authority, regulations, etc.

The phrase comes from running where every competitor in a race is expected to submit to the rules and put his toe on the starting line with everyone else.

The Queen's toed the line 25 years ago and formed a larger regiment. Since then it has lost one regular and two TA battalions.
MID SUSSEX TIMES, August 16, 1991.

Foreign Secretary Douglas Hurd helped pile pressure on rebels to toe the line by writing to every Conservative MP insisting Britain's place was at the 'heart' of the EC.
DAILY MAIL, November 20, 1991.

usage: To toe the mark is an alternative form, now less common. Interestingly, Partridge (1940) reverses the frequency of the expressions, claiming *to toe the mark* is the more common, and a cliché.

top: over the top

excessive, too much

The term originated in the trench warfare of the First World War. To mount an attack, soldiers had to climb out over the trench's protective wall of sandbags and charge into no-man's-land, the territory between allied and enemy positions. The full phrase originally was *Over the top and the best o' luck*, uttered to fellow soldiers just about to risk death. Because of the immensely high casualty rates and near certainty of death or injury, luck seemed irrelevant, so the second part was quickly dropped.

Since then, the meaning and context of use have broadened enormously. Anything excessive can now be described as *over the top*: a fashion, a remark, behaviour. It caught on in the entertainment world, where it described perform-

ances or material which were pushing the limits of accepted good taste. To exploit this meaning, and thereby gain an audience, a 1982 television series took the title O.T.T. What would Tommy Atkins make of that?

Does retirement always have to be this well planned? Weren't John and Evelyn going a little over the top, and being negative in anticipating future problems?
CARE MAGAZINE, Autumn, 1991.

Appearance *Very good, except that it was a bit over-the-top with the pepperoni – about 35 slices in all. It looked a lot better once some of the slices had been removed.*
TODAY, October 2, 1991.

It was like the best and worst qualities of his films, beautifully put together but rather over the top.
GUARDIAN, October 4, 1991.

usage: It is currently rather fashionable to say condescendingly that something is *OTT*. You are clearly in with the in-crowd to recognise the initials.

Topsy: like Topsy, it just growed

it has come out of nowhere and developed without encouragement

Topsy was a little slave girl in the book *Uncle Tom's Cabin* (1852) by Harriet Beecher Stowe. When Aunt Ophelia asks Topsy about her family, the child denies that she has one or that she was ever even born. 'I spect I *grow'd*. Don't think nobody ever made me,' she says.

. . . the idea of Notes and Queries was not an inspiration, but rather a development. It didn't spring, like Minerva in full

panoply, from the brain of its progenitor, but, like Topsy, it 'growed'.
NOTES AND QUERIES, Vol. 1 No. i, 1850s.

Like Topsy the Princess Royal's visit to Mid Sussex today has just grown and grown. So much so that the district has never known a red-carpet day like it.
MID SUSSEX TIMES, September 13, 1991.

The trouble with the society is that it has grown like Topsy.
GUARDIAN, October 4, 1991.

usage: There is a tendency to make *growed* into *grew* but the original still exercises a strong influence.

touch wood

words spoken by someone to avoid bad luck and be blessed with good luck

The words *touch wood*, by which the speaker hopes to stave off a reversal of present good fortune, are almost always accompanied by rapping on something wooden. Winston Churchill, probably tongue in cheek, said that he rarely liked *'to be any considerable distance from a piece of wood'*. Several theories are put forward for the practice.

In the ancient times of the druids it was believed that good spirits lived within the trees. People seeking particular help would rap on the tree to implore the spirit's aid or protection.

They'd knock on a tree and would timidly say
To the Spirit who might be within there that day;
Fairy fair, Fairy fair, wish thou me well;
'Gainst evil witcheries weave me a spell!

(Nora Archibald Smith, 1900)

Some authorities suggest that the expression is not pagan but of Christian origin and that the wood to be touched was originally that of the rosary or crucifix.

Finally, there is a children's game Touch-wood in which one child chases the others who are safe only when touching wood. Touch-iron is a well-known alternative but this has not entered the language and perhaps makes the theory of Touch-wood the least likely of the three.

Touch wood, I've managed to steer clear of controversy so far.
MID SUSSEX TIMES, September 6, 1991.

Graham Seymour is a successful plumber, untroubled 'touch wood' by the recession, with enough work to keep three vans and half a dozen people on the go every day of the week.
BT BUSINESS NEWS, Spring, 1992.

usage: An American variant is *to knock on wood*.

trim one's sails, to

to restrain one's activities in line with present circumstances

The full expression is *to trim one's sails before the wind*, but the shorter *to trim one's sails* is now more commonly heard. The term is obviously nautical, referring to sailing ships and alludes to the setting of the sails according to the strength of the wind. Sails would be reefed when the wind was strong and let out in gentler conditions. In the same way someone who metaphorically *trims his sails* restricts his activities or expectations according to prevailing circumstance.

The Cecils were seriously alarmed, and Burghley, trimming his sails to the changing wind, thought it advisable, at the next Council, to take the side of Essex in the matter of the Spanish ransoms.
LYTTON STRACHEY, Elizabeth and Essex, 1928.

It's been more a question of trimming our sails because our overheads have grown.
GUARDIAN, October 4, 1991.

trip the light fantastic, to

to dance

This comes from John Milton's *L'Allegro* (1632). The relevant lines read:

Haste thee Nymph and bring with thee
Jest and youthful Jollity . . .
Sport that wrinkled Care derides,
And Laughter holding both his sides.
Come, and trip it as ye go
On the light fantastick toe.

The expression was not extracted from Milton's verse in the seventeenth century, however, but was picked out in the late nineteenth century, possibly in America, and popularised from there.

Somerset Maugham used the full expression correctly in *Cakes and Ale* (1930) when he wrote: 'The muse does not only stalk with majestic tread, but on occasion trips on a light fantastic toe.' Present-day use mostly confines itself to *to trip the light fantastic*, which has become a humorous cliché for 'to dance'.

He was a telephone man who fell in love with long distances; he gave up his job with the telephone company and skipped the light fantastic out of town . . .
TENNESSEE WILLIAMS, The Glass Menagerie, 1944. .

'I thought you'd all be on the floor by now. Now, Mr Gore-Urquhart; I'm not going to permit any more of this skulking about in here. It's the light fantastic for you; come along.'
KINGSLEY AMIS, Lucky Jim, 1954.

usage: jocular

trumps: to come/turn up trumps

unexpectedly to produce just what is needed at the last moment

A number of card games are played with trump cards in the deck. Trump is an anglicised version of the French *triomphe* meaning 'triumph' and a trump is a valuable card to hold. The allusion in this expression is to someone with a mediocre hand unexpectedly turning up a trump card and finding his bad luck suddenly reversed.

Send your cv to all relevant organisations with a covering letter explaining circumstances and previous salary. The response may not be overwhelming, but they can come up trumps.
GOOD HOUSEKEEPING, September 1991.

The French police inspector, like his English counterparts, is not happy at the Moons' involvement but as always it's young Trevor who turns up trumps while Gladys fiddles with the Tarot cards.
WEEKEND TELEGRAPH, January 18, 1992.

'The fact that we drew was down to Chris Woods. He had more to do than in any other game for me and came up trumps. Had it been Peter Shilton out there he would have got rave reviews.'
SUN, May 18, 1991.

usage: informal

two-faced

hypocritical, saying one thing and meaning another

Two faces under one hood was the original expression of duplicity. It was in use in this form from the end of the fourteenth until well into the nineteenth century. The earliest record is from the *Romaunt of the Rose*, written around 1400: *'Two hedes in one hood at ones.'* A late example comes in the form of a rhyming couplet in Bohn's *Handbook of Proverbs* (1855):

> *May the man be damned and never grow fat,*
> *Who wears two faces under one hat.*

Present day usage has shortened the phrase to *two-faced*.
See *Janus-faced*.

Every player must, if he is to survive, become some kind of professional cheat, or hustler. Success is always with the two-faced: and one can no more enter the game innocently (though Dan did his best) than a house with BORDELLO in neon lights.
COBUILD CORPUS.

In the very bank Jefferson is publicly accusing of being a menace to the republic! Oh, he is as two-faced as Janus! Do you know why he is so eager for a war in Europe? Because it will increase the price of wheat.
COBUILD CORPUS.

usage: derogatory

ugly duckling, an

a gauche, awkward child who blossoms into beauty

The term refers to one of Hans Andersen's tales in which a swan's egg is mistakenly hatched by a duck, who cannot understand how she could have produced such an ungainly child so different from the rest of her brood. The cygnet, scorned for its dull feathers and its clumsiness, hides away in shame all winter, but then emerges from the reeds as a beautiful swan.

In the 1950s Danny Kaye had a hit song 'The Ugly Duckling', telling Andersen's story to a new generation.

Born in Madrid, he had grown up in a Boston family, a strange, alien, lonely child, a duckling, far from ugly, in whom perceptive eyes foresaw the swan.
V. W. BROOKS, New England: Indian Summer, 1940.

The Oliviers were rather puzzled that the ugly duckling they had known all their lives was being taken by so many people for a cygnet.
DAVID GARNETT, The Flowers of the Forest, 1955.

I used to spend hours looking through magazines and wishing I was beautiful. But I never thought I could do it. I thought I would be an ugly duckling for life.
SUN, August 13, 1991.

umbrage: to take umbrage

to take offence

Umbrage has a Latin root *umbra* meaning 'shade'. The word was specifically used in English to describe the shade given by a screen of trees, then figuratively to mean 'the shadow of doubt or suspicion'. It remains with us today chiefly in the expression *to take umbrage*, meaning that a person feels overshadowed by another, giving rise to offence and resentment. No one likes to live in another's shadow.

Umbrella shares the same Latin root. Originally umbrellas were used only as shade from the sun. Jonas Hanway is said to have introduced the umbrella as protection against the rain in about 1760, but its use in wet weather must have been recognised long before then, for Swift wrote in 1710:

The tucked-up sempstress walks with hasty strides,
While streams run down her oiled umbrella's sides.

Perhaps Hanway's contribution was to make the umbrella acceptable higher in society, for there is historical evidence that hackney-coachmen and sedan-chairmen *took umbrage* over this threat to their monopoly in protecting the moneyed from the elements.

Product comparisons in marketing materials are hardly unusual these days, but SYSTAT took umbrage. It reacted by preparing a 25-page booklet detailing its objections to StatSoft's literature and then sending it to the august American Statistical Association.
MACUSER, May 1, 1992.

I was trying to be funny, to lighten the odd five minutes for you, describing my batty behaviour with bargains, my compulsion to waste whatever money comes my way. Not surprisingly, in a time of fierce recession, a lot of you took umbrage. Your five minutes were not lightened, but darkened with rage.
GOOD HOUSEKEEPING, May 1992.

usage: Once somewhat formal, now standard. Regularly followed by the preposition *at* or, less commonly, *over*.

wagon: on the wagon

teetotal, not drinking alcohol

Water carts and wagons have been transporting water or sprinkling the streets since at least 1700. A person in the US who had given up strong drink was described in a colourful metaphor as needing to be *on the water wagon* (that is, drinking the copious quantities of water available there, not alcohol). The expression has been in use at least throughout the twentieth century.

Monty didn't drink, and Clifton James went on the wagon for the Empire.
THIS WEEK MAGAZINE, December 21, 1946.

usage: There is a good deal of flexibility in the use of the phrase. Doctors can *put* someone on the wagon. In a moment of weakness, non-drinkers can *fall off* the wagon. And so on.

The commoner contemporary US form and only current British one is *on the wagon. Waggon* is a more traditional British spelling.

see also: climb on the bandwagon, sign the pledge

wall: to drive someone to the wall

to force someone into a hopeless situation by circumstances

See *to go to the wall*

That indeede . . . shall driue him to the wall. And further than the wall he can not go.
THOMAS HEYWOOD, Proverbs, 1546.

Barry, pushed to the wall, realized that unless Field were silenced everything would be lost. He planned the murder.
ELLERY QUEEN, The Roman Hat Mystery, 1929

He set his grandmother up in the agency business and then turned around and drove her to the wall in a month's time.
ERSKINE CALDWELL, Love and Money, 1954.

wall: to go to the wall

to suffer failure, ruin

Four hundred years ago streets were narrow and unlit and invited crime. The innocent passer-by was in danger of being set upon by thieves. Once he *had gone to the wall*, that is once he had been cornered with his back to the wall in some dark alley, the victim knew he had no escape. Alternatively, some medieval chapels (such as the one in Dover Castle) provided stone seats around the walls for those who were ailing. Everyone else was required to stand. Hence, it is suggested, the old saying *The weak shall go to the wall*. Whichever explanation is correct, this expression has been in figurative use since the sixteenth century.

Other expressions share the same origins. *To have one's back to the wall*, means 'to be in extreme difficulty and have no way out'. Sir Thomas More, finding himself in grave difficulty, wrote: '*I am in this matter euen at the harde walle, and se not how to go further*' (*Works*, 1528). *To be driven to the wall* means 'to be forced into a hopeless situation by circumstances'.

. . . following the rules of capitalism, the inefficient will go to the wall and the efficient will reap their due reward.
BENEFITS AND COMPENSATION INTERNATIONAL MAGAZINE, September 1991.

Already the For Sale signs have started going up on guest houses and bed and breakfasts, while the receivers are running hotels that have gone to the wall. Rumours of who will be the next to go are rife up and down the coast.
OBSERVER, July 5, 1992.

wall: to have one's back to the wall

to be in a hopeless situation from which there is no escape

See *to go to the wall*

I'm in the position of a man with his back to the wall. I'm fighting for my life. Naturally, I'm going to fight. But you and I needn't be the worse friends for that. We may become the best of friends yet.
THEODORE DREISER, The Titan, 1914.

As for the dances and the fetish worship, the missionaries have not the power to stop them if they wished to; Christianity here has its back to the wall.
GRAHAME GREENE, Journey without Maps, 1936.

warpath: on the warpath

preparing to fight; in aggressive or vengeful mood

This expression originated among the North American Indians and described the route taken by a warlike tribe on its way to confront its enemy. Used figuratively the phrase applies to anyone spoiling for a fight or a show-down.

The veteran brave has come out of his tent and is in full cry. The Tories have come through their difficult rite of passage and are back on the warpath.
DAILY MAIL, October 11, 1991.

usage: informal

---

warts and all

making no attempt to hide defects

It was, and still is, the task of portrait painters of the rich and powerful to soften craggy features and paint their subjects in a kind light. Oliver Cromwell, good Puritan that he was, would have none of this. His order to Sir Peter Lely was: *'I desire you would use all your skill to paint my picture truly like me, and not flatter me at all; but remark all these roughnesses, pimples, warts, and everything as you see me, otherwise I will never pay a farthing for it.'* Those who know the painting will judge that Cromwell must have been pleased with the result.

But despite such hiccups, As It Happens *built up a following who liked the warts-and-all approach.*
OBSERVER, July 28, 1991.

The country watched as . . . the Conservative Party turned on their leader, Margaret Thatcher. This week, the fascinating drama documentary The Final Days *recounts the story behind the furore – warts and all.*
WHAT'S ON TV, September 1991.

All good travel agents should have copies of the ABC Agents' Gazeteers for 1992 *which you can ask to consult. These manuals contain descriptions of more than 13,000 hotels, apartments and resorts in the Mediterranean, the USA and Euro-*

pean cities. Researched by the publishers' local agents, the write-ups give warts-and-all descriptions of the property itself and its location.
SUNDAY TELEGRAPH, May 24, 1992.

usage: Used adjectivally immediately before a noun, it is often hyphenated.

Waterloo: to meet one's Waterloo

to suffer defeat after realising some success

The expression refers to the final and overwhelming defeat of Napoleon by the allied forces at Waterloo, Belgium, on June 18, 1815. The town of that name is just ten miles south of Brussels. The aftermath of the battle saw Napoleon's abdication and his captivity on the island of St Helena until his death in 1821.

An article in *Good Housekeeping* (May 1991) shows how the 'little Corsican' may meet his Waterloo for the second time: what has been suggested is a direct TGV link between Paris and London when the Channel Tunnel is finally opened. This, of course, will need to be given a suitably French and heroic title, and the preferred name at the moment is the Napoleon Line. However, someone in the railway bureaucracy, showing a rare sense of humour, has made a further suggestion about where the high-speed Napoleon should finish its journey. Where else but Waterloo?

The idiom emphasises total defeat, with no mention of the victory of the British. Perhaps their commander, the Duke of Wellington, can take comfort in being idiomatically overlooked since he found linguistic fame elsewhere as the origin for the wellington boot!

In the opinion of editors Mortimer Ellis had obviously been a news item of value. The cutting was headed, Contemptible Scoundrel meets his Waterloo.
W. SOMERSET MAUGHAM, First Person Singular, 'The Round Dozen', 1931.

wheat: to separate the wheat from the chaff

to separate the good from the bad, the valuable from the worthless

The expression refers to the farming practice of threshing corn in order to separate the worthless husks from the good grain. Someone who, figuratively speaking, separates the wheat from the chaff identifies what is worthwhile in an undertaking and discards that which is a waste of time.

A similar allusion is used in the Bible. This time the wheat refers to those who belong to Christ and are judged worthy and the chaff to those who have rejected him and have no place in his kingdom. Luke 3:17 reads: *'His winnowing fork is in his hand to clear his threshing-floor and to gather the wheat into his barn, but he will burn up the chaff with unquenchable fire.'*

The entry *to separate the sheep from the goats* discusses another biblical analogy which conveys the same spiritual message but is also widely used in secular contexts to describe the separating of something good from something bad.

So MI6 wheeled on Doug and Dave to do their stuff, confusing the public so that they couldn't distinguish the wheat from the chaff.
MID SUSSEX TIMES, September 27, 1991.

But, on health and safety particularly, it's the job of governments and not individuals to sort the research wheat from the chaff to protect our wellbeing.
GOOD HOUSEKEEPING, September 1991.

usage: literary

see also: to separate the sheep from the goats

wheeler-dealer, a

an entrepreneur, usually dishonest

Someone who frequents casinos or saloons *wheels and deals* there, at roulette and cards, constantly chancing his luck and skill and perhaps his ability to cheat. From the original context the application is now more commonly to the businessman who likes to make deals and live by his entrepreneurial acumen. The suggestion is often that the schemes he dreams up are of dubious honesty.

The policy is being marketed after some last-minute suggestions by Dr Penny O'Nions, a former hospital doctor who gave up medicine to become a financial adviser, a career change that broke a long family tradition.
She says: 'The family was done out of a lot of money by a financial wheeler-dealer and I thought it would be nice if one of us knew something about money.'
THE SUNDAY TIMES, August 11, 1991.

usage: Often derogatory, but not always so. Colloquial.

whipping boy, a

one who suffers the punishment for the wrong done by another, a scapegoat

A *whipping boy* was an unfortunate child who shared the rich benefits of the nursery and schoolroom with a young prince but who was beaten in his royal companion's place whenever the latter misbehaved. Edward VI's punishments fell upon Barnaby Fitzpatrick and Mungo Murray suffered for Charles I. Presumably it was considered inappropriate for a servant or tutor to punish a child from a family who ruled by divine right. However, not all princes were so fortunate. George Buchanan was the Latin master of James I. He punished his royal charge, despite the presence of a whipping boy, and threatened to repeat it if he carried on being lazy.

The practice was international. King Henry IV of France, on his adult conversion to Catholicism, sent two ambassadors to the Pope in 1593, where they were symbolically whipped to atone for his previous Protestantism. Their reward was to be made cardinals shortly afterwards!

The allusion has survived the practice for, although royal children now have to bear the consequences of their misdeeds themselves, we still call someone who suffers for someone else's bad behaviour a *whipping boy*.

[Life in] modern cities is more stressful than life on the brink of starvation in the developing nations. Pollution is another popular whipping boy, scapegoat for almost any national ill in the post-war era.
COBUILD CORPUS.

The Financial Times *says in its special article that Libya has been bugbear and whipping boy for the Americans ever since the Reagan administration was elected.*
COBUILD CORPUS, BBC World Service, 1989.

white elephant, a

an unwanted object, especially something cumbersome

The devious kings of Siam invented an ingenious way of ridding themselves of any courtier who irked them. They would present the hapless fellow with a white elephant, a rare and sacred beast. The cost of maintaining the creature, which was not permitted to earn its keep as a working animal, was excessive and gradually ruined its new owner.

A *white elephant* has taken on much more diminutive proportions in modern use, where the reference is often to unwanted items, encumbering bric-à-brac. These are sold off at *the white elephant stall* at the local church bazaar or school fete.

When we got rid of the white elephant of a house in Lexham Gardens my mother took her six sons, three daughters, a cook, a parlour-maid, and a housemaid to a house in Colinette Road, Putney.
LEONARD WOOLF. Sowing. 1960.

I found no dark horses here, only white elephants for recycling.
DAILY EXPRESS. August 29, 1991.

whited sepulchre, a

a hypocrite, something outwardly presentable but inwardly corrupt

This is a biblical expression and comes from the words Jesus uses in Matthew 23:27 when he condemns the scribes and Pharisees for being outwardly orthodox and beyond reproach but inwardly corrupt, full of self-indulgence and greed: *'Ye are like unto whited sepulchres, which indeed appear beautiful outward, but are full of dead men's bones, and of all uncleanness'* (Authorised Version).

In biblical times, contact with dead bodies or tombs was considered ritually unclean, so Jewish sepulchres were whitewashed to make them clearly visible to any passer-by who feared defilement. It seems unlikely, however, that Jesus would call such tombs beautiful since attractiveness was not the reason for the whitewashing. It is more likely that he was referring to the ornamental plasterwork which adorned the sepulchres of the rich.

The same with love. This white love that we have is the same. It is only the reverse, the whited sepulchre of the true love. True love is dark, a throbbing together in darkness, like the wild-cat in the night, when the green screen opens and her eyes are on the darkness.
D. H. LAWRENCE, 'The Ladybird'.

So that I consider myself a better woman than you are. Oh yes! I know you don't stand alone. I know there are plenty like you in the best society – whited sepulchres, fair without, and rottenness and dead men's bones within.
FLORENCE MARRYAT.

usage: literary

wicket: to bat on a sticky wicket

to be faced with a difficult situation requiring tact and diplomacy to resolve it

The term is from cricket and alludes to the problems faced by a batsman when performing on a wicket that has been saturated by rain. The fearsome West Indians fell prey to the difficulties of a *sticky wicket* in 1935: *'A Test at Kensington is akin to entering the lion's den, West Indies having a remarkable record here. They have won every one of the last 10 Tests on the ground, having lost only once – to England by four wickets in 1935 on a "sticky" pitch.'* (*Daily Telegraph*, April 18, 1992). These days the covers are put on overnight and come out again at the first sign of a shower so the problem scarcely arises, for professional cricketers at any rate.

No one has ever doubted the Health Secretary's class, elegance, style and culture. What has been suspect is his defensive solidity and technique on a sticky wicket, his judgement on which balls to leave alone rather than wafting them airily into the slips.
DAILY MAIL, October 11, 1991.

Yesterday the doubters were silenced by a performance on a very sticky wicket which was solid, thorough and resolute.
DAILY MAIL, October 11, 1991.

wild goose chase, a

a purposeless errand, a pointless exercise, a waste of time

The phrase can be traced back to the sixteenth century. Its meaning is obscure, although distinguished ornithologists

It's not cricket!

The vocabulary of general English is enlarged, even enriched, by the assimilation of words from the jargon, slang, cant or argot of subcultures in society. The special lexicons of business, the military, jazz musicians and thieves amongst many others have contributed words and phrases that are used far beyond their original confines, often with a somewhat different meaning. It would be surprising, then, if that very English game of cricket hadn't provided English speakers in general, and not just cricketers, with quite a few interesting idioms.

For instance, the wicket is the central part of the playing area in the middle of the ground where all the action is. In ordinary informal British English to be or **to bat on a sticky wicket** means 'to be in a difficult situation'. The entry for this term has examples of its narrower and general meanings.

The quickest way to score runs in cricket is to hit the ball up in the air and right out of the playing area. For that, you get six runs, you *hit the ball for six*. In general English, however, the expression is used with a different meaning. You might hear, for instance:

My wife's death hit me for six, it took me months to recover.
The news knocked me for six, I just didn't believe it.

The sense here is that the event or happening overwhelmed me, shattered me, dealt me as severe a blow as the batsman hitting the ball over the boundary.

There are quite a few more idioms from cricket: *off one's own bat*, for instance, which means 'on one's own, independently, without help or assistance'. Then there's that lovely phrase *It's not cricket*, 'it's not fair, honest and honourable', that's so often said slightly humorously or satirically, as perhaps A. A. Milne meant in this extract from *Year in, Year out* (1952):

Had Mr Mullins lit a cigarette, the ladies would have swooned and the men muttered that it wasn't cricket. 'Parkinson,' the Host would have said, 'remove Mr Mullins.'

have testified to the erratic movements of wild geese which, apparently, make them extremely difficult to catch.

The *OED*'s suggested origin is a game from the Middle Ages, mentioned at some length in Shakespeare's *Romeo and Juliet* (Act II Scene iv). The game opened with a race on horseback, the winner earning the right to lead the rest, who then followed on at measured distances, over a totally unpredictable course. The winding path and the intervals between the players were said to imitate the flight of wild geese. We do not know how the game ended, but that is the nature of a wild goose chase – fatigue eventually makes one call a halt.

My mind now began to misgive me that the disappointed coachmaker had sent me on a wild-goose errand.
CHARLES DICKENS, The Uncommercial Traveller, 1868.

I advertise for antique footstools. There are four replies and four wild goose chases, the last one on a hilltop farm.
WEEKEND TELEGRAPH, May 9, 1992.

willies: to give someone the willies

to arouse nervousness, uneasiness, fear in someone

The origins of the phrase are shadowy but, although the *OED* says it dates back to the nineteenth century, it is possible to make a reasonable case for much earlier origins. It has been suggested that the word comes from 'willow tree', of which the word *willy* is an old form. The willow has long been a symbol of grief and mourning, and there are many references to it in English literature. The saying 'She is in her willows . . .' was used of a woman who had lost her lover or spouse. More than one authority has pointed out that Giselle, the heroine of the nineteenth-century ballet of that name, is possessed by the Wilis, or spirits of beautiful young girls who have died before their wedding day and who dance to express their anger at death.

The current sense is not one of grief but of apprehension or nervousness.

One pregnant lady, about to deliver, went to her pit latrine to relieve herself, and the baby started coming out. It was a near catastrophe; just thinking about it gave me the willies.
THOMAS HALE, On the Far Side of Liglig Mountain, 1989.

Sir Gordon Borrie, outgoing director-general of Fair Trading, is not free of red tape yet. Borrie's final report to his 13th and last boss, Michael Heseltine, was initially addressed to the Trade and Industry Secretary. This was hurriedly changed
to President of the Board of Trade . . . – which is where the lawyers come in. They say the legislation governing the operations of the Office of Fair Trading specifically mentioned the Secretary of State for Trade and Industry, and that is how Heseltine is described in the final report, published yesterday. A Fair Trader sums it up: 'Our production people have had the willies.'*
DAILY TELEGRAPH, June 4, 1992.

usage: colloquial

willy-nilly

whether one likes it or not

The term is a contraction of the words *will I, nill I* (similarly *will he, nill he; will ye, nill ye*) and means that the business will take place whether it is with the will of the person concerned or against it.

A similar expression is *shilly-shally*.

An imprudent marriage is a different thing, for then the consequences are inevitable when once the step has been taken, and have to be borne, will he, nill he.
MRS OLIPHANT, c1870.

usage: Usually written as two words, though may still be hyphenated. Informal.

see also: shilly-shally

win hands down, to

to gain a resounding victory

The phrase is from the world of racing. When a jockey feels assured of certain victory, he stops whipping and forcing his horse on, and relaxes, dropping his hands and allowing his mount to run on past the winning post.

Men always approve of dowdy women – but when it comes to brass tacks the dressed-up trollops win hands down! Sad, but there it is.
AGATHA CHRISTIE, Murder in the Mews, 1925.

There was nothing that you could really call a war between his higher and lower selves. The lower self won hands down.
P. G. WODEHOUSE, Mulliner Nights, 'Cats' Will Be Cats', 1933.

usage: informal

wing: to take someone under one's wing

to provide someone with help, encouragement, protection

In a passage to be found in Matthew 23:37, Jesus laments over Jerusalem declaring how, like a mother hen who spreads her wings wide so that her brood can creep safely beneath them, he had longed to offer its people protection but they turned away.

O Jerusalem, Jerusalem, thou that killest the prophets, and. stonest them which are sent unto thee, how often would I have gathered thy children together, even as a hen gathereth her chickens under her wings, and ye would not!

Psalm 63:7 carries the same idea: *'Because thou hast been my help, therefore in the shadow of thy wings will I rejoice.'* Reference to the wings of protection have been used in English literature since the thirteenth century.

He took Gordon under his wing in a friendly way, showed him the ropes and was even ready to listen to his suggestion.
GEORGE ORWELL, Keep the Aspidistra Flying, 1936.

They had met through Labour Party activities, when Mor had been teaching in a school on the south side of London, and Mor and Nan had to some extent taken Tim, who was a bachelor, under their wing.
IRIS MURDOCH, The Sandcastle, 1957.

usage: Wing might occasionally be found in the plural

wolf in sheep's clothing, a

someone who is not as pleasant and harmless as first appears

Aesop tells a fable about a wolf who, wrapped in a fleece, manages to sneak into a sheepfold by pretending to be one of the flock. Once inside he falls upon the sheep and devours them. Our present-day expression, like many others, may have come from Aesop's cautionary tales, though probably its source is the Bible. Matthew 7:15 says: *'Beware of false prophets, which come to you in sheep's clothing, but inwardly they are ravening wolves.'* However, such has been the popularity of Aesop's fables from ancient times until the present day that Funk (1950) suggests it is even quite possible that the fable was the origin of the biblical simile.

There is the meekness of the clergyman. There spoke the wolf in sheep's clothing.
HENRY FIELDING, Amelia, 1751.

204 · wolf ·

I know Andrews. He's a wolf who doesn't even bother to put on sheep's clothing.
JAMES HADLEY CHASE, The Double Shuffle, 1952.

The 'philanthropic Mr Owen' suddenly appeared as a wolf in sheep's clothing; and his plans for the unemployed took on quite a new aspect when they were seen as merely one part of a vast and sinister design against the established order in both Church and State.
G. D. H. COLE, Socialist Thought, 1953.

wolf: to keep the wolf from the door

to ward off hunger

The *wolf* here is hunger. Since ancient times, the wolf has been a symbol of poverty and want. Fables depict the wolf as ravenously hungry, in desperate need of sustinence. The French say *'manger comme un loup'* (to eat like a wolf) and the Germans have an expression *'wolfs-hunger'*. In English someone who eats ravenously is said to 'wolf' their food. *Keeping the wolf from the door*, then, means to ward off gnawing hunger and starvation, which our ancestors in the fifteenth century who first used the phrase would have understood far better than we do.

That hungry Wolf, want and necessity, which now stands at his door.
JOHN GOODMAN, The Penitent Pardoned, 1679.

It makes a lot of difference to . . . one's happiness if the wolf is not scratching at the door.
HENRY HERMAN, His Angel, 1891.

I take it your uncle cut off your allowance after that Goodwood binge and you had to take this tutoring job to keep the wolf from the door?
P. G. WODEHOUSE, The Inimitable Jeeves, 1924.

wool: to pull the wool over someone's eyes

to deceive someone

At one time anyone who considered himself a gentleman would wear a powdered wig. Such creations were humorously referred to as 'wool' because the curls looked rather like a fleece. The wigs tended to be ill-fitting and cumbersome and were easily pushed over the wearer's eyes so that he could not see what was going on around him. This made him an easy victim of theft or pranks.

Judges wear wigs to the present day and some authorities suggest that the expression may have been used in courts of law when lawyers, who had succeeded in a skilful deception, would boast at having *pulled the wool over the judge's eyes.*

The first thing she's going to do when she meets you is to try to pull the wool over your eyes and persuade you that he's as sane as I am.
P. G. WODEHOUSE, Uncle Fred in the Springtime, 1939.

They are suspicious people over whose eyes no coloured Festival wool can possibly be pulled, the great undiddleable.
DYLAN THOMAS, Quite Early One Morning, 'The Festival Exhibition, 1951', 1954.

see also: a big wig

writing is on the wall, the

downfall or ruin is imminent

In Daniel, chapter 5, the Bible tells how Belshazzar, King of Babylon, showed his contempt of the Lord by holding a great feast where wine was served in goblets taken from the temple in Jerusalem. During the feast a human hand appeared, writing on the wall. The inscription read: *Mene, mene, tekel, parsin*. The only one able to interpret the sign was the Jewish exile, Daniel, who voiced the Lord's anger and prophesied the downfall of Belshazzar and his kingdom. Just as Daniel had said, that very night Belshazzar was slain and his kingdom taken by a foreign power. These days the message of doom is likely to apply to a failing enterprise, a politician or a football manager.

The writing on the wall is clear: if Man behaves like an animal and allows his population to increase while each nation steadily increases the complexity and range of its environment, nature will take her course and the Law of the Jungle will prevail.
J. GRAY, 'The Proper Study of Mankind is Man', The Listener, September 3, 1959.

Collective belt-tightening threatens to bring down not only Blitz but its style-conscious competitors. The writing has been on the wall for some time now. The style press actually started dying when newspapers like this one launched their own style pages.
GUARDIAN, September 2, 1991.

Rights for animals!

Animals often play a gruesome part in idioms. There are a number of accounts in the entries of this book where they usually meet a grisly death. A cat might get away with its life on its discovery in a bag (see **pig in a poke** for how it got there), but a cat in a bag in Shakespeare's time might well not escape with its life if there were any bowmen about. For the full story of that one, see **no room to swing a cat**. Many animals up to the nineteenth century met a judicial death through no fault of their own – dogs were by no means the only ones who could properly wear **a hangdog look**! Other animals have been actively pursued for sport: fox-hunting may give us a **red herring**, stag-hunting **to keep at bay**. The long-banned bear-baiting spawned phrases such as *to stave off*. See **Hammer horror stories** (page 93) for more macabre idioms.

BIBLIOGRAPHY

A select list of some books to which reference has been made.

APPERSON, George Latimer, 1929:
English Proverbs and Proverbial Phrases

BACCHUS and VENUS, 1737:
A New Canting Dictionary

BARTLETT, John, 1st edition 1855, 14th edition 1968:
Familiar Quotations *(Little, Brown Boston and Toronto)*

BENHAM, Sir William Gurney, 1st edition 1907, revised edition 1948:
Book of Quotations, Proverbs and Household Words *(Cassell, London)*

BERG, Paul C. 1953:
A Dictionary of New Words in English *(Allen & Unwin, London)*

BERRY, Lester V. and VAN DEN BARK, Melvin, 1st edition 1942, 2nd edition 1952:
American Thesaurus of Slang *(Crowell, New York)*

BOATNER, Maxine Tull and GATES, John Edward, 1966:
A Dictionary of Idioms for the Deaf

BOMBAUGH, C. C., 1905:
Facts and Fancies for the Curious from the Harvest Fields of Literature (Lippincott, Philadelphia and London)

BRANDRETH, Gyles, 1990:
Everyman's Modern Phrase and Fable *(Dent, London)*

BREWER, Ebenezer Cobham, 1970:
Dictionary of Phrase and Fable *(Cassell, London)*

BROPHY, John and PARTRIDGE, Eric, 1931, revised edition 1965:
The Long Tail – Soldiers' Songs and Slang 1914–1918 *(Deutsch, London)*

BURVENICH, Arthur, 1905:
English Idioms and Colloquialisms *(Thieme, Zutphen, Ad Herckenrath Ledeberg-Gent)*

COLLINS, Vere Henry, 1st edition 1956, 3rd edition 1958:
A Book of English Idioms *(Longman, London)*

COLLINS, Vere Henry, 1958:
A Second Book of English Idioms *(Longman, London)*

COLLINS, Vere Henry, 1960:
A Third Book of English Idioms *(Longman, London)*

COWIE, Anthony P. and MACKIN, Ronald, 1975:
Oxford Dictionary of Current Idiomatic English Volume 1 (Oxford University Press)

COWIE, Anthony P., MACKIN, Ronald and McCAIG, Isobel, 1983:
Oxford Dictionary of Current Idiomatic English Volume 2 *(Oxford University Press)*

CURRAN, Peter, n.d.:
Beware of Idioms. An audio-active course for students of English *(Tudor-Tape Co., London)*

DIXON, James Maine, 1891:
English Idioms *(Nelson, London)*

DONALDSON, Graham and ROSS, Maris, 1990:
The Complete Why Do We Say That? *(David and Charles, Newton Abbot)*

EDWARDS, Eliezer 1882, revised 1911:
Words, Facts and Phrases *(Chatto & Windus, London)*

EWART, Neil, 1983:
Everyday Phrases *(Blandford, Poole)*

FARMER, John Stephen, 1888 and 1889:
Americanisms – Old and New *(Thomas Poulter, London)*

FARMER, John Stephen, 1890–1904:
Slang and its Analogues, past and present *(Thomas Poulter, London)*

FARMER, John Stephen and HENLEY, William Ernest, 1905, USA 1966:
A Dictionary of Slang and Colloquial English *(Routledge and Sons, London)*

FREEMAN, William, 1951–1952:
A Concise Dictionary of English Idioms *(The English University Press, London)*

FUNK, Charles Earle, 1950:
A Hog on Ice and other curious expressions *(Harper Bros, New York)*

FUNK, Charles Earle, 1950A:
Thereby Hangs a Tale: Stories of Curious Word Origins *(Harper Bros, New York)*

FUNK, Charles Earle, 1955:
Heavens to Betsy! and other curious sayings *(Harper Bros, New York)*

FUNK, Charles Earle, 1958:
Horsefeathers and other curious words (Harper Bros, New York)

FUNK, Wilfred John 1950:
Word Origins and their Romantic Stories (Wilfred Funk, Inc., New York)

GROSE, Francis, 1963:
A Classical Dictionary of the Vulgar Tongue (Routledge and Kegan Paul, London)

HARGRAVE, Basil, 1911:
Origins and Meanings of Popular Phrases and Names (Werner Laurie, London)

HENDERSON, B. L. L. and G. C. E., 1964:
A Dictionary of English Idioms (Blackwood, London)

HILL, Robert H., 1963:
A Dictionary of Difficult Words (Arrow, London)

HOLT, Alfred Hubbard, 1961:
Phrase and Word Origins (Dover, New York)

HOTTEN, John Camden, 1874 and 1922:
The Slang Dictionary, etymological historical and anecdotal (Chatto & Windus, London)

HYAMSON, Albert Montefiore, 1922 and 1970:
A Dictionary of English Phrases (Routledge & Sons, London, E. P. Dutton & Co., New York)

JOHNSON, Trench Henry, 1906:
Phrases and Names; their Origins and Meanings (Werner Laurie, London)

KIRKPATRICK, John, 1912 and 1914:
Handbook of Idiomatic English (Carl Winter, Heidelberg and Edinburgh)

KNOX, Thomas, 1856:
Dictionary of Familiar Sayings and Phrases, with Anecdotes illustrating their Origins (Sutherland & Knox, Edinburgh)

KWONG, Ki Chiu 1880:
A Dictionary of English Phrases with Illustrative Sentences (Barnes & Co, New York)

LEVITT, J. and J. 1959:
The Spell of Words (Darwen Finlayson, Beaconsfield)

LONGMAN, 1979:
Longman Dictionary of English Idioms (Longman, Harlow)

MACKAY C., 1887:
Glossary of Obscure Words and Phrases in the writings of Shakespeare and his contemporaries, traced etymologically to the ancient language of the British people as spoken before the irruption of the Danes and Saxons (Sampson Low, London)

MANSER, Martin, 1983:
Dictionary of Contemporary Idioms (Pan, London)

MANSER, Martin, 1990:
Dictionary of Word and Phrase Origins (Sphere, London)

MARCH, Francis Andrew and MARCH, Francis Andrew Jr., 1902 and 1958:
March's Thesaurus – Dictionary (W. H. Allen, London)

McMORDIE, W., 1909, 3rd edition 1954:
English Idioms and how to use them (Oxford University Press)

METHOLD, Kenneth, 1964 and 1969:
English Idioms at Work (University of London Press)

MORRIS, William and Mary, 1962:
Dictionary of Word and Phrase Origins (Harper and Row, New York)

MOSS, Walter, 1956:
English Idioms – selected and explained (Nauck & Co., Koln and Berlin)

MURPHY, M. J., 1968:
Test Yourself on English Idioms (University of London Press)

NARES, Robert, 1822:
Glossary of Words, Phrases, Names and Allusions, particularly of Shakespeare (Routledge, London)

NEAMAN, Judith and SILVER, Carole, 1991:
In Other Words: A Thesaurus of Euphemisms (Angus & Robertson, London)

NORTHEY, James, 1985:
My Best Togs (Salvation Army)

NOTES AND QUERIES 1849–1935:
for readers and writers, collectors and librarians. Editors: E. G. STANLEY (Oxford University Press, London)

PALMER, Harold E. 1938 and 1965:
A Grammar of English Words (Longmans, London)

PARTRIDGE, Eric Honeywood, 1940, 5th edition 1950:
A Dictionary of Clichés with an Introductory Essay (Routledge & Kegan Paul, London)

PARTRIDGE, Eric Honeywood, 1949, 3rd edition 1968:
A Dictionary of the Underworld, British and American (Routledge & Kegan Paul, London)

PARTRIDGE, Eric Honeywood, 8th edition, 1984:
A Dictionary of Slang and Unconventional English (Routledge & Kegan Paul, London)

RADFORD, Edwin, 1946:
Crowther's Encyclopaedia of Phrases and Origins (A John Crowther Publication, Bognor Regis)

RADFORD, Edwin, 1946:
Unusual Words and how they came about (Philosophical Library, New York)

REES, Nigel, 1987:
Why do we say . . . ? (Blandford Press, Parkstone)

REES, Nigel, 1990:
Dictionary of Popular Phrases (Bloomsbury, London)

ROGET, P. M., 1962:
Roget's Thesaurus (Longman, London)

ROGET, P. M., 1963:
Roget's International Thesaurus: The complete book of synonyms in British and American usage (Crowell, New York)

SMITH, J. L., 1916 and 1942:
English Phrases and Idioms

SMITH, Henry Percy, 1883:
Glossary of Terms and Phrases (Kegan Paul, London)

SMITH, William George, 1948:
The Oxford Dictionary of English Proverbs (Clarendon Press, Oxford)

STEVENSON, Burton Egbert, 1949:
Book of Proverbs, Maxims and Familiar Phrases (Routledge and Kegan Paul, London)

SUTCLIFFE, Herbert and BERMAN, Harold, 1978:
Words and their Stories (Voice of America)

VANONI, Marvin, 1989:
Great Expressions (Grafton, London)

VIZETELLY, Francis Horace and de BEKKER, Leander Jan, 1923 and 1970:
A Desk-Book of Idioms and Idiomatic Phrases in Eng-

lish Speech and Literature (Funk & Wagnalls, New York and London)

WALL, C., 1969:
Words and Phrases Index (The Pierian Press, Ann Arbor, Michigan)

WALSH, William Shepard, 1892:
Handy Book of Literary Curiosities (Lippincott, Philadelphia)

WEEKLEY, Ernest, 1927:
More Words Ancient and Modern (Murray, London)

WEEKLEY, Ernest, 1926 and 1946:
Words Ancient and Modern (Murray, London)

WENTWORTH, Harold and FLEXNER, Stuart Berg, 1960:
Dictionary of American Slang (Harrap, London)

WHEELER, William Adolphus, 1882:
Familiar Allusions: A hand-book of Miscellaneous Information (Osgood, Boston)

WHITEHEAD J. S., 1937:
Everyday English Phrases. Their Idiomatic meanings and origins (Longman, London)

WHITFORD, Harold C. and Dixson, Robert J., 1953:
Handbook of American Idioms and Idiomatic Usage (A Regen Publication, Simon & Schuster, New York)

WOOD, Frederick Thomas, 1964 and 1967:
English Verbal Idioms (Macmillan, London)

WOOD, Frederick Thomas, 1967:
English Prepositional Idioms (Macmillan, London)

WOOD, Frederick Thomas, 1969:
English Colloquial Idioms (Macmillan Lang, London)

WORRALL, Arthur James, 1932, 3rd edition 1938:
English Idioms for Foreign Students (Longman, London)

WORRAL, Arthur James, 1953:
More English Idioms for Foreign Students (Longman, London)

YULE-BURNELL:
Hobson-Jobson (London)

INDEX